Thomas Maissen and Barbara Mittler
Why China did not have a Renaissance – and why that matters

Critical Readings in Global Intellectual History

Edited by
Susan Richter, Milinda Banerjee, Sebastian Meurer,
Li Xuetao

Volume 1

Thomas Maissen and Barbara Mittler

Why China did not have a Renaissance – and why that matters

An interdisciplinary Dialogue

Supported by the German Research Foundation

ISBN 978-3-11-071006-9
e-ISBN (PDF) 978-3-11-057639-9
e-ISBN (EPUB) 978-3-11-057403-6
ISSN 2568-843X

Library of Congress Cataloging-in-Publication Data
Names: Maissen, Thomas, 1962- author. | Mittler, Barbara, 1968- author.
Title: Why China did not have a renaissance - and why that matters : an interdisciplinary
    dialogue / Thomas Maissen and Barbara Mittler.
Description: First edition. | Berlin ; Boston : Walter de Gruyter, [2018] |
    Series: Critical readings in global intellectual history, ISSN 2568-843X ;
    volume 1 | Includes bibliographical references and index.
Identifiers: LCCN 2018009488 (print) | LCCN 2018024804 (ebook) | ISBN
    9783110576399 | ISBN 9783110573961 (hardback) | ISBN 9783110576399 (ebook)
Subjects: LCSH: Renaissance. | China--History--Ming dynasty, 1368-1644. | BISAC: HISTORY /
    Renaissance. | HISTORY / Asia / General. | HISTORY / Asia / China. | HISTORY / Europe /
    General. | HISTORY / Europe / Western. | HISTORY / Study & Teaching. | HISTORY / Modern /
    General.
Classification: LCC CB361 (ebook) | LCC CB361 .M28 2018 (print) | DDC
    909/.4--dc23
LC record available at https://lccn.loc.gov/2018009488

Bibliographic information published by the Deutsche Nationalbibliothek
The Deutsche Nationalbibliothek lists this publication in the Deutsche Nationalbibliografie;
detailed bibliographic data are available on the Internet at http://dnb.dnb.de.

© 2018 Walter de Gruyter GmbH, Berlin/Boston
This volume is text- and page-identical with the hardback published in 2018.
Printing and binding: CPI books GmbH, Leck
Cover image: Raphael, The School of Athens, around 1510 / Zhu Jianqiu 诸健秋 (ca. 1891–
1964) Three Vinegar Tasters 三嚐酸 Sanchangsuan.
Collage: Gregor Stiebert, Christiane Illius

www.degruyter.com

To our stimulating colleagues in Heidelberg and especially at the Heidelberg Centre for Transcultural Studies/Cluster of Excellence "Asia and Europe in a Global Context"

Contents

List of illustrations —— IX

Milinda Banerjee, Sebastian Meurer, Susan Richter
Series editors' note —— XI

Prologue

Barbara Mittler & Thomas Maissen
Periodization in a global context —— 3

Introduction

Barbara Mittler
Epochal changes in a global context – Toward a History-in-common —— 11

Thomas Maissen
Defining epochs in global history – Can we write a History-in-common without shared concepts? —— 25

Part I **Periodization**

Thomas Maissen
Europe: Secularizing teleological models —— 37

Barbara Mittler
China: Engendering teleological models —— 45

Part II **Renaissances**

Thomas Maissen
The view from Europe: The Renaissance —— 53

Barbara Mittler
The view from China: r/Renaissances —— 83

Conclusion

Thomas Maissen
The Renaissance and the rise of the West —— 123

Barbara Mittler
Renaissance-in-common? History-as-dialogue —— 133

Epilogue

Thomas Maissen & Barbara Mittler
Why China did not have a Renaissance – and why that matters: Conflicting approaches to periodization —— 161

Appendix —— 165
    Sources from the European Renaissance —— 166
    Sources from the Chinese Renaissance —— 190

Acknowledgements —— 221

Works cited —— 223

Index of names and places —— 235

List of illustrations

Cover: Raphael, *The School of Athens*, around 1510 / Zhu Jianqiu 诸健秋 (ca. 1891–1964), *Three Vinegar Tasters* 三嚐酸 *Sanchangsuan*.
Fig. 1   Title Page Hu Shi. *The Chinese Renaissance* 中国的文艺复兴 (*The Haskell Lectures*, 1933). Chicago: The University of Chicago Press; London: Cambridge University Press, 1934. (New York: Paragon Book Reprint Corp., 1963).
Fig. 2   Frontispiece of Johannes Albinus (Giovanni Albino), *Excerpta ex Blondi decadibus*, Naples, 1494. Bayerische Staatsbibliothek, Munich, Clm 11324.
Fig. 3   Justus of Ghent, *Euclid*, ca. 1474, Oil on Panel, 102 x 80 cm, Urbino, Galleria Nazionale delle Marche. / Justus of Ghent, *Vittorino da Feltre*, ca. 1474, Oil on Panel, 94 × 63 cm, Paris, Musée du Louvre. / http://www.destinazionemarche.it/wp-content/uploads/2015/03/tavole-uomini-ilustri.jpg.
Fig. 4   Giorgione, *The Three Philosophers*, 1508/09, Oil on Canvas, 125,5 cm × 146,2 cm, Vienna, Kunsthistorisches Museum Wien, Gemäldegalerie (GG 111).
Fig. 5   Raphael, *The School of Athens*, around 1510, Stanza della Segnatura, Palazzo Apostolico, Vatican.
Fig. 6   Edith Sichel, *The Renaissance* (London: Williams & Norgate, 1914), Table of Contents.
Fig. 7   Edith Sichel, *The Renaissance* (London: Williams & Norgate, 1914), 7–8.
Fig. 8   Bilingual Cover Page of a journal edited by Fu Sinian 傅斯年 (1896–1950), entitled *Xinchao* 新潮 (New Tide) and *The Renaissance*, 3.2.1919.
Fig. 9   Bilingual Cover Page of a journal published by Zhang Junmai 张君劢 (Carsun Chang, 1887–1969), with the English title *National Renaissance*, vol. 1 No. 1, 20.5.1932.
Fig. 10 Zhu Jianqiu 诸健秋 (ca. 1891–1964), *Three Vinegar Tasters* 三嚐酸 *Sanchangsuan*.

Milinda Banerjee, Sebastian Meurer, Susan Richter
Series editors' note

Starting the critical readings: Renaissances in dialogue and global intellectual history

The dialogue is a form of expression with a long history. Highly valued and differentiated during European Antiquity, it continued as a didactic tool of monastic learning throughout the Middle Ages. However, the rediscovery and revitalization of the antique culture of dialogue during the Renaissance stands out. According to Bodo Guthmüller, the Renaissance dialogue exemplifies a culture that considered every form of verbal statement, elaboration, or communication to be firmly rooted in its social context. It is in dialogue that the affable interaction of individuals and their diverse opinions, positions, or aesthetic judgments became manifest. Scholars holding erudite colloquies and courtiers cultivating conversation equally staged the Humanist ideal of a free exchange of arguments and positions; they performed this spirit of amity and tolerance, even when, in reality, dialogues often expressed agonistic tensions. Therefore, we may justly understand the European Renaissance in terms of a "dialogical cultural era."[1]

Peter Burke states, "The rise of rhetoric during the Renaissance was another stimulus to the dialogue, which offered a dramatic presentation of arguments pro and contra [...]."[2] Renaissance literature took up the ancient form of the characterizing oration (*sermocinatio*) in order to mark opposing positions, either to marginalize them, or to set the stage for balanced consideration of differing (yet acceptable) notions. The dialogue allowed for the weighing of arguments according to their strength (*soliditas*) or weakness (*debilitas*). In *A Defence of Poetry* (1579), Thomas Lodge (1558–1625) thus considers it an effective rhetorical strat-

---

1 Guthmüller, Bodo, Müller, Wolfgang G. Einleitung. In *Dialog und Gesprächskultur in der Renaissance*, ed. Bodo Guthmüller (Wiesbaden: Harrassowitz, 2004), 7. See also Buron, Emmanuel. *Les états du dialogue à l'âge de l'humanisme* (Tours: Presses univ. François-Rabelais de Tours, 2015). Cox, Virginia. The changing form of the Italian Renaissance dialogue. In *The Renaissance Dialogue: Literary Dialogue in its Social and Political Contexts, Castiglione to Galileo*, ed. Virginia Cox (Cambridge: Cambridge University Press, 1992), 61–69. Heitsch, Dorothea. *Printed Voices. The Renaissance Culture of Dialogue* (Toronto: University of Toronto Press, ²2014). Marsh, David. Dialogue and discussion in the Renaissance. In *The Cambridge History of Literary Criticism*, vol. 3, ed. Glyn P. Norton (Cambridge: Cambridge University Press, 1999), 265–270.
2 Burke, Peter. "The Renaissance Dialogue," *Renaissance Studies* 3 (1989): 1–12, here 7.

egy first to strengthen an opposing standpoint, only to thoroughly defeat it the more effectively. As a pedagogical genre, fictitious conversations had the purpose to encourage autonomous thinking in a dialogue partner, to engage with and, if need be, refute his or her argumentation.[3] Conversations were held between teachers and pupils as well as between friends – generally between men. Published dialogues invited contemporary readers to scrutinize or challenge the presented line of thought. The genre offered an argumentative interplay of erudite examples combining established teachings and contemporary tendencies, while leaving room for the articulation of current needs or unease.

The philosophical as well as the fictitious dialogue have their place in Chinese culture, too; for instance, as an element of the long-time engagement with Buddhism.[4] The transcultural heritage of dialogue is visible, for example, in the legacy left by ancient Indian formats of dialogue over wide spaces, with Buddhism being an important cultural transmitter.[5] Dialogical forms of exchange between scholars also feature prominently in Confucianism, often while treating speculative or moral philosophy. Confucian teaching centres on *ren* 仁, referring to man in his benign dealings with other humans. For Confucius, *ren* was also at the heart of all communication, of any interaction; an ideal he expressed in the dialogues with his disciples, which, as *Lunyu* (Analects of Confucius), became the key work of his written heritage. As early Confucians specified, such dialogues ideally lead to "zhongyong 中庸," the "mean,"[6] i.e. action in harmony and balance that could be attained by jointly pondering circumstances and different courses of action. Unlike Plato's Socratic dialogues, these colloquies are only loosely connected. Among them are not only doctrinal conversations between teacher and pupil but also debates among peers.[7] Ever since such begin-

---

3 Hösle, Vittorio. *Der philosophische Dialog. Eine Poetik und Hermeneutik* (Munich: Beck, 2006), 84.
4 Hösle, *Der philosophische Dialog*, 80.
5 For a recent example of transcultural scholarship on dialogue, see Sick, David H. "When Socrates Met the Buddha. Greek and Indian Dialectic in Hellenistic Bactria and India," *Journal of the Royal Asiatic Society* 17, 3 (2007): 253–78.
6 The *Doctrine of the Mean* attributed to Zisi or Kong Ji, the grandson of Confucius. See the translation by Legge, James. *The Doctrine of the Mean*, 1893. http://www.sacred-texts.com/cfu/conf3.htm.
7 Even class distinctions should not be of any importance in conversations. Wei, Yuqing. *Das Lehrer-Schüler-Verhältnis bei Rousseau und Konfuzius. Eine vergleichende Untersuchung zu zwei klassischen Erziehungsparadigmen* (Münster: Waxmann, 1993), 141–143. Reich, Kersten. Der Garten moralischer Vernunft. Gespräch mit Meister Kong (Konfuzius) und einigen seiner Schüler. In *Zweifeln bis zum Tor der letzten Herrschaft. Chinas Intellektuelle zwischen Despotie und Demo-*

nings, the dialogue remained an important format taken up by successors and mediators of Confucian lore: The *Shengyu* 聖諭 (Words of the Sages) refers to the doctrinal conversations of Mencius, advisor of princes and arbiter of Confucian teachings in the fourth century BC.[8]

Taking up both strands this book's cover image shows a fictitious dialogue between the philosophical cultures of Europe and China. Raffael's fresco *La scuola di Atene* (The School of Athens, fig. 5) dating from 1510/11 provides the framing hinting not only at the architecture of the agora but also at Aristotle, one of the most prominent philosophers of European Antiquity. As his dialogue partner, a (Zen/Chan-)Buddhist monk called Foyin 佛印 (Xie Duanqing 谢端卿, 1032–1098) takes Plato's place, leaning on a barrel of vinegar. These elements are taken from a late nineteenth-century Chinese drawing by Zhu Jianqiu, an artist of the New Culture Movement. This generic subject titled *Sanchangsuan* (Three Vinegar Tasters, fig. 10) joins prominent representatives of Buddhism, Confucianism, and Taoism in conversation.[9]

Joining the European Renaissance in fruitful dialogue and exchange with Chinese thought perfectly fits the approach of this series. As its opening volume, the productive, discipline-crossing dialogue between historian Thomas Maissen and sinologist Barbara Mittler on questions of periodization in different cultural contexts makes a wonderful start. This series strives to bring together intellectual debates from different world regions. Moreover, besides traditional academic formats like research monographs or collections of articles, the series welcomes less conventional forms. We look forward to fruitful debates on global ideation, the transfer and entanglement of ideas, and the methodological challenges, which need to be addressed in this field of study.

In recent years, global intellectual history has rapidly emerged as one of the most dynamic academic fields in the humanities, with the potential to revolutionize the ways in which we imagine key categories of thought, in relation to politics, economy, social relations, law, theology, or temporality. Intel-

---

kratisierung, eds. Heike Mallm, Kersten Reich (Cologne: Verlag Demokratie, Dialektik und Ästhetik, 1989), 54–95.
8 Phan, Peter C. Catholicism and Confucianism. An intercultural and interreligious dialogue. In *Catholicism and interreligious dialogue*, ed. James Heft (New York: Oxford University Press, 2012), 169–207.
9 In the original image, the Buddhist monk Foyin (Xie Duanqing) is lost in discussion with the Confucian Su Shi (Su Dongpo) and the Daoist Huang Luzhi (Huang Tingjian). We would like to thank the graphic designer Christiane Illius as well as Gregor Stiebert, research associate at the Chair for history of the early modern period, Heidelberg, for image acquisitions and the design of this fitting collage.

lectual and conceptual histories, in both Anglo-American and German traditions in the post-World War II decades, remained mainly focused on Europe and North America. In parallel and with an ironic simultaneity, subaltern studies and postcolonial scholarship emerged to foreground the agency of extra-European actors in realms of concept-production. There were some intersections between these parallel strands, such as when Anglo-American scholars wrote about intellectual histories of colonialism,[10] or when Indian postcolonial historians expropriated European philosophical traditions, from Hegel to Foucault and beyond.[11] A more comprehensive convergence only appeared in the twenty-first century. The publication of the volume *Global Intellectual History*, edited by Samuel Moyn and Andrew Sartori (2013),[12] marks something of a watershed. The last few years have seen a burgeoning of volumes, which deal, with greater or lesser degrees of explicitness, with transregional, transnational, and global frames in relation to intellectual production. Several volumes now carry "Global Intellectual History" (or some variant) as part of their title; they deal with a wide variety of themes including evangelicalism, notions of culture, international law, positivism, or ideas about the Muslim world.[13] The scholarly world proved receptive to these endeavours. A new journal, titled *Global Intellectual History*, has emerged in 2016 while older journals, such as *Modern Intellectual History*, have expanded their focus on the extra-European world. There are now regular series of academic events, including at the University of Cambridge ("Global Intellectual History Seminar") and Ludwig-Maximilians-Universität Munich ("Global Intellectual History as Polit-

---

10 For example: Stokes, Eric. *The English Utilitarians and India* (Oxford: Clarendon Press 1959). Travers, Robert. *Ideology and Empire in Eighteenth-Century India. The British Bengal* (Cambridge: Cambridge University Press, 2007).
11 For example: Chatterjee, Partha. *The Nation and its Fragments: Colonial and Postcolonial Histories* (Princeton: Princeton University Press, 1993). Spivak, Gayatri Chakravorty. *A Critique of Postcolonial Reason. Toward a History of the Vanishing Present* (Cambridge: Harvard University Press, 1999). Guha, Ranajit. *History at the Limit of World-History* (New York: Columbia University Press, 2002).
12 Moyn, Samuel, Sartori, Andrew, eds., *Global Intellectual History* (Columbia Studies in International and Global History) (New York: Columbia University Press, 2013).
13 Ward, William R. *Early Evangelicalism. A Global Intellectual History, 1670–1789* (New York: Cambridge University Press, 2006). Sartori, Andrew. *Bengal in Global Concept History. Culturalism in the Age of Capital* (Chicago: University of Chicago Press, 2008). Becker Lorca, Arnulf. *Mestizo International Law. A Global Intellectual History, 1842–1933* (Cambridge: Cambridge University Press, 2016). Aydin, Cemil. *The Idea of the Muslim World. A Global Intellectual History* (Cambridge: Harvard University Press, 2017). Feichtinger, Johannes, Fillafer, Franz L., Surman, Jan, eds., *The Worlds of Positivism: A Global Intellectual History, 1770–1930* (Cham: Palgrave Macmillan, 2018).

ical and Ethical Critique.")[14] The graduate school "Global Intellectual History" jointly run by Freie Universität Berlin and Humboldt-Universität Berlin, represents yet another sign of academic enthusiasm about this nascent field.[15]

Still, one should refrain from painting too rosy a picture of a global academic community jointly researching and discussing a common intellectual heritage. Due to socio-economic inequalities and the intensive funding that archival research surrounding global history often requires, the fulcrum of global intellectual history scholarship – at least in an institutionalized way – remains in Europe and North America. Undoubtedly, there are significant exceptions. Increasingly, scholars located beyond Europe and North America are making significant interventions in the field, drawing on rich extra-European intellectual traditions. Global intellectual history increasingly features in university curricula: the introduction of courses on early modern and modern global intellectual history in Presidency University, Kolkata, represents an important trend.[16] Certainly, a comprehensive democratization of scholarship in this field is dependent on the reduction of socio-economic inequalities on a worldwide scale. Within such obvious material limits, there are hopeful trends.

One way in which global intellectual history scholarship can contribute to widening the scope of extra-European contributions, and to reducing inequalities of knowledge (and beyond), is by establishing a more profound relation with critical thinking and critical politics. It is worth remembering that radical transformations in scholarly enquiry have generally been nourished by, and fed into, radical political movements, such as decolonization, peasant and working class struggles, feminism, and environmental movements. In this series, we hope to intensify some of these connections between critical thinking and practice, and global intellectual history. While it is not to be expected – nor necessarily desirable – that every volume in the series will bear its politics on its sleeve in the same manner, we hope and expect that they will contribute to reducing the staggering epistemic as much as material inequalities that structure the world we inhabit. Obviously, this does not imply a departure from academic probity. There is still a great need for foundational research and especially the deconstructivist reversal of normalized ideological usurpations, methodological nationalism, and modernist marginalization since the nineteenth century. These general methodological concerns are especially demanding for global intellectual history, which faces considerable challenges

---

14 www.hist.cam.ac.uk/seminars/global-intellectual-history; www.japan.uni-muenchen.de/personal/gastwissenschaftler/banerjee/banerjee_intellectual_history/index.html.
15 www.gih.global-history.de/.
16 www.presiuniv.ac.in/web/ugphhistsyl16.pdf.

on how to conceptualize the multifarious modes of interaction including migration, transculturation, adaption, imitation, and translation of ideas. Knowledge production and intellectual debate do not stop at borders, but intellectual history often has. The older history of ideas has contributed its fair share to the naturalization and petrification of seemingly enclosed national "cultures," to which a canon of great (male) thinkers provided useful building blocks. Global intellectual history needs to take a critical stance and reflect, test and refine recent advances in methodology and theory that deal with the complexities of a transcultural world. Moreover, a growing body of international research has demonstrated that global history cannot be confined to the contemporary or modern periods. Rather, it has become clear that the early modern world has been shaped distinctively by global interconnections and entangled processes.[17] Globally oriented intellectual histories equally need to account for dissonances, ruptures, and breakdowns (or deliberate occlusions) in connection, as much as issues of intellectual transfer and entanglement. No consensus is in sight as to just how exactly existing narratives need to be modified to take these critical reorientations into account. The epithet "critical" in the series consciously alludes to these objects as a field of tension. The academically sound way of dealing with tensions that may arise is to keep up the conversation, to cherish a dialogue of many voices, without blanking out structural, political, or epistemological concerns.

The pathways through which these challenges will be addressed may open in unfamiliar ways. They may open up through methodological debates, for instance, on time and periodization – the concern of this first volume in the series; they may happen through explicit engagement with decolonial insurgencies; they may happen through the unearthing of forgotten strata of thought or their intersections. Thereby the series hopes to be of interest not only to scholars whose regional or temporal specialization matches a particular volume, but also to both experts and graduate students aiming for general orientation in the emerging field of global intellectual history. The series does not believe that it is possible to identify particular factors as single causes, which overdetermine

---

[17] In fact, this holds true also to the ancient and medieval periods. See, e.g. Scott, Michael. *Ancient worlds. A global history of antiquity* (New York: Basic Books, 2016). Borgolte, Michael, Tischler, Matthias M., eds., *Transkulturelle Verflechtungen im mittelalterlichen Jahrtausend. Europa, Ostasien, Afrika* (Darmstadt: Wissenschaftliche Buchgesellschaft, 2012). For the various ways in which a transcultural perspective can reorient multi-disciplinary scholarship on Asia and Europe since ancient times also see Abu-er-Rub, Laila, Brosius, Christiane, Meurer, Sebastian, Panagiotopoulos, Diamantis, Richter, Susan, eds., *Engaging Transculturality. Concepts, key terms, case studies* (New York: Routledge (in press)).

trajectories of globalized intellectual production. Instead, it aims at exploring variegated pathways of comparative and connected histories, and hopes that such diversified argumentation may ultimately even open up new ways of imagining decolonial futures for a world to come, a world that welcomes many voices.

Prologue

Barbara Mittler & Thomas Maissen
Periodization in a global context

By producing and reproducing periodization schemes, naming and renaming epochal moments, scholars structure and delimit narratives of temporality. Periodization is comfortable and may even be unavoidable. Yet it is problematic, not least because any criterion demarcating periods of time is necessarily arbitrary. Periodization schemes tend to be far too general to encompass all the important phenomena in a given time or region. They are neither inert nor innocent. Often, they have normative or teleological implications, and they bear the risk of ideologizing or essentializing. Many historians, among them prominent scholars such as Jacques Le Goff or Reinhart Koselleck, have questioned, therefore, not only the arbitrary choices of particular periodizations, but the very practice of using periods in general.[1] Historicizing the issue itself, the historian of philosophy Kurt Flasch went so far as to state: "The concept 'epoch' had its time, and its time is over."[2]

Problems of periodization are particularly apparent in world history as it has been conceived since the Enlightenment. To "take up ownership of the past"[3] can be seen as a manipulation, an imperialist "theft of history" even.[4] If specific "regimes of historicity"[5] are imposed upon others, they are "dictating particular ways of seeing and thinking."[6] World history has for a long time been written by historians looking for an explanation of the "rise of the West."[7] Accordingly, the occidental experience and its periodization schemes have been used as a matrix for judging the progress – and often the backwardness – of other regions of the world. This world has been interpreted for a long time as exclusively determined and structured by the European states which, since the late fifteenth cen-

---

1 Jacques Le Goff, *Faut-il vraiment découper l'histoire en tranches?* (Paris: Seuil, 2014), 187–91, argues especially against the Renaissance as an epoch and in favor of "long" Middle Ages. The case of Koselleck is more ambiguous, see Helge Jordheim, "Against Periodization: Koselleck's Theory of Multiple Temporalities," *History and Theory* 51 (2012).
2 Kurt Flasch, "Epoche," in *Philosophie hat Geschichte*, vol. 1: *Historische Philosophie. Beschreibung einer Denkart* (Frankfurt am Main: Klostermann, 2003), 134.
3 Janet L. Nelson, "The Dark Ages," *History Workshop Journal* 63 (2007): 191–92.
4 Jack Goody, *The Theft of History* (Cambridge: Cambridge University Press, 2006).
5 François Hartog, *Régimes d'historicité. Présentisme et expériences du temps* (Paris: Seuil, 2002).
6 Serge Gruzinski, *Quelle heure est-il là-bas? Amérique et islam à l'orée des temps modernes* (Paris: Seuil, 2008), 81; quote on 184.
7 William H. McNeill, *The Rise of the West: A History of the Human Community* (Chicago: Chicago University Press, 1963).

tury, had brought – often in violent ways – the six continents into commercial, political and cultural exchange. By the twenty-first century, the European preponderance for explaining past and present on a global scale is no longer a given and the same is true for the epochal frames coined in Europe. On the other hand, European attempts at structuring *the* History in a linear and often teleological way have become hugely successful models globally, as have particular periodization schemes. These are not transnational or even universal, however, for they all reveal clear cultural, social, and national leanings and predispositions.

Our aim in this interdisciplinary dialogue, which brings together a scholar of early modern (European) history and a scholar of (modern) Chinese history,[8] is modest. We do not claim to solve these problems of periodization.[9] Indeed, we recognize the epochal frames as useful pragmatic tools. In this, we agree with Johan Huizinga, who was rightly suspicious of "every name for a period which is taken too literally, or behind which too much is sought," but also declared, "We cannot do without the names of periods, because they have become filled with meaning that is valuable to us, even though every attempt to motivate their validity only demonstrates the contrary."[10] In this light, we do not try to develop – and even less impose – new, or more valid periodization schemes, but instead reflect upon their cultural framings, and thus the possibilities and limitations of their transfer. We do so in order to rethink some of the dynamics behind the particular cultural and historical uses of periodization schemes as concepts for ordering the past and "devised to think the world."[11] One of our starting points is a set of questions formulated by Jerry Bentley in 1996 about periodiza-

---

8 Already the fact that one of our disciplines is defined with a focus on a clear time frame (early modern) and the other with a focus on a very broad regional frame (China), (Sinology – includes much more than just millennia of Chinese history, but also China's languages, literatures, music, economy, politics, etc.), speaks to fundamental differences in thinking about the world in each of our disciplines.
9 For a recent discussion of the problems, see Stéphane Gibert, Jean Le Bihan and Florian Mazel (eds.), *Découper le temps. Actualité de la périodisation en histoire* (= *Atala. Cultures et sciences humaines* 17, 2014) and especially Gibert's introduction "Les enjeux renouvelés d'un problème fondamental: la périodisation en histoire," (7–31), but also Christian Grataloup's reflections on global history in "Les périodes sont des régions du Monde," (65–81, and especially 77–81).
10 See Jan Huizinga, "The Task of Cultural History," in *Men and Ideas: History, the Middle Ages, the Renaissance*, trans. James S. Holmes and Hans van Marle (London: Eyre and Spottiswoode, 1960), 75, 69.
11 This formulation is taken from a recent controversial debate about a parallel term "Enlightenment" and its use in a global context, see Sebastian Conrad, "Enlightenment in Global History: A Historiographical Critique," *The American Historical Review* 117, no. 4 (2012): 1011.

tion in world history: "To what extent is it possible to identify periods that are both meaningful and coherent across the boundary lines of societies and cultural regions? What criteria or principles might help historians to sort out patterns of continuity and change and to distinguish such periods?"[12] Our answers to this, each from our specialized perspectives, will diverge considerably.

In our dialogue, we will focus on the Renaissance. With all the controversy it engenders and the many uses to which it is put, the Renaissance may be seen as an emblematic case to study the advantages and shortcomings of periodization as a practice. Joan Kelly's famous article "Did women have a Renaissance?" and the negative answer she must give, highlights one significant shortcoming mentioned above: epochal frames are clearly not all-inclusive, neither generalizable nor applicable as a common experience to all.[13] Our dialogue proposes to expand this argument and add another – the global – dimension. By asking how and why the Renaissance, as a powerful epochal frame and idea, moved to China and what that means, we are seeking to test whether and how "Renaissance" can be applicable as a common experience across social, cultural, and even historical boundaries. Thus, we take up the question formulated by the late Jack Goody in his last book *Renaissances – The One or the Many* in 2010: are "renascences," as Goody chooses to calls them, a common historical pattern or generic model – an anthropological constant even – and is the Western claim for the superiority of their particular Italian and occidental Renaissance, therefore, just part of a Eurocentric "theft of history"?[14] In 1954, Arnold Toynbee suggested that the Renaissance in Italy was "no more than one particular instance of a recurrent historical phenomenon."[15] More cautiously, and in a more comparative vein, Peter Burke, too, has pondered to what extent the Italian Renaissance can be "globalized" – that is, compared as an analytical type or category not only with other periods in Europe but also with other parts of the globe.[16]

---

12 Jerry H. Bentley, "Cross-Cultural Interaction and Periodization in World History," *The American Historical Review* 101, no. 3 (1996): 749.
13 Joan Kelly-Gadol, "Did Women Have a Renaissance?" in *Becoming Visible. Women in European History*, ed. Renate Bridenthal and Claudia Koonz (Boston: Houghton Mifflin, 1977).
14 Jack Goody, *Renaissances: The One or the Many* (Cambridge: Cambridge University Press, 2010). Goody develops an argument introduced first in his *The Theft of History*, 125–153, in the chapter on "Science and civilization in Renaissance Europe." See also Peter Burke, "Jack Goody and the Comparative History of Renaissances," *Theory, Culture & Society* 26, no. 7–8 (December 2009).
15 Arnold J. Toynbee, *A Study of History*, vol. 9 (London: Oxford University Press, 1954), 4.
16 Peter Burke, "Renaissance Europe and the World," in *Palgrave Advances in Renaissance Historiography*, ed. Jonathan Woolfson (Basingstoke: Palgrave Macmillan, 2005). See also his commentary on "Jack Goody and the Comparative History of Renaissances," mentioned above, and

Other scholars are no longer describing the particularities and inventions of the fifteenth and sixteenth century as an exclusively European phenomenon but as a product of cultural exchanges. In 1995, Claire Farago invited art historians to "reframe" the Renaissance, reevaluating the Eurocentrism of Italian Renaissance art history by envisioning how the history of Renaissance art would look if cultural interaction and the conditions of reception became the primary focus.[17] In *Florence and Baghdad: Renaissance Art and Arab Science* (2011), Hans Belting points to the role of Muslim theoreticians in the development of central perspective. In her current book project on *The Global Renaissance*, Anne Dunlop uses a similar point of departure, while Bernd Roeck studies European developments from an entangled comparative perspective.[18]

Another alternative to writing a global history of the Renaissance has been suggested by Patrick Boucheron and Serge Gruzinski. They do not ask how a "type" that could be called "renaissance," or "renascence," has played out globally. Instead, they suggest writing a global history of the time when Europe experienced the Renaissance; thus, Boucheron deliberately substitutes "Renaissance" with "Fifteenth Century,"[19] and Gruzinski's narrative, where Renaissance becomes merely a particular (axial?) time frame (the fourteenth to sixteenth centuries), seeks to be "less stubbornly Eurocentric" and "more in tune with our age."[20] Even while remaining faithful to the European time frame, Gruzinski does not take the European experience as a central starting-point, but instead sets out to scrutinize and rethink European feelings of superiority, all the

---

his outline "Western Historical Thinking in a Global Perspective – 10 Theses," in *Western Historical Thinking. An Intercultural Debate*, ed. Jörn Rüsen (New York: Berghahn Books, 2002), 15–30, 189–196 (Reply), where he maintains that the linear view of the past as development or progress is the most important characteristic of Western historiographical thought.

17 Claire Farago (ed.), *Reframing the Renaissance: Visual Culture in Europe and Latin America 1450 to 1650* (New Haven and London: Yale University Press, 1995).

18 Anne Dunlop's forthcoming book on *The Global Renaissance: a Survey* is an introduction to the global movement of artistic images, objects, and ideas about art in the period between about 1400 and 1700; Bernd Roeck, *Der Morgen der Welt. Geschichte der Renaissance*, (Munich: C.H. Beck, 2017); Roeck also convened the conference at the German Historical Institute in Rome on "Renaissancen global? Die europäische Renaissance im transkulturellen Vergleich," 13–14 October 2016; see the review in *Quellen und Forschungen aus italienischen Archiven und Bibliotheken* (2017), 96(1): 513–515.

19 Patrick Boucheron (ed.). *Histoire du monde au XVᵉ siècle* (Paris: Fayard, 2009); see also Patrick Boucheron and Nicolas Delalande, *Pour une histoire-monde* (Paris: PUF, 2013).

20 Serge Gruzinski, *The Eagle and the Dragon: Globalization and European Dreams of Conquest in China and America in the Sixteenth Century*, trans. Jean Birell (Cambridge: Polity Press, 2014), 4.

while reconsidering the history of the Renaissance as the history of a time of global "discoveries" and mutual (re-)cognition.[21]

Reframing Renaissance from our particular interdisciplinary perspective, between the "early modern" history of Europe and the "modern" history of China, we will further deliberate on "*the* Renaissance" and its travels to China as part of a broader discussion about (new) vocabularies used to study history within a global context. We ask ourselves how to write global history or global histories in terms that are both adequate for the respective contemporary experiences and understandable to audiences all over the world. To what extent can we avoid that only particular (and essentialized) associations and interpretations linked with particular terminologies by particular interpretive communities are accepted as a standard, without, on the other hand, losing these same particular meanings for a term in overarching universalizing generalization?[22] To what extent are the term Renaissance and the periodization scheme it stands for – not unlike the term Enlightenment discussed recently and controversially by Sebastian Conrad – equally "heavily invested with notions of European uniqueness and superiority"?[23] We will debate whether such terms could and should be used to describe phenomena in places other than particular parts of occidental Europe where these epochal frames and the concepts surrounding them were once engendered and if so, what this entails for our schemes of ordering the past here and elsewhere. We will do so in deliberately dialectic fashion. In our dialogue, each of us will be retaining their own disciplinary stance and subjective voice, presented as thesis and antithesis, and thus clearly drawing out the contradictions and inconsistencies between them that are caused by our own disciplinary myopia and *déformations professionnelles*.

Our dialogue will be organized in three parts: after the introduction, in which each of us will present some of our main arguments, we begin, briefly, by contextualizing uses of the "Renaissance" within different models for periodization in Western Europe and China – cyclical and linear, religious and secular. The particular historical and historiographical contexts in which "Renaissance" appears and is used in Western Europe and in China will then be discussed in the second part of our dialogue. Our disagreement on fundamental issues

---

[21] Gruzinski, *The Eagle and the Dragon*, 2. For a summary of his argument, see especially the conclusion, "Towards a Global History of the Renaissance," 238–244. Characteristically, he begins his study by citing the Chinese servant in Paul Claudel's *The Satin Slipper* (1929), saying to Don Rodrigo, Viceroy of the Indies: "We have captured each other, and there is no way of getting unstuck."
[22] See Conrad, "Enlightenment in Global History."
[23] Conrad, "Enlightenment in Global History," 1005.

about why China did not have a Renaissance and why that matters, will be exposed in each of our conclusions. We share an awareness of the problems in writing a new kind of global history which no longer takes the European case as a singular and monolithic central matrix and which does not treat other historical developments as deficient copies thereof, but we do not agree on how best to solve them. The synthesis engendered from the kind of interactive rather than additive, interdisciplinary dialogue that we are presenting here may be a first step towards developing a new form of transdisciplinary hermeneutics for the writing of global history – one that goes across and thus beyond disciplinary borders.

To our readers, we present the dialogue as a new form of decentered antagonistic intervention that may help to open up new avenues of thinking. It may seem appropriate that we have chosen a form that was also popular with the humanists of the Renaissance – namely, a dialogue that not only spans over centuries, but that hopes to link areas and disciplines which still have a lot to learn from each other. The structure of a dialogue allows us to scrutinize one another and enables us to rethink our premises and standpoints and, even while remaining firm on some or even all of these positions, to transform ourselves (as did the humanists) in an effort to learn from what is far removed in space, time and language but is nonetheless relevant to understanding the present.

If through dialogue, we are willing to open ourselves to the logic of others and to the always complex and internally contested intellectual communities from which other voices and texts emerge, we will allow their lines of argument and concerns to lead us to unexpected forms of knowledge and towards the possibility of reconfirming as well as criticizing our own disciplinary positions.[24]

Not unlike the humanist dialogue, our endeavor is ultimately analytical and not didactic, then:[25] we do not set out, primarily, to find a final answer to our particular question but instead to stimulate further discussion. This dialogue does not aim at defending and propagating one "true" definition of "Renaissance" – such a thing does not exist – but intends, rather, to open our eyes to the specific historiographical background and the particular preconditions of our disciplines and, in a larger sense, the (trans-)cultural contexts we are working within.

---

[24] See Leigh K. Jenco, "Recentering Political Theory: The Promise of Mobile Locality," *Cultural Critique* 79 (2011): 55.
[25] For an extensive discussion of the significance of dialogue in the Renaissance, see Thomas Maissen, below, p. 64–66.

Introduction

Barbara Mittler
Epochal changes in a global context – Toward a History-in-common[1]

The beginning of the sixteenth century ... presented at the same time the greatest spectacles that the world had ever seen.... At that time Nature produced extraordinary men in almost every field, especially in Italy. What is still striking in that outstanding century is that despite the wars caused by ambition and the religious disputes which had begun to disturb European states, that same genius which made the fine arts flourish at Rome, Naples, Florence, Venice, Ferrara, and brought their light from Italy to Europe, first refined men's manners over almost all Christendom.... Prosperity made its contribution ... Industries were stimulated everywhere.... in a word, Europe saw the birth of great days. F. M. A. DE VOLTAIRE: *Essay on Universal History, the Manners, and Spirit of Nations*, 1756[2]

When Renaissance men and Enlightenment *philosophes* attacked Christianity, scholasticism, and the "Dark" Middle Ages, they were armed with the classics of Greek and Roman antiquity. In other words, they were guided by an inner light. By contrast, May Fourth intellectuals had to go out of their darkened cave – China – in order to see the light of day; they were guided by a light from outside – the West. YU YING-SHIH "Neither Renaissance, nor Enlightenment," 2001[3]

If Johan Huizinga was convinced that "we cannot do without the names of periods,"[4] the protagonists both of the Chinese and the European Renaissances and

---

[1] I am adapting the phrase "History-in-common" from a parallel usage by Japan historian Carol Gluck who, during her keynote lecture, at the Heidelberg Cluster of Excellence "Asia and Europe in a Global Context" Annual Conference, October 9–11, 2013, spoke on "Modernity in Common: Japan and World History." She summarized her use of the term as follows: "Just as the modern history of a society cannot be explained in isolation from the world, it is also possible to explore the history of the modern world from the vantage point of any particular place in the existing 'globeful of modernities.' Here, that place is Japan, which because it shares commonalities and connections with other modern societies offers the opportunity to think about the 'modern' on empirical bases different from the European experiences that underlay earlier theories of modernity."
[2] F.M.A. de Voltaire, *An Essay on Universal History: the Manners, and Spirit of Nations, from the Reign of Charlemagne to the Age of Lewis XIV.* Written in French by M. de Voltaire. Translated into English, with additional notes and chronological tables, by Mr. Nugent. The second edition, revised, and considerably improved by the author (London: printed for J. Nourse at the Lamb opposite Katherine-Street in the Strand, 1759), Chapter xcvii, 377–378. Voltaire was translated into Chinese by Fu Lei among others, see *Modern China and the West: Translation and Cultural Mediation*, ed. Hsiao-yen Peng and Isabelle Rabut (Leiden: Brill, 2014).
[3] Yu Ying-shih, "Neither Renaissance nor Enlightenment: A Historian's Reflections on the May Fourth Movement," in *The Appropriation of Cultural Capital: China's May Fourth Project*, ed. by Milena Doleželová-Velingerová and Oldřich Král (Cambridge: Harvard University Press, 2001), 312.
[4] Huizinga, "The Task of Cultural History," 69.

the scholars studying these movements appear ready to support this idea. The term itself, 'epoch' *shidai* 時代 or 'period,' had become, by the mid-1920s one of the most important catchwords among the protagonists of the New Culture Movement 新文化運動 *Xin wenhua yundong* – a movement which they also called The Chinese Renaissance.[5]

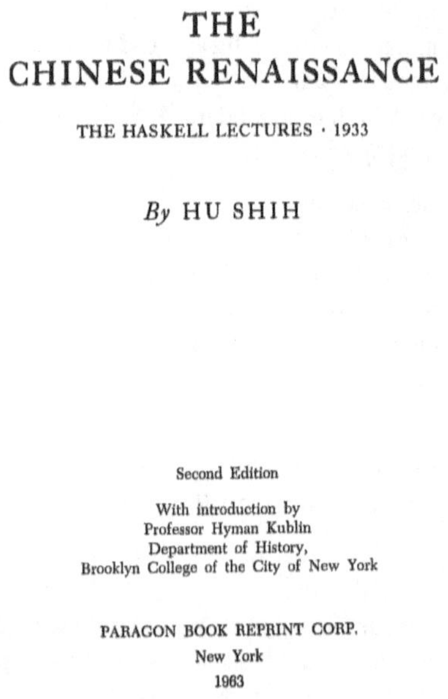
THE
CHINESE RENAISSANCE

THE HASKELL LECTURES · 1933

By HU SHIH

Second Edition

With introduction by
Professor Hyman Kublin
Department of History,
Brooklyn College of the City of New York

PARAGON BOOK REPRINT CORP.
New York
1963

Fig. 1 Title Page Hu Shi. *The Chinese Renaissance* 中国的文艺复兴 (*The Haskell Lectures*, 1933).

Indeed, the prefaces to one of its seminal works, a 1933 book entitled *The Chinese Renaissance* (see fig. 1), by Hu Shi 胡適 (1891–1962), are unanimous in seeing "epochal changes then overtaking China."[6] In their view, the protagonists of the Chinese Renaissance, not unlike those of the European Renaissance, staged themselves and their movement as one of unprecedented importance: the New Culture Movement was considered by contemporaries to be the "ushering in of a brand new age,"[7] one that was destined to be as brilliant as the European

5 Yu, "Neither Renaissance nor Enlightenment," 31.
6 Hyman Kublin, preface to *The Chinese Renaissance*, by Hu Shi (New York: Paragon Book Reprint Corp., 1963), no page (quote is on 2nd page of preface).
7 Zhao Jiabi, preface to *The Great Series of China's New Literature* (*Zhongguo xin wenxue daxi*), vol. 1 (Shanghai: Liangyou tushu gongsi, 1935), 1.

Renaissance.⁸ Hu Shi writes in his own preface: "I want my readers to understand that cultural changes of tremendous significance have taken place and are taking place in China.... Slowly, quietly, but unmistakably, the Chinese Renaissance is becoming a reality."⁹ He admits, that to compare oneself with the European Renaissance "may sound a little conceited, especially from the lips of one who has taken a personal part in this new movement. The Renaissance is, of course, the term usually associated with that great movement in Western history which heralded modern Europe." But still, he considers the use of the term adequate and therefore, in his own words: "The same name has been accorded to the far-reaching changes in thought and action which have swept over China during the last ten years."¹⁰ Hu Shi is also sure to distinguish "his" Renaissance, the New Culture Movement, from other movements in Chinese history that had been called "renaissances" before.¹¹ All of those, so he states,

> suffered from one common defect, namely, the absence of a conscious recognition of their historical mission. There was no conscious effort nor articulate interpretation: all of those were natural developments of historical tendencies and were easily overpowered or swept away by the conservative force of tradition against which they had only dimly and unconsciously combated. Without this conscious element, the new movements remained natural processes of revolution, and never achieved the work of revolution.¹²

In his mind, "his" Renaissance was distinctive. It was aware of its own import and, accordingly, it "was capturing the imagination and sympathy of the youth of the nation as something which promised and pointed to the new birth of an old people and an old civilization."¹³ It was this quality which, according to him, formed its likeness with the European Renaissance, since it is only certain periods and times which feel themselves to be "epochal."

Thus, the protagonists both of the Chinese and the European Renaissance appear to have been conscious that their break with the (medieval) past was deliberate and unprecedented in their own history. Hans Blumenberg sees the development of early modern times (*Frühe Neuzeit*) in Europe as a direct conse-

---

8 Kyle D. Anderson, "Promises of Modern Renaissance. Italian Presences in Chinese Modernity" (PhD diss., Pennsylvania State University, 2010), 63.
9 Hu Shi, preface to *The Chinese Renaissance* 中国的文艺复兴 (*The Haskell Lectures*, 1933) (Chicago: The University of Chicago Press; London: Cambridge University Press, 1934), no page.
10 Hu Shi, "The Renaissance in China," *Journal of the Royal Institute of International Affairs* 5 (1926): 265–266.
11 See Hu, *Chinese Renaissance* (1963), 45.
12 Hu, *Chinese Renaissance* (1963), 45–46.
13 Hu, *Chinese Renaissance* (1963), 44.

quence of Renaissance rhetorics – their conscious break with the past – and he considers their awareness of rupture unique in European history.[14] Moreover, he considers the self-exegesis, or the performance of self by early modern protagonists, to be crucial to this epochal formation.[15] Renaissance men thought of themselves as living in a new kind of age, an *aetas nova*. Not unlike the protagonists in the New Culture Movement, they used the verb *renascere* (among other metaphors) to refer to their achievements because they were convinced that they were reviving the creative spirit of the ancients. The very use of the term "Renaissance" – a new or a re-birth – thus became a "significant element of the epoch,"[16] and this characteristic was important to those inspired by *the* Renaissance in China.

The idea of Renaissance (first known as *rinascita*) in Europe was invariably connected with (and caused, or enabled by) the notion of an age of darkness and obscurity that preceded it – the Middle Ages – and thus, engendered a need to "break free" from this age and all its implications. In emphasizing the darkness of this previous age, just as in *chiaroscuro*, the brightness of the new age shines ever more brightly.[17] Only differential analysis can show what separates two eras beyond an epochal breaking point.[18] And indeed, it was by stressing this strong opposition between dark and bright, between dead and (newly) alive etc. that Europe's and China's Renaissances actually became the epochal breaks described both by contemporaries and by later scholars.[19]

---

14 Hans Blumenberg, *Aspekte der Epochenschwelle* (Frankfurt am Main: Suhrkamp, 1976), 13: "Ein Bewußtsein der entschiedenen Trennung von einer Vergangenheit, wie es die frühe Neuzeit ausgebildet hat, kann keiner anderen Epoche in ähnlicher Weise abverlangt werden." He continues (ibid., 18): "Für den Beginn der Neuzeit könnten die Bedingungen einzigartig sein. Und sie sind es. ... Vielmehr darf das Programm der Neuzeit nicht als kontinente Urzeugung angenommen werden: die Entfaltung ihrer begrifflichen Voraussetzungen reflektiert schon die singuläre Struktur der Bedürfnisse, die sich in der Autokatalyse des mittelalterlichen Systems zwingend herausgebildet hatten."
15 Blumenberg, *Epochenschwelle*, 19: "Die Neuzeit also ist, im Unterschied zum Mittelalter, nicht eher da als ihre Selbstauslegung, durch die sie zwar nicht hervorgetrieben wird, deren sie aber ständig zu ihrer Formierung bedarf."
16 Blumenberg, *Epochenschwelle*, 19: "Das macht den Epochenbegriff selbst zum signifikanten Element der Epoche."
17 Hans Blumenberg "Licht als Metapher der Wahrheit," in *Ästhetische und metaphorologische Schriften,* ed. Anselm Haverkamp (Frankfurt am Main: Suhrkamp, 2001), 143.
18 Blumenberg, *Epochenschwelle*, 20–21.
19 For a short discussion of how different intellectual and political groups in Europe and China have used the imagery of light and dark in the making of historical periodizations and how the use of these metaphors has changed from the analogy to natural circularity (the day following the night) to a more linear evolutionary structure (towards Enlightenment), see Thomas Maissen

For the Italian Renaissance, the "dark Middle Ages" were constitutive because they had obscured an idealized cultural reference that lay in the distant past of Antiquity – their "inner light" as Yu Yingshi, a historian of the New Culture Movement, would have it.[20] When Chinese authors in the early twentieth century took up the metaphor of overcoming darkness as part of their effort to change China's politics, society and mentality, their condemnation of the structures of their so-called feudal past were inspired by their particular understanding of the European Renaissance, or the "light from outside – the West," as Yu Yingshi had put it. In a famous 1915 letter by Huang Yuanyong 黃遠庸 (1885– 1915) to Hu Shi, in which he advocates the use of the vernacular as the solution to all of China's problems, this model is directly addressed: "Have we not seen that historians regard the European Renaissance as the foundation of the overthrow of medievalism in Europe?"[21] The idea, that China had become caught in a "medievalism" similar to the Europe of several centuries earlier, and that a "renaissance" was, therefore, the only means by which "modernity" could be achieved, was based on this understanding of historical development and epochal change in Europe. In China, "Renaissance" thus came to be understood as a rebirth, a forward-looking, transformation – a movement from shade towards the light.[22]

To Hu and his contemporaries, the protagonists in the New Culture Movement in China were like their counterparts in Europe whose Renaissance put an end to "unfathomable darkness and mystery."[23] China would move, inevitably, towards an ever-brighter future. The imagery of light and dark enabled these self-conscious historical actors to present themselves as the intellectual torchbearers in a fight against antagonists who in many cases were their own contemporaries, but whose thoughts were styled as representing those of an outlived past. Thus, their polemics against the "dark" Middle Ages[24] is a self-referential hint at the epochal change which these two "rebirth movements" were convinced that they embodied. In their pragmatic use of contrasting self-dram-

---

and Barbara Mittler, "Aus dem Dunkel ins Licht. Epochale Umbrüche in China und Europa," *Ruperto Carola Forschungsmagazin*, 7 (2015).
20 See the epithet at the beginning of this chapter.
21 The letter is cited in Hu Shi, "The Literary Renaissance," in *Symposium on Chinese Culture*, ed. Sophia H. Chen Zen (New York: Paragon Book Reprint Corp., 1969), 129. So far, I have been unable to locate the original letter in Chinese.
22 Irene Eber, "Thoughts on Renaissance in Modern China: Problems of Definition," in *Studia Asiatica: Essays in Asian Studies in Felicitation of the Seventy-Fifth Anniversary of Professor Chen Shou-yi*, ed. Laurence G. Thompson (San Francisco: Chinese Materials Center, 1975), 193.
23 Hu, *Chinese Renaissance*, 77.
24 Lucie Varga, *Das Schlagwort vom "Finsteren Mittelalter"* (Baden: Rohrer, 1932), 2.

atization, the "Fathers" of China's and of Europe's renaissances would structure (and make use of) this epochal break, as one that was made by great men. Engels's poetic description of the Renaissance in the preface to his *Dialektik der Natur* (1873), which was well-received in China in the early twentieth century, also suggests this: "It was the greatest progressive revolution that mankind has so far experienced, a time which called for giants and produced giants."[25] This view (which also echoes Voltaire's "extraordinary men," quoted in the epithet above) is crucial for a reading of Renaissance in China.

When Hu Shi describes the European as well as China's Renaissance in terms of great individuals, he constructs himself as one of the 'cultural giants' *wenhao* 文豪 who was pushing forward China's Renaissance.[26] In so doing, Hu was taking up a traditional pose – that of the outstanding intellectual concerned for his country's well-being – but it is important to note that when he called upon his people to follow him by writing in the vernacular he was also doing so in the name of the (European) Renaissance. Indeed, poised, as he felt himself to be, at the threshold of a vernacular age, he sought "to become a *figura Dantis*." By casting Dante as the paradigmatic "renaissance man" (*l'uomo universale*) and "anti-Latin hero"[27] fighting for vernacularism, he thus positioned himself as a prime mover in China's Renaissance and thus in China's modern history. He thus fulfills the new order of the times, something Liang Qichao 梁啟超 (1873–1929) had already preached in 1902 in his *New Historiography* – which we will return to below[28]– namely, that China's past millennia were a time "without history," while the new period of "people's history" would begin imminently. As the foundational historian of China's rebirth and her modernity at large, Liang also presented himself as one of its "cultural giants." Likewise, in 1905, Kang Youwei 康有為 (1858–1927) reflected in his *Italian Travelogue* 義大利遊記 *Yidali Youji* that what he was seeking for when traveling through Italy in 1904, was "not Italy as such, but an elixir (*yue* 葯) for China's rebirth (*huisheng* 回生)."[29] What he was practicing, so he wrote, was the domestication of Dante's

---

25 Mark Gamsa, "Uses and Misuses of a Chinese Renaissance," *Modern Intellectual History* 10, no. 3 (November 2013): 648 gives evidence for how frequently this quote was used in contemporary debates at the time, in Chinese.
26 Anderson, "Promises of Modern Renaissance," 64, 61.
27 Zhou Gang, *Placing the Modern Chinese Vernacular in Transnational Literature* (New York: Palgrave Macmillan, 2011), 10, 59–60 discusses Hu's rather hyperbolic descriptions of the importance of Dante in his "Modest Proposals for the Reform of Literature."
28 More below, on p. 47.
29 Kang Youwei, "Yidali Youji 義大利遊記," in *Ouzhou Shiyi Guo youji* 歐洲十一國遊記, orig. Shanghai 1905 (reprint: Beijing: Shehui kexue wenxian, 2007), 12. See Anderson, "Promises," chapter 1 passim.

"pane degli angeli" (Dante's metaphor for the knowledge he imparted to his countrymen in his *Convivio* 'The Banquet').[30] He (Kang) would cut from it "delectable strips" (*yi luan* 一臠) that he, as the privileged Chinese intellectual, would then serve up to his countrymen: "I am the cook for my dining countrymen 吾為廚人而同胞坐食之."[31]

A decade later, Guo Moruo 郭沫若 (1892–1972), in one of his dramatic poems (from the collection 'Goddesses' *Nüshen* 女神, 1916–1921), entitled "Rebirth of the Goddesses" 女神之再生 *Nüshen zhi zaisheng*, makes a similar declaration. In a powerful allegory, the poem tells the story of two goddesses who decide to return to the world to bring back the sun which had fled from the world (China) during man's incessant wars and fights. In a self-referential passage at the end of the poem, the audience is told that the poet has already disappeared in order to search for the whereabouts of the sun; everyone in the theatre is then called upon to follow him and search for the sun, ultimately to build new hope and a new future – modernity – for China. In its particular rhetoric, this dramatic poem is again typical of the kind of staging that protagonists of the New Culture Movement chose for themselves: the poets and intellectuals lead the way; they are models and saviors showing the path toward the light; they enlighten those who, benighted as they are, still languish in darkness.

And in all of this, the protagonists of the New Culture Movement were inspired by renaissance men: Huang Shi 黃石 and Hu Zanyun 胡簪雲, the translators and editors of Giovanni Boccaccio's *Decamerone* (The Decameron *Shiritan* 十日談, published in Shanghai by Kaiming shudian in 1930),[32] for example, speak of Boccaccio (as well as Luther) as men who were ahead of their times and as "well-informed seers" (*da zhi* 大智), and "daring heroes" (*da yong* 大勇).[33] They declare the *Decamerone* a vital tool in the liberation of Europe from the "Dark Ages" (黑暗時代 *hei'an shidai*) – a period which, in their words, was marred by superstition and a paucity of reason and critical thought, a time that gave "no room to breathe," and was an epoch of "murkiness and without any light of day" (暗無天日 *an wu tianri*)[34] that was characterized by political oppression and intellectual bondage. Europe's "age of darkness" was seen in parallel to China's oppressive "feudal" Confucian past and accordingly, they compared themselves – the intellectuals, politicians and military struggling to modernize the na-

---

30 For Dante's *Convivio* I, 7 as discussed by Kang Youwei, see Anderson, "Promises," 73.
31 Kang Youwei "Yidali Youji 義大利遊記," 12.
32 Anderson, "Promises," 223–224.
33 Giovanni Boccaccio, *The Decameron* 十日談 *Shiritan*, trans. Huang Shi and Hu Zanyun (Shanghai: Kaiming shudian, 1932), V; for a lengthy discussion, see Anderson, "Promises," 219.
34 Boccaccio, *Decameron*, VI; see Anderson, "Promises," 223.

tion – to Boccaccio in "penetrating" this darkness (the Chinese character 透 *tou* – to penetrate – is constantly repeated).³⁵

Everything and everyone who could possibly be "seen as having contributed to the subversion of traditional cultural and power structures (e.g. Latin, Classical Chinese, the Catholic Church, monarchy, feudalism, etc.) was hailed, in China, as taking part in a glorious spirit or age of modern progress."³⁶ To China, this reading of heroic renaissance men and the Renaissance itself as a fundamental and epochal break with the traditions and orders of the past, was important: they saw that those living in the Renaissance wanted to get rid of certain (medieval and Christian) traditions; that they had been convinced that rebirth would only be possible through a release from the bonds of medieval traditions, and that they must instigate a fundamental break with this past in order to retrieve and reconsider, under a new light and from a new perspective, the glories of Antiquity.³⁷ This Chinese interpretation thus highlighted, in particular, the Renaissance's conscious and epochal rupture with its immediate past and the fact that this allowed for a new beginning, which in turn made possible a new view of all that was (and had ever been) Chinese history.³⁸

China's leading figures in the early twentieth century thus invoked the Renaissance as a key term and the fundamental logic for the construction of their own modern national culture. For instance, Hu Shi read the Renaissance as the "root of Western modernity;"³⁹ Jiang Fangzhen in his *History of the European Renaissance* 歐洲文藝復興史 *Ouzhou wenyi fuxing shi*, written in 1921, agrees: "With regard to modern culture and society, all industry finds its begin-

---

35 Boccaccio, *Decameron*, V; see Anderson, "Promises," 220. In spite of his apparent snub to the lowest strata of society, Boccaccio, in the introduction to a later 1958 Chinese translation, is even cast as having promoted democratic ideals during the struggles between merchants and aristocrats played out on the streets of Florence in 1342. In this interpretation, Boccaccio becomes the chief supporter of the people, a preserver of republican freedom, a strict antagonist of "feudalism." He is even said to have detested the blind arrogance of the aristocracy so much, that he had himself adopted the status of a common citizen (*renmin shenfen* 人民身分) in order to perform government services. See Giovanni Boccaccio, *The Decameron/Shi ri tan*, trans. Fang Ping and Wang Keyi (Shanghai: Xin wenyi, 1958), IV and the discussion in Anderson, "Promises," 232.
36 Anderson, "Promises," 3.
37 See Matei Calinescu, *Five Faces of Modernity: Modernism, Avant-garde, Decadence, Kitsch, Postmodernism*, orig. 1977 (Durham: Duke University Press, 1987), 20.
38 Blumenberg, *Epochenschwelle*, 24 formulates this particular epochal consciousness for early modern Europe as follows: "Wenn die Neuzeit durch einen radikalen Bruch mit ihrer Vergangenheit eingeleitet worden sein sollte, so impliziert dies allemal das Zugeständnis, dass erst von diesem Neubeginn her gedacht und erkannt werden konnte, worauf es seit jeher hätte ankommen müssen."
39 Anderson, "Promises," 64.

nings in the Renaissance."⁴⁰ He continues that, therefore, "to research the Renaissance is to study the origins of contemporary European culture."⁴¹ These thinkers were recognizing the Italian Renaissance as the origin (發祥地 *faxiangdi*), the engine, even,⁴² of all "modern" developments in Europe, something which they perceived as sorely lacking in their own nation.

Their view echoes Voltaire's appraisal who, in the *Essays on Manners* cited in the epithet above, speaks of the sixteenth century as the beginning of prosperity, of industries, in short of "the birth of great days"⁴³ for Europe. The division of European history into three eras, Antiquity, the Middle Ages, and the (early) Modern Age, beginning with the early Renaissance, brought with it value judgements that were expressed in the metaphors of light and darkness, day and night, wakefulness and sleep – where classical Antiquity came to be associated with resplendent light, the Middle Ages identified as a nocturnal and oblivious "Dark Age," and the Modern, a time of re-emergence from darkness, of awakening and renascence, heralding a luminous future. This periodization scheme acquired great significance in redressing the apparently pressing problems of the Chinese nation-state.⁴⁴

The role that Renaissance played in narratives of modern Chinese developments is, in and of itself, significant: Chinese intellectuals evidently felt compelled to transplant European ideas and periodization schemes into Chinese contexts for their own reasons.⁴⁵ They adopted a specific moment from Europe's past, the Renaissance, to interpret their own history, to present their special predicament, their distinctive future perspectives as well as their particular perceptions and characteristic attitudes towards historical time. In some of the following, I will explain in more detail how and why they appropriated the explicit and latent meanings attributed to an epochal movement such as the Renaissance in order to propagate their own ideas and institutions and how, therefore, the dark

---

40 Jiang Fangzhen, *A History of the European Renaissance* 歐洲文藝復興史 *Ouzhou wenyi fuxing shi* (= Collection of Republican Texts Minguo congshu, vol. 61), orig. Shanghai: Shangwu Press 1921 (Shanghai: Shanghai shudian, 1989), 1.
41 Jiang Fangzhen, *European Renaissance*, 3.
42 Jiang Fangzhen, *European Renaissance*, 1.
43 Voltaire, *Essay on Manners*, Chapter xcvii, 377–378. For a discussion, see Peter Burke, "The Idea of Renaissance," in *The Renaissance* (London: Longman, 1964), www2.idehist.uu.se/distans/ilmh/Ren/ren-burke-the-idea.htm.
44 I follow Prasenjit Duara, *Rescuing History from the Nation: Questioning Narratives of Modern China* (Chicago: University of Chicago Press, 1995), 34. Cf. also Calinescu, *Five Faces of Modernity*, 20; Kathleen Davis and Nadia Altschul, eds., *Medievalisms in the Postcolonial World: The Idea of "The Middle Ages" Outside Europe* (Baltimore: John Hopkins University Press, 2009).
45 See Anderson, "Promises," 255.

pasts and bright presents they began to construct through use of Renaissance as a particular "chronotype" – that is, a "model" or a "pattern" through which historical time "assumes practical or conceptual significance"[46] – were shaped through global circulations of meaning.

The case of the Chinese Renaissance illustrates that, in spite of the fact that obviously, epochs do not remain the same when read transculturally,[47] this need not mean that we can let go of them altogether. Indeed, Huizinga's point that "We cannot do without the names of periods" remains a valid one.[48] Reading the Chinese Renaissance – as depicted by its own protagonists – may have taken us quite far from European conceptions of the period, however. And here, Huizinga's suspicion of "every name for a period which is taken too literally, or behind which too much is sought" may lead us to ask more of such periods and periodization schemes. It is my purpose therefore, in this dialogue to rethink their potential for fluidity and growth and for variation and differentiation in a global context. I will argue that the particular significance that specific epochal movements acquire in different times and localities, can be understood as the result of situated co-productions that transgress continental boundaries and affect perceptions of historical time in the non-European world – if not yet in Europe itself. Indeed, the question of how such reflection may in turn inspire a new perception of the European past in Europe proper, still remains to be asked and answered.[49] Did China have a "Renaissance" after all? And does that matter? While some would reserve such vocabulary for the European experience, one might also argue that, while not universal, a term such as "Renaissance" has in fact been fruitfully applied to describe other cultural and historical experien-

---

[46] John B. Bender and David D. Wellbery, eds., *Chronotypes: The Construction of Time* (Stanford: Stanford University Press, 1991), 4.

[47] See Robert D. Hume, "Construction and Legitimation in Literary History," *Review of English Studies*, new series 56, no. 226 (2005): 646: "the idea of uniformity across a period of decades is convenient but too silly even to be worth attacking." For a discussion on whether or not to discard periodization altogether, see David Feldman and Rebecca L. Spang, "Periodization, Then and Now," *History Workshop Journal* 63, no. 1 (Spring 2007).

[48] Huizinga, *Men and Ideas*, 75, 69. Further defence of periodization as a valuable intellectual enterprise can be found in Theodore K. Rabb, *The Last Days of the Renaissance & The March to Modernity* (New York: Basic Books, 2006), xx–xxi.

[49] A project conducted at the Heidelberg Centre for Transcultural Studies, *East Asian Uses of the European Past: Tracing Braided Chronotypes*, under the direction of Joachim Kurtz (Heidelberg), Tatiana Fisac (Madrid) Leigh Jenco (LSE, London) and Martin Dusinberre (Zurich), will probe some of these questions in greater detail. See http://heranet.info/eau-tbc/index.

ces – the Chinese modern being only one among the lot.⁵⁰ Even within Europe, there were indeed many (national/regional) renaissances, not just one,⁵¹ and there is also a long tradition, going back to eminent scholars such as Erwin Panofsky, of establishing medieval renaissances.⁵² It might be useful, therefore, to begin enriching our vocabularies such that we are able to include these alternative readings of "r/Renaissance" in established systems of historical periodization. Any such use of a term such as "r/Renaissance" can no longer adequately be described, in a negative sense, as "second-hand" and "derivative," even when, historically, actors may have been inspired by particular models from else-when and else-where. This is not to say, that the term "r/Renaissance" should be used arbitrarily, nor is it to say that it did not once have European roots, which it certainly did. But I would contend that it may be even more interesting to focus on the dynamics of its global interactions, to observe the processes of translation, adaptation, reinvention (or even the "renaissance") of these terms rather than to discuss how and from where a particular terminology "originated."⁵³

---

50 For a regional/cultural expansion, see Jerry Brotton, *The Renaissance Bazaar: From the Silk Road to Michelangelo* (Oxford: Oxford University Press, 2002), republished as *The Renaissance: A Very Short Introduction* (Oxford: Oxford University Press, 2005); for still more radical claims and a list of publications exemplifying the "trend toward an increasingly cross-cultural, global perspective on Renaissance Europe," see the editor's introduction in Jyotsna G. Singh, ed., *A Companion to the Global Renaissance: English Literature and Culture in the Era of Expansion* (Malden, Mass.: Wiley-Blackwell, 2009); as well as Brenda D. Schildgen, Zhou Gang and Sander L. Gilman, eds., *Other Renaissances: A New Approach to World Literature* (New York: Palgrave Macmillan, 2006).
51 See, for instance, Roy Porter and Mikulas Teich, eds., *The Renaissance in National Context* (Cambridge: Cambridge University Press, 1992); Peter Burke, *The European Renaissance: Centres and Peripheries* (Oxford: Blackwell, 1998).
52 For these proto-renaissances, or renascences as they have also been called, see Erwin Panofsky, *Renaissance and Renascences in Western Art* (Stockholm: Almqvist & Wiksell, 1960); Charles Homer Haskins, *The Renaissance of the Twelfth Century* (Cambridge, Mass.: Harvard University Press, 1927); and the special issue Jennifer Summit and David Wallace, eds., "Medieval/Renaissance after Periodization," *Journal of Medieval and Early Modern Studies* 37, no. 3 (Fall 2007).
53 Conrad, "Enlightenment in Global History," 999, questions narratives of uniqueness and diffusion in rather wholesale fashion. He writes: "The assumption that the Enlightenment was a specifically European phenomenon remains one of the foundational premises of Western modernity, and of the modern West. The Enlightenment appears as an original and autonomous product of Europe, deeply embedded in the cultural traditions of the Occident. According to this master narrative, the Renaissance, humanism, and the Reformation 'gave a new impetus to intellectual and scientific development that, a little more than three and a half centuries later, flowered in the scientific revolution and then in the Enlightenment of the eighteenth cen-

Taking co-creation as a concept seriously, would be to begin scrutinizing different uses of terms such as "r/Renaissance" in conjunction – with the scholar specialized in studying the European Renaissance and the scholar specialized in studying other "r/Renaissances," both in space and in time, working together – and in a joint effort not simply of comparing but of understanding different uses of the same vocabulary, both in the discourse of historical actors and in the writings of historians narrating particular historical periods and cultural constellations. Thus, rethinking "r/Renaissance" from inside and outside would "enrich" the term with multiple meanings – Chinese or otherwise; it would allow us to reconceive "r/Renaissance" in new ways, both for China and for Europe.

In this dialogue, my own approach to "r/Renaissance" as a term within a larger system of categories that categorize particular stages in history, is one such attempt at getting away both from generalization and essentialization, and moving toward greater differentiation and demarcation. I will consider r/Renaissance as an epochal frame on three levels, (1) as *the* Renaissance (in Italy and then, Western Europe – something that Thomas Maissen will describe thoroughly in this dialogue), with a capital R; (2) as chronotype Renaissance(s) which are inspired adaptations and co-creations of *the* Renaissance by historical actors, such as the New Culture Movement intellectuals, which are still written with a capital R but are "qualified" by the actors involved (Chinese or otherwise); and (3) as renaissance/renascence, a generic, typological or epistemological category, marked in the lowercase.[54]

I would argue that if we begin to read history jointly and in a global context, all *H*istory becomes *regional* (as well as time-bound) and empirically-based history. *H*istory (if read in a global context) thus becomes histor*ies*, and periodization schemes are relativized and thus released both from their alleged "universalist" and "imperialist" burdens. Rethinking periodization in terms of how it structures narratives and representations of temporality or in terms of it offering "chronotypes" inspiring historical actors' temporal thinking, we are then able to read appropriations of European periodizations such as "*the* Renaissance" as creative acts in their own right. We can read them as reformulating (rather than reproducing or vindicating – as in the case of medieval renaissances, for example – with something one could call a "we had it first" attitude) the

---

tury'." He then continues to argue (1009): "From such a vantage point, it is less instructive to search for alleged origins – European or otherwise – than to focus on the global conditions and interactions in which the 'Enlightenment' emerged."

54 Thomas Maissen is using capital R and lowercase r differently, see his definition below on p. 30.

terms of European epistemological and political domination, which will then no longer play an exclusively important role.⁵⁵

By contextualizing uses of "r/Renaissance" within different models of periodizations in China – cyclical and linear, religious and secular – in the first part of this dialogue, and by explaining uses of "*the* Renaissance" by Chinese actors in its second part, I offer to rethink such terms in the writing of a new and global History-in-common. This new History-in-common is interested in these, as well as other, European experiences as regionally and chronologically specific and thus "authentic" histories but also as part of one global trajectory. In the end, I will be deliberating on whether and how scrutinizing China's (and other) r/Renaissances may also change our understanding of "*the* Renaissance." What does it mean, for example, that women have a Renaissance in China, but not in Europe? Such considerations, I would argue, will eventually allow us to safely move, in a final step, from (local) histor*ies* to *H*istory, a History-in-common – that is, a History written with a greater common awareness of the other (but distinctly not the History of a shared past that we all have "in common"). Instead, this History is based on a joint reading "in-common" of different kinds of empirical evidence that we are then able to situate within a global context and on a global scale, along with a new view of epochal frames (no longer the emblematic and hierarchical chronotypes of old) that is empirically and comparatively based and thus characterizes these epochal frames not with sameness and universality, but instead with variation and differentiation.

---

55 See the description of a project to be conducted at the Heidelberg Centre for Transcultural Studies, *East Asian Uses of the European Past: Tracing Braided Chronotypes*, cited above in note 49 on p. 20.

Thomas Maissen
Defining epochs in global history – Can we write a History-in-common without shared concepts?

History as the practice of collecting and writing down events of the past has for a long time been a widespread and often sophisticated cultural practice. History – that is, historiography – as a methodologically controlled and professionalized scholarly activity is a recent occidental invention. The discipline was essentially established at universities in the nineteenth century when it was closely linked to the rise of the nation-state. The state institutionalized and financed the discipline that delivered, not least, narratives that legitimized the internal and external claims of a particular nation that was grounded in a distant but no longer mythical past, usually in what was called the "Middle Ages." History as a scholarly discipline has therefore developed its critical tools, its problematics, and its questions, but also its blind spots, which are to a large extent based on those (often archival) sources that helped us to understand and to write down national histories. This was a competitive endeavor in the competitive system of occidental states which then dominated large parts of the globe. Accordingly, the explanation of that political system and its superiority, at least in military terms, was a natural focus of much historical research. It complemented an interest in (world) history, already established in the Enlightenment in the eighteenth century, that wondered about the rise and decline of civilizations and, in order to explain their development, divided into periods the history of states as well as of civilizations.

Consequently, it does not come as a surprise that in universities and schools, periodization is used as a popular tool for reducing historical variety and complexity to a series of epochs explaining the historical evolution of humankind. It is also not astonishing that periodization, even if and especially when it refers to world (or global) history, reflects almost exclusively the experiences and perspectives of the Europeans or rather of some particular European nations. After all, the plurality of often very small but autonomous states is so characteristic of Europe that one must guard against juxtaposing it as if it were a homogenous unit to the single empire that China has been for millennia in spite of its internal diversity and changing borders. Indeed, when we discuss "Europe" in this book, we are not speaking of Finland, the Ukraine or Ireland, but of a handful of countries in the south and in the west of the continent, possibly reaching – when we speak of the Renaissance – as far as Poland in the east: in other words, the usual suspects of the occidental master narrative. Typically, as the author of these

https://doi.org/10.1515/9783110576399-005

lines, I would introduce myself as a scholar of early modern history, without any further specification, as if my Western European field of research covering the period from the fifteenth to the eighteenth century was *the* History of that time. Still, if I had granted my colleague's wish, a specialist in Sinology (significantly, without a subtler specification),[1] and were to accept the denomination of "Early Modern European History," this would pose another problem: it would suggest that there is early modern history elsewhere, not just in Europe. Early modern history entails not just a history of the sixteenth to eighteenth centuries (or other figures covering the same time span in a different kind of calendar), it also denominates as "early modern" something that logically precedes, prepares and – not least – helps us to understand the "modern" period, which started around 1800 and is characterized, for example, by the industrialization and urbanization of mass societies in nation-states. These are, however, phenomena that remained for a considerable time limited to very particular places, even in Europe and North America, and *a fortiori* elsewhere on the globe. Take just one decisive characteristic of the epoch of early modern history, as developed in and for (western and central) Europe: where else did a homogeneous religious culture break apart in a Reformation and allow different confessions and their churches to become the ideological base for competitive state-building? The fact that there were Christian missionaries all over the world is, of course, one by-product of the religious scission in Europe; however, it also shows us exactly that their efforts had decidedly different structural effects in other regions of the world. As there is no Reformation and no Confessionalization beyond Europe, can there be an early modern history elsewhere?

And can there be a Renaissance elsewhere? Or an Enlightenment? Both are core concepts in a positive interpretation of the (European) path towards modernity, which is based on individualism, emancipation, rationality, secularization, democratic participation, and so on. There is an obvious danger that a superiorist Eurocentric interpretation continues to do what it has done for centuries – namely, claiming these and other positive aspects of civilizational development and change as properly and only European qualities; or worse, as the exclusive qualities of specific occidental nations. However, the question remains: Is the antidote to such claims for cultural and political superiority and hegemony to be found in proclaiming a historiographic "not you, we too": your European Renaissance (or Enlightenment) is not as bright as you think, and it is not unique, because we had one, too? This is one core element of Jack Goody's ap-

---

[1] See above p. 7, note 8.

proach in *Renaissances – The One or the many*.[2] Barbara Mittler's assertion – following Sebastian Conrad's lead[3] – that the use of such periodization schemes should not be described as "second-hand" and "derivative" goes even further.[4] Speaking of "second-hand" uses of terms implies that there could be some kind of original, first-hand, and non-derivative correspondence between a universal term – for example, "Renaissance" – and an equally universal phenomenon it describes – that is, renaissances across time and space whose denomination is not derivative although they occurred later. I would emphasize the unique and particular historical and cultural context that allowed for the invention of such terminologies, and the unique and particular historical and cultural contexts of their transfer and adaptations. The fear of being "derivative" is political because it can suggest inferiority. In a scholarly context, "derivative" has a completely different and positive connotation, however: better, which is to say more precise knowledge, is always "derived" from or built upon earlier, less precise knowledge.

In order to understand the "multiple modernities" (Eisenstadt)[5] of the twenty-first century, can it really be helpful to export concepts and periods that describe particular European developments (or rather those of some particular European countries) to other geographic areas with different developments? The battle against a Eurocentric master narrative is not won if one transfers concepts or epochs that originate in Europe to other areas where they do not correspond to historical and cultural long-term developments. No one ever proposed using an epochal name such as the Zhou Dynasty to describe historical change in Europe. *The* Renaissance is as particular as the Zhou is, with its equally particular pre-

---

[2] Goody asserts that the occidental narrative of the Renaissance illegitimately claims an exclusive European path towards modernity (including capitalism, secularism, individualism etc.), implying that other civilizations were or are backward. He stresses, on the one hand, the importance of extra-European borrowings in shaping the European Renaissance and, on the other, claims that the latter was not unique, because other civilizations experienced similar movements with a cultural output of comparable quality. See Goody, *Renaissances*, e.g. 38, 43, 61, 185, 198, 213, 222, 254.

[3] Although definitely not monomaniac like Goody, Sebastian Conrad sometimes also follows the "not you, we too" scheme, see for example Conrad, "Enlightenment in Global History," 1004, where he points out that during the Enlightenment "popular social practices such as occultism, mesmerism, and magic not only survived, but were enmeshed with elite culture, empirical science, and the celebration of reason."

[4] The quotations from Mittler in these paragraphs stem from the preceding section, here above p. 21.

[5] Shmuel N. Eisenstadt, ed., *Multiple Modernities* (New Brunswick: Transaction Publishers, 2002).

ceding and succeeding dynasties. Epochs are not isolated, they are linked to each other by an internal logic: the Renaissance was characterized by the humanists' passion for original classical sources. The ensuing Reformation inherited this legacy and developed it further and humanists such as Erasmus (1466–1536) and Melanchthon (1497–1560), who focused their philological skills on the Bible and on early Christian authors such as Augustine (354–430), prepared and accompanied the Reformer's turn against the existing church. Periodization schemes try to conceive and explain socio-cultural change over millennia in a particular region. Although this is an intellectually hazardous and always somewhat arbitrary task in itself, in this book we do not discuss the well-known problems of periodization in general but rather the advantages and risks of transferring them to other cultural regions.

The "exportability" of particular periodization schemes depends on how narrowly they are defined and thus historically contextualized. Scholars of German literature (and generations of pupils in high schools) call the time when Goethe and Schiller wrote their first works "Sturm und Drang," thus defining a kind of a youth movement, a literary generation with a specific impetus and with stylistic particularities. Unlike the following period of romanticism, the German literary epoch "Sturm und Drang" cannot be exported, neither to German music nor to French literature, let alone to general history or to other continents. To speak of an "age of imperialism," on the other hand, with its very broad meaning of establishing far-reaching domination over different nations, fits well the European experience of the nineteenth century, but also with Rome in Antiquity or China during the Qing.

To decide whether "Renaissance" (or "renaissances") has actually been "fruitfully applied to describe other cultural and historical experiences," as Barbara Mittler claims above,[6] depends essentially on how broadly or how narrowly the concept is defined and thus linked to just one precise historical context or to more general phenomena. There is no God nor History herself who could dictate such definitions. They stem from human interpretative efforts and are exposed to criticism and contest. This is already manifest in the Occident where many scholars would agree with Mittler that "there were indeed many renaissances, not just one."[7] This is regularly the case among those who understand Renaissance (only) as an increased interest in the art and literature of a distant, "classical," and exemplary past. Such moments of interest are indeed a widespread cultural, even a common human experience. It may not be a coincidence that an anthro-

---

6 See p. 20.
7 See above, p. 21.

pologist like Jack Goody insists that the many renaissances worldwide be understood as "looking back" and a "revival."[8] While this is not my definition of "Renaissance," it is a legitimate position which has provoked and stimulated scholarly debates and produced many insights for over a century now. Hence the concepts of a "Carolingian Renaissance" (Erna Patzelt), an "Ottonian Renaissance" (Hans Naumann), and the "Renaissance of the twelfth century" (Charles Homer Haskins), all of which can be seen as products of the 1920s "revolt of the medievalists" (Wallace K. Ferguson) against Jacob Burckhardt and his vulgarized claim that modernity had its origins in the Italian Renaissance.[9] To some extent, this "revolt" followed a line of argument similar to the "not you, we too" trend in current claims about renaissances or enlightenments beyond Europe: classical references were numerous in medieval cultures, and modernity had many different origins. Given that Burckhardt (to whom we will return) was very skeptical about what he experienced as modernity and given that he started his book and reflections on individuality with the illegitimate despots of the Renaissance, this contestation is somewhat paradoxical. But it is characteristic for a turn that sees modernity as well as individuality and other phenomena traditionally linked to the Italian Renaissance as essentially positive elements in the history of humankind and claims that other periods (the Middle Ages) or other areas of the world (China) may also have contributed, and considerably, to such a success story.[10] It is not my aim here to contest this, but did they do this through a Renaissance?

To insist on the particularity of, first, the Italian, then, the Western European Renaissance with a capital R is not a claim of occidentalist property or copyright over a term or concept with positive connotations. The insistence stems from the historian's wish to understand the particularities of a phenomenon he studies – in this case, the Renaissance – and of his conviction that these particularities

---

8 Goody, *Renaissances*, 5–10.
9 Wallace K. Ferguson, *The Renaissance in Historical Thought. Five Centuries of Interpretation* (Boston: Houghton Mifflin Co., 1948). My position is close to Ulrich Muhlack in his programmatic article "Mittelalter und Humanismus. Eine Epochengrenze," in *Staatensystem und Geschichtsschreibung. Ausgewählte Aufsätze zu Humanismus und Historismus, Absolutismus und Aufklärung* (Berlin: Duncker & Humblot, 2006), who also provides a good overview of the German debates in the ninteenth and early twentieth century; for a summary which uses a geographically and chronologically broader framework, see also Paul F. Grendler, Art. "Renaissance," in *Encyclopedia of the Renaissance*, vol. 5 (New York: Charles Scribner's Sons, 1999), and the articles in Jonathan Woolfson, ed., *Palgrave Advances in Renaissance Historiography* (Basingstoke: Palgrave Macmillan, 2005).
10 Eisenstadt, *Multiple Modernities*; Erica Brindley, *Individualism in Early China: Human Agency and the Self in Thought and Politics* (Honolulu: University of Hawaii Press, 2010).

contribute to a better understanding of aspects that, in a very tortuous way, have indeed contributed to the "rise of the West," to "modernity" or just to the temporary relative advantages that give answers to a still fascinating and tricky question: why, around 1800, did (only) some European countries engage in a rapid process that changed largely agrarian and locally bound societies into industrialized and urbanized mass societies?

The advantage of using a word such as "renaissance," with a lowercase r, in a wide and open sense is arguably that it allows for easy comparison with similar phenomena. Then *the* Renaissance with a capital R would eventually become just the "Italian renaissance," and thus only one among many "renaissances." For pragmatic reasons only, the lowercase character will indicate, in my chapters, such generic as well as – in Mittler's words – chronotypical uses of "renaissance," which, however, are not mine. My real message is to avoid them altogether and to employ only one term in only one limited context: *the* Renaissance, as I will spell it, with a capital R, in my chapters.[11] Insisting on the importance of the one and only Renaissance of the fourteenth to sixteenth century, is legitimized by at least two other factors presented in detail in my "View from Europe" in Part II of this book: unlike their medieval "predecessors," the humanists of that period were very conscious that reawakening Antiquity meant and was intended to mean a rupture in cultural practice that also produced and necessitated a set of other concepts such as the "Middle Ages." Furthermore, the way they effected this reawakening has been experienced by the *umanisti* (who themselves coined this label) as well as described by more recent research as a very particular treatment of the past. It goes far beyond a simple renewed interest in Antiquity, as will be explained later.

Can we come to a global concept or conception of Renaissance or other epochs by "enriching our vocabularies" with "multiple meanings – Chinese or otherwise," as proposed by Mittler?[12] She maintains that rethinking our definitions by taking into consideration a wider and more pluralistic range of phenomena will allow us to sharpen our vision by seeing more variety and hence enable a better description of phenomena which are, precisely, various in different times and geographic areas. To me, this "enriching" sounds like defining an epoch or its denomination in a very wide sense in order to make it as inclusive as possible – that is, to include a large number of historical experiences that somebody has once called "renaissance." Thus, "renaissance" would become

---

11 Differently, Mittler distinguishes three, not two types of "renaissance" or "Renaissance," as explained above on p. 22.
12 Above p. 21–22.

a universal term like, for example, "imperialism." And in order to fit a particular historical situation it would always require an adjective such as "classical Greek imperialism" and "modern American imperialism" or "Italian renaissance of the fifteenth century" and "Chinese renaissance of the early twentieth century." For the historian that I am, collecting material evidence to form a corpus for comparison seems to be a good starting point, but it is not the desired result. Unlike (arguably) the social sciences, the purpose of historical research is not to produce a collection of generally applicable terms, but to forge an analytical vocabulary, one that is as precise and as specific as possible, to describe and distinguish concrete historical phenomena and their integration into more encompassing explanations about historical change.[13] For the purposes of comparison and the distinction of similar phenomena, it can be helpful to use Weberian ideal types which emphasize some characteristics of a phenomenon and disregard others of lesser importance. Yet in order to accentuate comparative distinctness, ideal types reduce the quantity of a concept's possible contextual aspects – quite the opposite of "enriching" it, which to me corresponds to a broadening of its meanings, thus making them fuzzier rather than more distinct. My impression is that "enriching" a term such as "Renaissance" would be to pretend that "Renaissance" is not a particular term that can be localized historically and culturally, but that it is a universal process to be found over all times and in many civilizations, with distinctions of course, but with distinctions that matter less than the commonalities. My assertion is therefore quite the opposite: what distinguished the Italian renaissance of the fourteenth to sixteenth century, therefore, merits an exclusive claim to the title "Renaissance."

If the historian highlights the particularities of individual historical phenomena, how does he come to a History-in-common, the final postulation in Mittler's introduction?[14] To me, it remains vague what exactly amounts to the "in-common" in such a history. It does not seem to be a shared past, a criterion that would reduce global history to nothing if it means that people all over the world experienced the same event, or, at best, to a rather thin book if by "shared" one understands transcontinental or transcultural encounters such as the crusades, the discoveries, overseas trade, or mission work. It has been suggested that such moments of cross-cultural exchange between historical actors coming from distant areas of the globe could "provide a foundation for a genuinely global periodization of world history."[15] I am afraid that the criterion of

---

13 Ulrich Muhlack makes the same point against a universal concept of "humanism," see Muhlack, "Mittelalter und Humanismus," 11.
14 Above, p. 23.
15 Bentley, "Cross-Cultural Interaction," 750–751.

such commonalities is too selective to allow for a reasonable global history, because it reduces "global" to "interactive." The world we are living in is not only the product of globally shared experiences, far from it, and here, we seem to agree.

We disagree, however, on the feasibility of Mittler's suggestion that "History-in-common" could consist essentially in a new, shared perspective that is put in practice by scholars working together on global history. Developing such a perspective and a corresponding heuristic practice requires, in my view, very thorough reflection on what could be the common objects and methodological procedures of such historiography. What Mittler calls "a joint reading of different kinds of empirical evidence"[16] is, of course, an important plea for interdisciplinary work, but as in any individual or collaborative research, it is still left up to the scholar (or a group of them) to define which empirical evidence they will consider in their global History-in-common. Working together, "in common," necessitates – even more than individual research – a clear definition of the field of research, the questions, the methods, tools and concepts or vocabularies that are jointly used. I suppose that in a History-in-common, concepts and, in particular, epochs would be a commonality – why else would Mittler develop our discussion of periods into a claim for a History-in-common? But using a word such as "Renaissance" in joint research to describe and analyze historical phenomena requires and denotes much more than just sharing a perspective. The scholars involved will have to define, explicitly or implicitly, the interconnected fields of historical research and the criteria for selecting and comparing them.

Agreement on such conceptual tools seems to me a reasonable claim and an indispensable condition for interdisciplinary research. It is easier, however, for scholars to apply a concept such as the "uncertainty principle" all over the world without confusion than to expect a similar common understanding for "democracy." In the humanities, concepts are the result of long and culturally framed scholarly debates. To what extent, on the one hand, can they be applied to phenomena from other cultures? And, on the other hand, how much "empirical evidence" from other cultures can they integrate without becoming blurry? The answer will always depend on the concrete concept and its cultural background. In what follows, we are actually testing the advantages and disadvantages of using particular concepts of time (i. e. epochs) in cultural and geographical areas that they were not originally coined for. This can be helpful if we better understand a phenomenon by bringing it close to a similar and comparable phenomenon, but it can be confusing if it subsumes phenomena within one category

---

16 See above p. 23.

that does not fit all of them. This is what I am afraid will happen if one uses, as Mittler demands, "a new view of epochal frames" that characterizes these "precisely not by sameness and universality, but instead, by variation and differentiation."[17]

Sameness and similarity are, on a more general level, indispensable in constructing historical narratives; not only, but also in global history. Any historical narrative brings its actors into a logical or rhetorical relationship when it develops scientific problems and provides answers to them. There is a link from Martin Luther (1483–1546) to Ignatius of Loyola (1491–1556) and from the Jesuits fighting Protestantism in Europe to those on mission in Japan or Latin America. What is valid on the level of the historical actors is also valid for the readers of their histories. While the Reformation was for many reasons a German event, if one looks at its starting point, the spread of Protestantism became a European and later a global enterprise. Such posteriority is not at all a reason why Korean or Argentinian Protestants today should not see Martin Luther as part of their own history, or at least as much as an agnostic German does. In historiography as well as in collective memory, a shared past is unavoidably a construction: no German living nowadays has experienced the Reformation, nor has any Italian experienced the Renaissance. They share or don't share memories of the past that are based on narratives that stress (and thus construct) local, regional, national, religious, social, gender-based, mental, intellectual (and so on) commonalities and continuities. To some extent, such constructions and their corresponding causalities are always arbitrary. Whether they are convincing and valid depends, in the end, on their reception and acceptance in the scientific community and by interested readers.

One may wonder whether the use of a particular terminology, for example "Renaissance," by some authors is sufficient to create convincing links between phenomena that are separated by centuries and enormous distances. To my understanding, the New Culture Movement's interest in the Renaissance is a (minor) chapter in the history of learning: how did some Chinese adapt aspects of a *Weltanschauung*, which they saw as a key element of both Europe's success and of its success story, which they viewed with a mixture of admiration and repulsion? I fully agree with Barbara Mittler that it is worthwhile studying the "processes of translation, adaptation, reinvention" of terms such as "renaissance" in China and other areas of the world; and we can leave it to any individual scholar to decide whether this is more interesting than studying the origins

---

[17] See above p. 23.

of such terms.[18] But studying the aftermath, the *Nachleben*, of a concept such as "renaissance" in other cultural contexts is something completely different from appropriating it as a methodological tool to analyze and describe exactly these different cultural contexts. Modern scholars, who describe Italy and Western Europe in the fifteenth and sixteenth centuries as the period of *the* Renaissance, consciously adopt the self-fashioning terminology used by their sources, the humanists, as an appropriate analytical tool to interpret that time. Do modern scholars of the New Culture Movement, when they quote their sources' claim for a Chinese renaissance, really want to use this self-stylization as an analytical tool? This is one of the questions to which I hope to receive an answer in the following chapters.

---

[18] See above p. 21

Part I **Periodization**

Thomas Maissen
Europe: Secularizing teleological models

Structuring the past is an important element of any historical narrative and to some extent an anthropological phenomenon, since we distinguish what we have experienced ourselves from what has happened before we were born. As a cultural practice, history is not least the aggregation and structured transmission of such individual narratives. In the beginning, this can happen orally, but in the long run, only written texts guarantee a continuous transmission of histories. When the number and variety of historical narrations grows, one feels an increasing need to combine them and bring them into a chronological and thematic order. For political entities, a founding moment can be the point of reference, such as the Roman dating since the origins of the city (*ab urbe condita*), or the reference to the rulers, again in the Roman case by dating according to the acting counsels of a particular year (*Pompeio et Crasso consulibus*) or to the reign period of an emperor (as was also the case in China). Using dynasties of emperors or kings to demarcate a longer period of time in hereditary monarchies is a consistent way of imposing order. As dynastic change usually implies struggles for succession and political turmoil, these moments often also become memorable ruptures in historical time frames.

The religious realm offers alternative reference points that can be combined with political dates. Again, the moment of creation, in this case of the world (*Annus mundi*), is one possible point of reference, as in the Jewish calendar (6/7 October 3761 BCE) or in the Byzantine calendar (1 September, 5509 BCE). The deeds of the eminent intermediaries (Jesus, Mohammed) have become the key elements of other monotheist chronologies. It was relatively late, however, that the birth of Christ (*Annus Domini*) became the decisive point of reference in the Christian Occident, thanks to erudites such as Dionysus Exiguus (ca. 470–ca. 544) and the Venerable Bede (672/673–735). Since the Bible (Luke 2: 1) itself dated the birth of Christ to the times of "Caesar Augustus," salvific history was indissolubly linked to Roman history, which, in the Middle Ages, was congruous with "world history" because very little was known about the past of other areas of the globe.

Dating events in the past and referring them to each other is one important task of historiography. Periodization is a different challenge and reveals theological, philosophical or methodological predispositions about the development of humankind during historical change.[1] In models of descendency, humankind

---

[1] For what follows, see Karl Löwith, *Meaning in History. The Theological Implications of the Phi-*

loses its original perfection and ends in decadence; examples are the fall of man after the original sin and the expulsion from paradise in the Judeo-Christian tradition, or the pagan theory of ages as presented by Hesiod (eighth–seventh century BCE) or Ovid (43 BCE–17/18 CE), where an original Golden Age gave place to an age of silver, ore and iron. On the other hand, theories of ascendency maintain that the history of humankind aims at perfection and a better end, which can be salvation in a religious sense, such as the Christian paradise after the Last Judgment. Christian theology thus contains both a rationale of descendency and ascendency, with the same pre- and post-historical goal: paradise. The past is therefore integrated into an overarching interpretive scheme that includes the future as well. But paradise is beyond this world. This, in the traditional Christian perspective of the Middle Ages, devalued secular history. The only truly important events for humankind were those that led to salvation as described and announced in the Bible: from the creation of the universe and the fall of man to the revelation of Christ, the Redeemer, and eventually, the Last Judgment. This Christian understanding of time was thus linear and teleological, distinguishing essentially between the time "before the law" (the Decalogue of Moses), "under the law" (the Old Testament), and the time "under grace" after the coming of the Christ, as narrated in the New Testament. What happened on earth was but an inevitable muddling through a vale of tears – that is, a retribution for the human fall through original sin. The *telos*, the goal and purpose of humankind, would only be fulfilled beyond human histories and beyond this world in the eternal Heaven.

In the linear narrative of salvific history, the era of humankind on earth was characterized by an unstructured collection of facts, deeds, and events that historians transmitted for centuries as "histories." These "histories" played a pedagogical role and were used to teach morals, but they did not really contribute to an understanding of humanity's final destination, which depended on God's will alone. The Christian attempts to create subdivisions of earthly time into several ages (*aetates*) included events past and present only as the building stones for this metaphysical truth as it was revealed in the Bible. The most influential interpretations reacted to the pagan accusation that the emperor's conversion to Christianity in the fourth century CE was responsible for the decline of the Roman Empire, which was manifest in the temporary conquest of Rome by the Vandals in the year 410.

---

losophy of History (Chicago: University of Chicago Press, 1949); also Justus Fetscher, Art. "Zeitalter/Epoche," in *Ästhetische Grundbegriffe, Historisches Wörterbuch in sieben Bänden*, vol. 7, eds. Karlheinz Barck et al. (Stuttgart: J. B. Metzler, 2005), 774–810.

In his *Historiae adversum Paganos* (*Histories against the Pagans*), Orosius (ca. 375–ca. 418) interpreted historical facts in order to demonstrate that the world had improved and human misery had decreased since the appearance of Christ. This teleological narrative stemmed from his teacher Augustine, the most important church father. In an analogy to the history of creation, Augustine divided world history into six ages of decline, which would be followed by a seventh age of eternal life in the City of God, thus combining descendency and ascendency with the revealed Truth of the Bible. For Augustine, humankind was living in the sixth age and thus awaiting the Last Judgment, the *telos* of earthly life and the moment when there would be a definitive separation between those damned members of the Earthly City and those redeemed in the City of God.

A different, yet also influential mode of structuring the past maintained that there was no general and complete change over time, but a constant return of similar patterns. This concept was already a potential in Hesiod and Ovid or his contemporary Virgil (70 BCE–19 BCE) who dreamed, after a long decline of humanity, of the return of a Golden Age. Other classical authors, such as Aristotle (384 BCE–322 BCE) and Polybius (ca. 200 BCE–ca. 118 BCE), conceived of a cyclical succession of political constitutions: the *anakyklosis* or *metabole politeion* (the cycle or change of constitutions). A virtuous monarch would build a strong and just kingdom, but his reign would inevitably give way to that of less virtuous heirs who would be spoilt by an easy and luxurious life. Thus, monarchy slowly degenerated into selfish tyranny to be replaced, when it had become insupportable, by aristocracy, the collective government of the best, wise and virtuous men, that itself would degenerate because of an easy life in a stable constitution, ending in oligarchy, the rule of only a few, without respect for the commonwealth and the common good. This unbearable government would eventually be toppled by a democracy (*politeia*, in Aristotle's terms), the rule of many virtuous citizens willing to sacrifice their life and wealth for the common good. In due course, their successors would yield to temptations and vice again and end in a government of the selfish multitude, ochlocracy. Then the cycle begins again, with misrule giving rise to a new strong man, a virtuous king who would build a just monarchy again.

This cyclical model established in Greece became popular again during the Renaissance with authors such as Machiavelli (1469–1527). At first glance, there are similarities with the Chinese interpretation of dynastic cycles, which pass from the moment when their founder has gained the Mandate of Heaven to a period of decline under his successors. But these were existing monarchical dynasties, while the particularity of the Greek cyclical theory lies precisely in the fact that it moves through the six different types of constitutions. The European monarchies of the Middle Ages, then, resolved their legitimation problems through dynastic change and rupture in ways that were different from China. They insisted either on legitimacy through election (by the estates or the electors, as in the Holy Roman Empire in Germany) or through familial continuity. Genealogists could be quite creative in proving the latter. The Frankish and French pointed at more or less alleged kinship between Merovingian, Carolingian, and Capetian kings to legitimize new ruling dynasties. For the elective monarchy in the Holy Roman Empire, what mattered most was to underline the continuity with the legitimizing institutions of (late) Antiquity. In order to emphasize the links to classical Rome and its first emperor, Augustus, the new or renewed empire kept the word "Roman" in its name, even when, from 800 CE onwards, the rulers were Franks and later on Germans.

With this focus on uninterrupted Roman traditions, the concept of transfer (*translatio* in Latin) was paramount to medieval authors: on the one hand, the *translatio studii* for the continuity of erudition and scholarship that was handed over from one nation to another and eventually became institutionalized in the Sorbonne University in Paris; and on the other hand, the *translatio imperii* that asserted the continuity between the Roman emperors of Antiquity and the German emperors in the medieval Holy Roman Empire. To metaphysically explain the *translatio imperii*, medieval authors referred to a dream by the Babylonian king Nebuchadnezzar, which is related by the biblical prophet Daniel (chap. 2: 31–44) and interpreted it in ways of descendency. In his dream, Nebuchadnezzar sees a composite statue made of four metals. Its head of gold, in Daniel's interpretation, stands for Nebuchadnezzar's own kingdom (Babylonia). This would be followed by the rise of another, inferior kingdom, represented by the silver chest, and later on by a third kingdom, symbolized by the belly of bronze, and a fourth, in the legs strong as iron. This will be the last kingdom on earth and when it is smashed, so the interpreters of Daniel predicted, the God of Heaven will set up his own kingdom there, one that will never be destroyed. In Christian interpretations since late Antiquity, the three latter empires were usually identified with Persia, Alexander's Greece, and the Roman Empire, which had obtained the decisive function in salvific history because Jesus was born under its first emperor, Augustus.

And so, continuity was established from that same Augustus to Charlemagne and on to the Habsburg rulers, such as Charles V in the sixteenth century. The "Holy Roman Empire" continued to exist for centuries – indeed, it still bore that name when, in 1806, Napoleon finally put an end to it.[2] However, the legit-

---

[2] Uwe Neddermeyer, *Das Mittelalter in der deutschen Historiographie vom 15. bis zum 18. Jahrhundert: Geschichtsgliederung und Epochenverständnis in der frühen Neuzeit* (Cologne: Böhlau,

imizing title could not hide the fact that, at least from the eleventh century onwards, Rome, the city of the popes, and the southern half of Italy were out of reach of direct rule by those emperors whose influence was gradually reduced to (parts) of Germany. The *translatio imperii* was an ahistorical interpretation of universal history as salvific history, one that subordinated contradicting historical evidence and did not care about those areas of the world not mentioned in the Bible. The notion of political continuity in an imperial order designed by God did not conflict with the medieval authors' conviction that they could draw a neat distinction between themselves as Christians and those they would call "heathen" or "pagans." Since Constantine the Great officially accepted Christianity in 313, it blossomed under official protection all over the empire. Confronted with what Emperor Theodosius established as the state religion in 380, the so-called pagan culture, (i.e. the ancient Roman and Greek heritage) was increasingly neglected unless it could be integrated into Christian learning and theories. Thus, a large part of the classical corpus was lost or forgotten. Pagan authors such as Sallust and Ovid, for example, were read only because their texts provided examples that could be used to offer moral advice within a Christian context.

This changed in the fourteenth to sixteenth centuries during the Renaissance, which will be discussed in the next chapter. In the sixteenth and seventeenth centuries, periodization became a "largely Protestant and German" endeavor (and has remained so ever since). It was used to examine, by way of philological techniques, the different existing calendrical calculations of time and to combine them within epochs that were believed to reveal the divine order of secular history.[3] In the eighteenth century, the age of Enlightenment, European philosophers began to consider History, now in the singular, as one continuous process and as something definitely different from the histories in the plural that had been narrated by Christian chroniclers but had remained meaningless ephemeral earthly facts as opposed to the eternal verity of revealed salvific history.[4] History in the singular, on the other hand, was human, mundane, and secular. Enlightenment authors such as Adam Smith (1723–1790)[5] or Nicolas

---

1988), 68–100, shows how regularly the *translatio imperii* was evoked in Germany even in the eighteenth century.
3 Anthony Grafton, *Joseph Scaliger. A Study in the History of Classical Scholarship*, vol. 2 (Oxford: Clarendon Press, 1993), 137.
4 Reinhart Koselleck, "Historia Magistra Vitae. The Dissolution of the Topos into the Perspective of a Modernized Historical Process," in *Futures Past. On the Semantics of Historical Time*, trans. Keith Tribe (New York: Columbia University Press, 2004), 26–42.
5 Adam Smith, *An Inquiry into the Nature and Causes of the Wealth of Nations* (London: W. Strahan and T. Cadell, 1776).

de Condorcet (1743–1794)[6] began to reconceive the past as a sequence of periods, referring to an end that humankind would accomplish imminently within this world: the progress of humanity and civilization in a succession of social stages, skills, and advancements in learning.

Such interpretations of the history of humankind can be understood as a secularization of the Christian model of linear ascendency.[7] However, they implied a decisive difference in teleology: the new *telos* – that is, the goal and the purpose of history in the singular – was an immanent (i.e. secular) process. History no longer had an origin or end in a revelation ordered by the Christian God. History now became the structured development of humankind advancing through time in establishing increasingly sophisticated political, economic, social and cultural structures and eventually making the world perfect since the capacity for perfection was considered to be part of the human potential that could itself be trained and developed through education.

G.W.F. Hegel (1770–1831) took up this idea of the past as a gradual sequence of development ("Stufen der Entwicklung") that aimed for a secular end – namely, the conscience of the liberty of the mind. In his "world history" four different empires or "worlds" took the lead during their time and dominated an epoch based on their particular principles: the oriental, the Greek, the Roman, and the German, culminating in the French Revolution.[8] They came to be used in a periodization scheme to describe stages within the "universal" progress of humankind, although they merely captured – at best – common experiences and processes within certain Western European countries. Hegel's idea that a period represented a particular stage of the *Weltgeist* became crucial in the systematic restructuring and specialization of scientific disciplines in Europe. Next to general and ecclesiastical history, new historical disciplines emerged: the history of literature, the history of philosophy, of art and of music. Each of these new disciplines asserted their own importance by claiming the capacity to systematize artistic production in successive periods such as the gothic, the baroque, or the romantic, always with particular reference to a specific *Zeitgeist*. The latter could be referred to the development of humankind in general or to occidental civilization as a whole. However, it was evident right from the beginning that

---

[6] Nicolas de Condorcet, *Esquisse d'un tableau historique des progrès de l'esprit humain*, eds. P.-C.-F. Daunou and Mme M.-L.-S. de Condorcet (Paris: Agasse, 1794).

[7] This is the core argument of Löwith's *Meaning in History*.

[8] Georg Wilhelm Friedrich Hegel, *Grundlinien der Philosophie des Rechts* (1821) (= *Sämtliche Werke*, ed. Hermann Glockner, vol. 7) (Stuttgart-Bad Canstatt: Frommann-Holzboog, 1964), 449 (§ 346); *Vorlesungen über die Philosophie der Weltgeschichte* (1837) (= *Sämtliche Werke*, ed. Hermann Glockner, vol. 11) (Stuttgart-Bad Canstatt: Frommann-Holzboog, 1971), 92, 557–558.

these histories were not a process in lockstep: heterochronic phenomena were very present at one and the same time. Historical stages and periods fitted best when they were attributed to a particular region. In the nineteenth century this seemed to be the nation. And accordingly, periodization in specific disciplines of the humanities became an essential element in nation-building: scholars claimed that there was German, French, English literature, art, music etc., and that they had developed and were further developing within specific epochs. The historiographical tradition of historism in the nineteenth century can thus be said to have structured the "natural" unfolding of societies by specific epochs, styling each epoch into the unique and singular cultural experience of a particular nation. After the experience of the French revolution, historism became more skeptical about the possibility of a general progress of humanity. In particular, Leopold von Ranke (1795–1886), in his famous lecture *Über die Epochen der neueren Geschichte* (1854), insisted on the specific value of every epoch because each was immediate to God (and not just one link in a linear chain of progress). Asian civilizations, on the other hand, served for Ranke as examples of how history could also mean decline.[9]

In the nineteenth century, periodization could also suggest another linear development: the revolutionary emancipation of humankind as a whole with a focus not on the homogeneity of the nation but on social inequalities in a history of classes. Karl Marx (1818–1883), Friedrich Engels (1820–1895), and later Marxist historians conceived a teleology of human development that was based in the control of capital goods – in a clear evolution from slaveholder society and feudalism, capitalist bourgeois society to socialism and full emancipation of the working class and any individual in a classless, communist society.

It is neither possible nor necessary to describe here the success stories that such periodization schemes experienced all over the world in the twentieth century, the national and Marxist foremost among them. Still, adopting patterns of periodization always means an – implicit – subjection to a historical teleology which only claims to be general and universal, but which immediately reveals, upon closer scrutiny, its very idiosyncratic cultural, social, and often national biases and prejudices. So the act of transferring the terminology of historical periods that have been coined for one particular socio-cultural experience to other nations and cultures, not only suggests that there could be something like uniform modes of historical change all over the world, but it also entails submitting the history of one nation or culture to the historiographical logic of another. I do

---

[9] Leopold von Ranke, "Über die Epochen der neueren Geschichte," in *Aus Werk und Nachlass*, ed. W. P. Fuchs and Th. Schieder (Munich and Vienna: Oldenbourg 1971), 56.

find this problematic and will explain why in my next chapter, by considering the concrete case of the Renaissance as an example for the patterns of periodization as they have developed in and for some European countries.

Barbara Mittler
China: Engendering teleological models

Chinese historiographical (chrono-)logics had for millennia been firmly grounded in the great observable cycles that formed the basis of a cosmology encompassing everything under the heavens. The beginning and end of these cycles were explained with a grand conjunction when the sun, moon, and planets came together in one division of the sky. History and the dynastic cycles were conceived to re-enact this cosmic rhythm.[1] A cyclical succession of order and chaos, developed by thinkers from Mencius 孟子 (c. 372–289 BCE) to Wang Fuzhi 王夫之 (1619–1692), in the form of dynastic cycles (*chaodai xunhuan* 朝代循環), became the backbone of writing official dynastic histories.[2] The historical cycle begins with a new ruler who gains the Mandate of Heaven *tianming* 天命, unites the country, and founds a dynasty; under the new dynasty, there is prosperity and the population increases. Slowly, bad habits develop, corruption occurs in the imperial court, the population is overtaxed, and natural disasters follow. This in turn causes the desperate population to rise in rebellion, and civil war ensues. All of these are signs that the ruler has lost the Mandate of Heaven. As the population decreases because of violence and war, a new ruler gains the Mandate of Heaven; he emerges victorious from the fighting, starts a new dynasty, and the cycle begins anew.[3] Dynasties are thus progressing in accordance with a predictable moral dynamic: men of ability and integrity, both emperors and their counsellors, are able to arrest the inevitable decline within the dynastic cycle for a time, and may even temporarily reverse it, but eventually the dynasty weakens and falls. This process inevitably led to general decline, since the sys-

---

1 Shigeru Nakayama, "The Chinese 'Cyclic' View of History vs. Japanese 'Progress'" in *The Idea of Progress*, eds. Arnold Burgen, Jürgen Mittelstrass and Peter McLaughlin (Berlin: De Gruyter, 1997).
2 See Jörn Rüsen, ed., *Time and History: The Variety of Cultures* (New York: Berghahn Books, 2007).
3 See Thomas H. Lee, "Must History Follow Rational Patterns of Interpretation? Critical Questions from a Chinese Perspective," in *Western Historical Thinking. An Intercultural Debate*, ed. Jörn Rüsen (New York: Berghahn Books, 2002), 173; Christoph Harbsmeier, "Some Notions of Time and of History in China and in the West," in Chun-Chieh Huang and Erik Zürcher, eds., *Time and Space in Chinese Culture* (Leiden: Brill, 1995); Bodde, Derk, "Cyclical and Linear Time," in *Chinese Thought, Society and Science. The Intellectual and Social Background of Science and Technology in Pre-modern China*, Derk Bodde (ed.), 122–133. (Honolulu: University of Hawaii Press, 1991); Hans Bielenstein, "Is there a Chinese Dynastic Circle?" *Bulletin of the Museum of Far Eastern Antiquities* 50 (1978).

tem would invariably repeat itself in a spiraling movement that followed this predictable pattern indefinitely.[4]

Next to this cyclical model, alternative notions of the stages that history could pass through existed. The *Gongyang Commentary* (*Gongyang zhuan* 公羊傳) to the *Spring and Autumn Annals* (春秋 *Chunqiu*),[5] for example, suggests that history moves forward in 'three stages' *sanshi* 三世,[6] leading from an epoch of 'decay and chaos' (*shuailuan* 衰亂), to 'rising peace' (*shengping* 昇平), followed by 'universal peace' (*taiping* 太平). It is no coincidence that when Chinese historians in the late nineteenth and early twentieth centuries first came across European theories of linear progression from ancient to modern civilization and from slaveholder society to classless communist society, and as they began to rethink their own history and to propose schemes for the periodization of Chinese history as well, these "Chinese linear models" had a role to play. One of the earliest attempts at writing such a history was Kang Youwei's *Datongshu* (大同书 *Book of Great Unity*), conceived between 1884–1902, but published posthumously in 1935. Beginning in the mid-nineteenth century, and inspired both by Chinese and European models – Christian as

---

[4] Lee, "Patterns of Interpretation."
[5] Along with the *Zuo zhuan* and the *Guliang zhuan*, the *Gongyang zhuan* is one of the three commentaries on the *Chunqiu* 春秋 *Spring and Autumn Annals*. The dating of the *Gongyang Zhuan* is unclear, see Joachim Gentz, "Long Live the King! The Ideology of Power between Ritual and Modernity in the *Gongyang zhuan*," in *Ideology of Power and Power of Ideology in Early China*, ed. Paul R. Goldin, Martin Kern and Yuri Pines (Leiden: Brill, 2005), 70–71. The *Spring and Autumn Annals* is the earliest surviving Chinese historical text to be arranged in the form of annals. As the official chronicle of the State of Lu, it covers a 241-year period from 722 to 481 BCE. Because it was traditionally regarded as having been compiled by Confucius (as Mencius claims), it was included as one of the *Five Classics* of Chinese literature. The primary assumption of the *Gongyang zhuan* is that Confucius authored the *Chunqiu* in order to criticize the politics of his time and set a constitutional guideline for future generations. Moreover, Confucius is not merely considered a transmitter of ancient scholarship but a charismatic sage (*sheng* 聖) who should have received the Mandate of Heaven and become a King himself. But since Confucius did not receive the kingship due to the political circumstances at the time, he compiled the *Spring and Autumn Annals* based on official chronicles, in which he criticized (*baobian* 褒贬) the events and historical figures of the Spring and Autumn Period according to a coherent philosophy. The *Gongyang zhuan* significantly influenced the political institution in the Han Dynasty but fell out of favor in the later Han. It is a central work of "New Text Confucianism" *jinwen jingxue* 今文經學 which advocates Confucius as an institutional reformer. *Gongyang zhuan* scholarship was reinvigorated in late Ming Dynasty and became a major source of inspiration for Chinese reformers from the eighteenth to early twentieth century, those who would be called upon as China's "renaissance men."
[6] See Seung-hwan Lee, *A Topography of Confucian Discourse: Politico-philosophical Reflections on Confucian Discourse since Modernity*, trans. Jaeyoon Song and Seung-hwan Lee (Paramus, NJ: Homa and Sekey Books, 2008).

well as secular, and here Smith's,[7] Hegel's,[8] and Marx's ideas in particular – cyclical concepts of the order of time thus came to be replaced by linear, evolutionary patterns. Indeed, teleological linearity became the exclusive mode in narrations of this new and "national" history now written in China.

The Christian model, on the other hand, also became influential, so, for example, in the making of Hong Xiuquan's 洪秀全 (1814–1864) so-called Heavenly Kingdom, the *Taiping Tianguo* 太平天國, which, for several decades at the end of the nineteenth century threatened the last ruling Manchu Dynasty. Inspired by a Protestant missionary tract, the core of the Taiping faith focused on the belief that *Shangdi* 上帝, the 'God on High,' had chosen the Taiping leader, Hong Xiuquan, who believed himself to be the younger brother of Jesus Christ, to establish his Heavenly Kingdom upon earth to replace the corrupt Manchu Dynasty and to fight those deluded by Confucianism. The Taipings also believed in the Chinese, being God's chosen people, would eventually live in paradise. This new teleology is captured in their influential *Three Character Classic* 三字經 which served as a history primer in schools.[9]

About half a century later, around the turn of the twentieth century, Liang Qichao – a student of Kang Youwei's – with his "New Historiography" (*Xin shixue* 新史學, first published in 1902 in his journal *Xinmin congbao* 新民叢報 *The New Citizen*) introduced a new, now secular, linear model of (world) historic development. In his essay, entitled "The New Historiography," he called on the Chinese to study world history in order to understand China better. The article includes all the critical impulses of a modernist re-examination and rejection of

---

[7] See Chen-chung Lai, ed., *Adam Smith across Nations: Translations and Receptions of The Wealth of Nations* (Oxford: Oxford University Press, 2000).
[8] See Tibebu, "The Orient."
[9] From Genesis 1–8: "The Great God, made heaven and earth, made land and sea, and all things complete. In six days, He made the whole Man, the Lord of all, was endowed with glory" to the flight of Israel (57–60), the Birth (121 ff.), Death (129 ff.) and Resurrection (133 ff.) of Christ. Next follows the history of China (149–286) which is described as a history of decline from the early ages when "the Chinese were looked after by God" (150) to an age, perhaps significantly at around the time of the European Middle Ages, when "What was spoken about God, Men have not understood. While the devil king of Hades has deluded them to the utmost." (207–210) So then, Hong Xiuquan is called upon and asked "to drive away the devilish demons, with the cooperation of angels" (233–234) and thus "God has set up his son; To endure forever" (275–276): 277 "To scatter corrupt schemes, By display of majesty and authority, … 279 Also to judge the world, To divide the wicked from the righteous, The one to the miseries of hell, The last to the joys of heaven. … 283 Heaven manages everything; Heaven sustains the whole, Let all beneath the sky, Come and acknowledge the monarch."

the past,[10] it attacks "old" (Chinese) historiographical methods, which, as Liang lamented, focused on dynasty over state, the individual over the group, and which highlighted the past but not the present, and facts instead of ideals. He declared the victory of 'evolution' *jinhua* 進化, for in his view a natural law or pattern could be found both in human history as well as the natural world. According to him, history must describe the process of human evolution and social transformations, such as the development from tribes to societies developed by, for example, Hegel who served as his explicit model. This alone suggested the advancement of humankind as a whole. Liang found Chinese historiography to be inadequate for advancing the goal of building a strong nation. He declared Chinese history up to his own day to have been merely "the history of (monarchic) rulers" and not a "people's history" (here, Marxist inspiration becomes evident) and concluded that therefore, China's past millennia had been a time "without history," while the new period of "people's history" would begin in his present, and position him as its foundational historian. Liang's openly self-aggrandizing but hugely influential *New Historiography* thus marked a new beginning in Chinese historical thinking, a "historiographical revolution" *shixue geming* 史學革命 as he would call it, and the rise of a nationalist historiography in China.[11]

Following the Taipings, Kang Youwei and his student Liang Qichao, with his *New Historiography,* thus introduced the new secular, linear model of (world) history to China. Indeed, linear forms of historical writing became integral to the generic set of tools and conceptions that China (not unlike many other Asian countries in these decades) turned to in their quest to become "enlightened" and "modern." Their use of European models can, of course, be called "self-orientalizing." It is true enough that European types of periodization, which, indeed, captured European experiences and processes, now came to be used as if they were able to describe China or even the universal progress of humankind. But do we have to be wary of such adaptations and find them problematic, as Thomas Maissen does? Admittedly, the use of any pre-fixed order of conceptualization may work like a cookie cutter – an analogy recently used by Henry Keazor: it produces a particular *Denkzwang* (a compulsion to think in certain ways). Cutting the dough of empirical evidence into prefabricated shapes means that

---

10 Xiaobing Tang, *Global Space and the Nationalist Discourse of Modernity: The Historical Thinking of Liang Qichao* (Stanford, Calif.: Stanford University Press, 1996), 48.
11 Wang, *Inventing China*. On later calls for a new "post-Confucian" historiography, see Brian Moloughney, "From Biographical History to Historical Biography: A Transformation in Chinese Historical Writing," *East Asian History* 4 (December 1992), 20–21.

everything which doesn't fit the form of the cookie cutter, everything that is heterogeneous and contradictory, is left over and pushed aside.¹²

But looking at each of these efforts a little more closely, one realizes that rather than simply adopting a model of allegedly "universal" (but really European) history, these were in fact *new* versions of thinking about history in the world. The restructuring of Chinese history in accordance with new and linear periodization patterns must be read as "derivative," but in the positive sense already established by Thomas Maissen above¹³ and not in the negative sense of "unauthentic." Such restructurings can be interpreted as creative acts of engaging with a particular cultural make-up that was developing and eventually became firmly rooted in many places in the world, East and West, and at around the same time, as part of something which Japan historian Carol Gluck has called "modernity-in-common."¹⁴

According to her, there is not one (European) "modernity" with multiple (non-European) alternatives (as the idea of "multiple modernities" by Shmuel Eisenstadt suggests)¹⁵ – on the contrary, the accouterments of modernity itself, in a "global synchronicity" or "actualization" described by Conrad in his essay on the Enlightenment in global history,¹⁶ are, from Gluck's perspective, common to everyone who partakes in them willingly – on the level of technology, materiality, as well as of knowledge. Chinese uses of a steamship or a train, their wearing of the two-partite suit, of jeans and high-heels or a perm, or the application of a linear concept of history in introducing something like a "new historiography" for China inclusive of new periodization schemes as well as their use of vocabularies such as "Renaissance," the last explained as the harbinger of modernity in the West, can all be considered such "actualizations." They are manifestations of a particular Chinese experience of this modernity-in-common. Analyzing these productive uses of technologies, materialities, and knowledge then, may help to further the writing of what could perhaps be called, by analogy, "Renaissance-in-common," a concept

---

12 Henry Keazor served as discussant to a dialogic keynote lecture which presented some of the deliberations that went into this book at the *Frühneuzeittag* 2015, in Heidelberg. In his discussion, he also referred to Ludwik Fleck's thoughts and his ideas of "Denkzwang," in particular, as discussed in Ludwik Fleck, *Entstehung und Entwicklung einer wissenschaftlichen Tatsache. Einführung in die Lehre vom Denkstil und Denkkollektiv* (Frankfurt am Main: Suhrkamp, 1980); for the idea of "Denkzwang," see especially 85–86.
13 See p. 27.
14 See footnote 1 on p. 11 above.
15 Eisenstadt, *Multiple Modernities*.
16 Conrad, "Enlightenment in Global History," 1027.

which recognizes how and why not just *a* modernity, but also *the* Renaissance became firmly rooted in many places in the world – China included.

Part II **Renaissances**

Thomas Maissen
The view from Europe: The Renaissance

The example of the Renaissance can illustrate why I hold that adopting patterns of periodization amounts to subjection to a historical teleology that immediately reveals, upon closer scrutiny, its very particular cultural or national imprint. For that reason, I do believe that transferring such concepts to other areas will inevitably blur differences that matter. The application of the identical terminology suggests not just a comparable, but a similar historical development in very distant regions. I do not think that this can help us in conceiving "History-in-common."

The term "Renaissance" emerged as the name for a particular historical period in an encompassing, broad sense only in the nineteenth century with two famous historians, the Frenchman Jules Michelet (1798–1874) in 1855, and the Swiss Jacob Burckhardt (1818–1897) in 1860.[1] Earlier uses of the same and similar terms, especially in the fifteenth and sixteenth centuries, had remained restricted to the realm of literature and arts and will be discussed below. This was still the common understanding when "renaissance" became popular in France during the Bourbon Restoration after 1814: Stendhal mentions a "renaissance des arts" in 1818; the rearrangement of the Louvre as a museum for sculpture since the "renaissance" is another example; as is Sainte-Beuve alluding, in 1828, to a "renaissance" in the letters; Balzac's hero's reasoning, in 1829, about Italian painting in the "renaissance"; Josquin Després questioning, in 1833, the "renaissance" as an "époque"; and the denomination of a part of the Louvre as a "Museé de la Renaissance" in 1834.[2] The literary historian Jean-Jacques Ampère (1800–1864) spoke in his lectures during the 1830s and in his *History of French Literature* (1840) of renaissances around 800 and 1100 CE and then mentioned "la grande renaissance" in the fifteenth and sixteenth centuries.[3]

---

[1] August Buck, *Zu Begriff und Problem der Renaissance* (= *Wege der Forschung*, vol. 204) (Darmstadt: Wissenschaftliche Buchgesellschaft, 1969).
[2] Honoré de Balzac, "Le bal de Sceaux," in *La Comédie humaine* (La Pléiade), vol. 1, ed. Marcel Bouteron (Paris 1951), 78. See Karlheinz Stierle, "Renaissance. Die Entstehung eines Epochenbegriffs aus dem Geist des 19. Jahrhunderts," in *Epochenschwelle und Epochenbewußtsein* (= *Poetik und Hermeneutik*, 12), ed. Reinhart Koselleck and Reinhart Herzog (Munich: Fink, 1987), 469–484, and Mignon Wiele, *Die Erfindung einer Epoche. Zur Darstellung der italienischen Renaissance in der Literatur der französischen Romantik* (Tübingen: Gunter Narr Verlag, 2003).
[3] Marie-Sophie Masse, "Présentation," in *La Renaissance? Des Renaissances? (VIIIe–XVIe siècles)* (Paris: Klincksieck, 2010), 8–9; see also Jean-Jacques Ampère, *Histoire littéraire de la France avant le XIIe siècle* (Paris: Hachette, 1840), and also his 1836 lecture with the same

It was during the Restoration, then, that the traditional "renaissance des lettres et des arts" shifted and became "les lettres et les arts de la renaissance" – an epoch of its own – denoting the sixteenth century in France or/and the decades preceding it in Italy. The ground work for the use of "renaissance" as an epoch and a concept not limited to France had already been prepared for some time. In his vision of the cultural development and progress of the human mind, Voltaire (1694–1778) in his *Le siècle de Louis XIV* (1751) distinguished four periods of blossoming: (1) the time from Pericles to Alexander in Greece; (2) of Caesar and Augustus in Rome; (3) the Medici in Florence and Rome; and finally, (4) Louis XIV.[4] Beginning in 1848, Paul Lacroix and Ferdinand Séré edited a collection on art and cultural history, titled *Le Moyen Âge et la Renaissance*. And yet, Jules Michelet was the first to use just Renaissance in a title and with a capital R, for the seventh volume of his 1855 *Histoire de la France*. The book deals with the political and military history of France from 1494 to 1516 with its obvious links to the Italian Wars which the French king Charles VIII started in 1494 – the decisive moment of cultural inspiration, according to Michelet. But in a general introduction, Michelet drafted an enthusiastic, yet arbitrary, overview of a period after the "bizarre and monstrous" Middle Ages had definitely ended, passing from Columbus to Luther and Copernicus to Galileo, and mentioning, very briefly, the printing press and the rediscovery of Antiquity, and the conquest of America as well as the role of the bourgeoisie. Michelet thus interpreted the Renaissance as a passageway to the modern world. He also coined the idea of "découverte du monde" and "découverte de l'homme," which would inspire Burckhardt's formulation of the "Discovery of the world and of man."[5]

Unlike Michelet, who did not even use the word "humanism" or, apart from some casual references to Petrarch, engage with the Italian humanists at all, Burckhardt's seminal *Die Cultur der Renaissance in Italien* (*The Civilization of the Renaissance in Italy*), published in 1860, focused on the country that since the fourteenth century had been stylized as the hotbed of artistic and literary renewal – Italy – neatly transferring the term that had by that time been well-es-

---

title in *Revue des Deux Mondes* 5 (1836), http://fr.wikisource.org/wiki/Histoire_litt%C3%A9raire_de_la_France_avant_le_XIIe_si%C3%A8cle.

4 F.M.A. de Voltaire, *Le siècle de Louis XIV* (Paris: Livre de poche, 2005), 121–122 (chap. 1, introduction).

5 Jules Michelet, *Histoire de France*, vol 7: *Renaissance* (Paris: Chamerot, 1855), I–CXXX, especially II, v. See also Lucien Febvre, "Comment Jules Michelet inventa la Renaissance," in *Studi in onore di G. Luzzatto*, vol. 3 (Milan: Giuffrè, 1950), 1–11, and Le Goff, *Faut-il vraiment découper l'histoire*, 61–70.

tablished in reference to France.⁶ But he did not stop there. The table of contents for Burckhardt's work illustrates how comprehensive his idea of the Renaissance was, especially when one recalls that he also planned a complementary volume on the art of the Renaissance. His *Civilization* does not start with the "The revival of Antiquity" (only chapter 3) and the humanist movement, but with two long chapters on issues that traditionally had not been associated with that scholarly enterprise. The first chapter is on the "State as a work of art," meaning the conscious creation of states as merely political structures regardless of moral norms. In this context, Burckhardt discusses despots, dynasts, resistance, republics, war and the papacy. The second chapter is on "The development of the individual," in which Burckhardt identified personality, glory, ridicule and wit as the keys to understanding the self-conscious modern man. Chapters 4 to 6 of his book deal with the "Discovery of world and man" (journeys, science, landscape, psychology, biography and description), "Society and festivals" (equality, costumes, language, social etiquette, education, music, gender equality, domestic life and festivals), and "Morality and religion" (immorality, daily life, subjectivity, superstition and doubt, leading to a loss of respect for religion and moral rules in general). Thus, for Burckhardt, the term "Renaissance" encompassed not just an artistic movement or the antiquarian studies of the humanists, but included some of the fundamental changes, both cultural and political, over a time span from about 1300 to 1600 when a group of (Italian) individuals began to create their personal and collective identities.

In the wake of Burckhardt's comprehensive scheme, the term Renaissance has been used and is still being used today, to refer to a general cultural movement that was not limited to Italy but cut across Western Europe and was conditioned by specific governmental, economic, and social structures. The success story in which the individual first appears in the Renaissance, thus making a decisive step towards modernity, soon became a popular one among the bourgeois readers of Burckhardt's book. This reductive interpretation was transmitted in compendia and textbooks, and it soon eclipsed his rather ambivalent judgment of, for example, the cruel tyrants who characterized the Renaissance.

Our modern understanding of "Renaissance" as an epoch of European history differs considerably from the concept of "rebirth" that was commonly used by the humanists of the fourteenth to sixteenth centuries. When they spoke of a "rebirth," the term was limited to describing new trends in literature and the

---

6 Jacob Burckhardt, *Die Cultur der Renaissance in Italien* (Basel: Schweighauser, 1860). "Renaissance" was used in German arguably for the first time by E. Koloff in an article on "Die Entwicklung der modernen Kunst aus der antiken bis zur Epoche der Renaissance," see Stierle, "Renaissance," 490–491.

arts, primarily in Italy.⁷ The self-description as *"umanista"* was also contemporary and designated a specialist of the *"studia humanitatis,"* "a scholarly, literary, and educational ideal based on the study of classical antiquity."⁸ Medieval erudition was structured as the seven *"artes liberales"* (grammar, logic and rhetoric, plus arithmetic, geometry, music and astronomy) and the university disciplines of theology, medicine and law. Using philological skills as a primary instrument, the humanists switched their focus to five disciplines in particular: grammar, rhetoric, poetry, ethics and history. Studying these subjects should teach both the scholars and their pupils how to correctly conduct their individual and social life. Promoting classical Latin, and later Greek, thus implicated concrete opposition to an existing model of scholarship and erudition that had existed for centuries and still dominated the field when the humanists appeared. The humanists polemically contrasted their own artistic and literary production with that of their antagonists, the *"scholastici"* and *"dialecti"* and belittled them as the antediluvian representatives of the "dark Middle Ages," a concept that originally goes back to Petrarch.⁹

Francesco Petrarch (1304–1374) first distinguished two historical periods – *aetas antiqua*, 'Antiquity,' on the one hand, and *aetas nova*, 'the new age,' on the other. He explained this to a friend after they had wandered through, significantly, the ruins of Rome: "Our conversation was concerned largely with history, which we seemed to have divided among us, I being more expert, it seemed, in the ancient, by which we meant the time before the Roman rulers celebrated and venerated the name of Christ, and you in recent times, by which we meant the time from then to the present."¹⁰ These "recent times" had begun with Constantine's conversion to Christianity and stretched into

---

7 Already around 1330, Guido da Pisa quoted by Orazio Bacci, *La critica letteraria* (Milan: Vallardi, 1910), 163, referred to Dante as having reawakened dead poetry and calling to memory the poets of Antiquity: "per istum enim poetam resuscitata est mortua poesis ... ipse vero poeticam scientiam suscitavit et antiquos poetas in mentibus nostris reminiscere fecit."
8 Paul Oskar Kristeller, "The Humanist movement," in *Renaissance Thought. The Classic, Scholastic, and Humanistic Strains* (New York: Harper & Row, 1961).
9 For the contempted "scholastici" see e.g. Francesco Petrarca, *Familiares*, 1, 2; 6, 8; 10, 1; 12, 3; 13, 6; 18, 1; 20, 7; 21, 14.
10 Petrarca, *Familiares*, 6, 2 = *Letters on Familiar Matters*, vol. 1, ed. Aldo S. Bernardo (New York: Italica Press, 2005), 290–295, here 294, for the opposition between antique and new history, as discussed between the ruins of Rome. For Petrarch see Theodore E. Mommsen, "Petrarch's Conception of the Dark Ages," *Speculum* 17 (1942) and Andreas Kamp, *Vom Paläolithikum zur Postmoderne. Die Genese unseres Epochen-Systems*, vol. 1: *Von den Anfängen bis zum Ausgang des 17. Jahrhunderts* (= *Bochumer Studien zur Philosophie*, vol. 50) (Amsterdam: Benjamins, 1982), 5–68.

Petrarch's own days – he acknowledged (and frowned upon) this divide, which was so dear to salvific history. Petrarch did, of course, see Christianization as a positive event in salvific history, but unlike his predecessors, his division of historical time was essentially secular. He therefore deplored the cultural loss that the decline of Roman (i.e. Italian) power had produced in artistic and literary production. Accordingly, when Petrarch described his impressions of Rome in 1341, he was interested mainly in the remains and history of the pagan capital and not in the Christian aspects of the eternal city.[11] While the concept of a *translatio imperii* or Augustine's theory of ascendency focused on continuity of the universe and humankind in general, Petrarch divided history and cultural traditions in order to isolate the Romano-Italian legacy and its decadence from the universal development of salvific history. In different texts, for example in his letter to Agapito Colonna in 1359, Petrarch completely overturned what had up to that point been seen as dark and light in the Christian tradition. From the cultural perspective that he now assumed, the lightness of the Christian revelation turned dark when the barbarians (i.e. the Germanic tribes) imposed their "darkness" ("*tenebrae*") on classical Rome.[12] In his epic poem *Africa* (1338–1343), Petrarch chose a slightly different approach: he explicitly called Antiquity the "age of light" and juxtaposed it with the "age of darkness" of his own time, while he hoped for a cultural revival in a near future: "When the darkness breaks, the generations to come may manage to find their way back to the clear splendor of the ancient past."[13]

And indeed, the generations that followed recovered the ancient past in a systematic collaborative enterprise of which Petrarch himself would be praised as the pioneer and trailblazer. In 1436, in the biography that Leonardo Bruni (1469–1444) dedicated to Petrarch, he maintained that the Latin language had been perfect in Cicero's time but lost its elegance under the rule of successive (Christian) emperors. Petrarch, according to Bruni, was the first to bring back to light the antique facility of style which had long since been lost and extinguished.[14] Implicitly, Bruni thus claimed a triadic arrangement for literature as

---

11 Mommsen, "Dark Ages," 231–232.
12 Mommsen, "Dark Ages," 234.
13 Petrarca, *Africa*, IX, 456–457: "Poterunt discussis forte tenebris ad purum priscumque iubar remeare nepotes"; trans. Burke, *Renaissance*, 2; also quoted by Mommsen, "Dark Ages," 240. See also Petrarca, *Rerum Memorandarum*, Libri 1, 19; he was also the first to adumbrate the concept of a Dark Age in *Familiares*, 20, 8 (13 April 1359) (= *Letters on Familiar Matters*, 145.)
14 See Leonardo Bruni, *Vita di Messer Francesco Petrarca nel 1436*, 65–66 = *Life of Petrarch*, in *The Italian Renaissance. The essential sources*, ed. Kenneth Gouwens (Malden: Blackwell Publishing, 2004), 43–48; see appendix for the full text. See also Leonardo Bruni, *History of the*

a substitute for Petrarch's dyadic: cultural flowering, decline and stagnation, and recent recovery. To Bruni, Cicero (106 BCE–43 BCE) was both a symbol of eloquence and freedom in the Roman Republic; decline began with the arbitrary rule of the Roman emperors, and eventually the barbarian invasions by Germanic tribes almost extinguished the knowledge of letters. This period of decay ended, however, when Petrarch recovered the works of Cicero and brought the classical style back to life. While his focus on republican liberty was a peculiarity of Bruni, his description of cultural change became the core element of the humanists' self-fashioning. Lorenzo Valla (ca. 1405–1457) is just one other example of this, when he states in his preface to *Elegantiae linguae latinae* (*The Elegance of the Latin Language*, 1449): "I do not know why those arts which most closely approach the liberal ones – painting, sculpture, modelling, architecture – had been so long and so greatly in decline, and had almost (together with literature) died out altogether; nor why they have revived in this age, and so many good artists and writers appeared and flourished."[15] For later authors, such as Niccolò Machiavelli, it had become a characteristic particularity of Italy to resuscitate what had seemed long dead.[16]

In the 1430s, the Florentine humanist Matteo Palmieri (1406–1475) thanked God in his dialogue *Civil Life – Vita Civile* "that it has been permitted to him to be born in this new age, so full of hope and promise, which already rejoices in a greater array of nobly-gifted souls than the worlds has seen in the thousand years that have preceded it." Palmieri explicitly employed the concept of rebirth to convey that the arts, after a decline of more than 800 years, were used again and thus born again ("rinascere le arti perdute quando vuole l'uso").[17] Rebirth as a metaphor not only referred to times of former glory, but also to a period of decline. With regards to the necessary conceptual complement of decline, Petrarch had already expressed the hope that his own era might one day, in a brighter future ("*felicius aevum*"), become in hindsight a 'medium' sc. *aevum*, or a 'middle'

Florentine people, vol. 1., ed. and trans. James Hankins and D.J.W. Bradley (Cambridge, Mass.: Harvard University Press, 2001, 48–55 (Book I, 37–40).
15 Lorenzo Valla, preface to *The Elegance of the Latin Language*, quoted by Burke, *Renaissance*, 4.
16 Niccolò Machiavelli, "Dell'arte della guerra," in *Opere*, vol. 1, ed. Corrado Vivanti (Turin: Einaudi, 1997), 689: "perché questa provincia pare nata per risuscitare le cose morte."
17 Matteo Palmieri, *Vita civile*, ed. Gino Belloni (Florence: Sansoni, 1982), 44–46, excerpts translated by David Rundle, bonaelitterae.files.wordpress.com/2015/01/seminar-1-reading-palmieri.pdf and www2.idehist.uu.se/distans/ilmh/Ren/ren-revival-palmieri.htm; see also Denys Hay, ed., *The Renaissance Debate* (New York: Holt, Rinehart, Winston, 1965), 9. For more and similar examples, see Burke, *Renaissance*, 4–9 and Martin L. McLaughlin, "Humanist Concepts of Renaissance and Middle Ages in the Tre- and Quattrocento," *Renaissance Studies* 2 (1988).

age.¹⁸ But it was Giovanni Andrea Bussi (1417–1475) who was arguably the first to explicitly use, in the dedicatory letter of his edition of Apuleius in 1469, "media tempestas" to designate an epoch. He meant the degenerate "middle time" that Petrarch, Bruni, Valla, and many others had already deplored.¹⁹ This middle time was both Christian and barbarian, and thus different from both the old authors ("*veteres*") of Antiquity and those of the humanists' own time ("*nostra aetas*"). Other humanists also began to talk about the "*medium aevum*" or "*media aetas*," the "Middle Ages" and thus implicitly established the new triadic periodization scheme: ancient history – medieval history – new history, the history of their own times, which appeared as a crucial period of resurgence and renewal.²⁰

These distinctions were exported to Northern Europe in the sixteenth century. Since 1518, the humanist Reformer Melanchthon had spoken about "*litterae renascentes*." In 1525, Albrecht Dürer (1471–1528) mentioned "*Wiedererwachsung*," the renewed growth of the arts in his own time. The Swiss humanist and Reformer Vadian (1484–1551) was not only the first to repeatedly use the Latin "*media aetas*" (from 1522 onwards) and later "*media antiquitas*" (1537), but also in 1545 the German "*mitler jare*" (middle years), especially for the time when monastic life had declined – hence with a Protestant bias.²¹ The German "*mittel alter*" appeared in 1538 with another Swiss, Aegidius Tschudi (1505–1572), and the French Pierre Pithou (1539–1596) used "*Moyen âge*" in 1572 for the first time.²² In 1553, Pierre Belon (1517–1564) introduced the "eureuse et desirable renaissance" into French, in order to describe the sleeping human spirit which awakes from the darkness ("s'éveiller et sortir des tenebres") in a way sim-

---

18 Francesco Petrarca, *Francisco priori Sanctorum Apostolorum de Florentia* in: id. *Epistulae metricae/Briefe in Versen*, ed. and trans. Eva and Otto Schönberger (Würzburg: Königshausen & Neumann, 2004), 322 (3, 33) "Vivo, sed indignans, quae nos in tristia fatum Saecula dilatos peioribus intulit annis. Aut prius, aut multo decuit post tempore nasci; Nam fuit, et fortassis erit, felicius aevum. In medium sordes, in nostrum turpia tempus Confluxisse vides; gravium sentina malorum Nos habet; ingenium, virtus et gloria mundo Cesserunt...".
19 Nathan Edelman, "The Early Uses of Medium Aevum, Moyen-Âge, Middle Ages," *Romanic review* 29 (1938): 22; Ludovico Gatto, *Viaggio intorno al concetto di Medioevo. Profilo di storia della storiografia medievale* (Rome: Bulzoni, ⁵2002), 63–65, relativizes the importance of Bussi; Neddermeyer, *Mittelalter*, 10; see also the list of denominations for the Middle Ages on 245–247.
20 This distinction was made explicit only in three books on the three epochs published by Christoph Keller (Cellarius) from 1688 to 1696, see Neddermeyer, *Mittelalter*, 153–160, and Kamp, *Paläolithikum*, 89–102.
21 Neddermeyer, *Mittelalter*, 110–124.
22 Neddermeyer, *Mittelalter*, 246; Kamp, *Paläolithikum*, 88, with further references.

ilar to plants that flower again in the spring sun after wintertime.²³ This remained, however, a rare evidence of the use of this terminology in France; it was only in 1695–1697 that Pierre Bayle's *Dictionnaire historique et critique* made the "renaissance des lettres" a more popular concept.²⁴ In his book on *Le Vite de' più eccellenti architetti, pittori, et scultori italiani* (*Lives of the Great Painters, Sculptors and Architects*), published in 1550, Giorgio Vasari (1511–1574), himself an artist and art historian, was the first to use the noun "*rinascita*" (rebirth) to describe his age ("*tempi nostri*") as opposed to a dark age with its "*maniera tedesca*" (German, i.e. Gothic art) and "*maniera greca*" (Byzantine art) that had begun after Constantine and had brought an end to the most virtuous Antiquity ("*virtuosissima antichità*").²⁵ Unlike Petrarch, Vasari was not looking into the future, hoping for a revival, but by now he was looking backwards in time: after Leonardo, Raphael, and Michelangelo, it was quite obvious that the arts had indeed been reborn and now even outmatched those of Antiquity, and furthermore that the triumph of Christianity had been responsible for their decline.²⁶

What the humanists stylized as a "renaissance" not only led the Middle Ages back to a reborn Antiquity, however. Even more importantly, it paved the way for the *aetas nova*, a "new time," which was characterized not least by a clear break with the old time, including Antiquity. This consciousness of an epoch-making rupture was an important change in historical thought. As mentioned above, Christians who had lived in what we now call the Middle Ages saw themselves as being in direct continuity with classical Rome, through the *translatio imperii* in the political realm and the *translatio studii* in the cultural arena. The humanists, on the other hand, fostered a new perception of time, history, and, in particular, of what they had begun to qualify as "*tempestas antiqua*." They discarded the idea of continuity with and since Antiquity and instead experienced a feeling of alienation and loss as a result of their distance from Antiquity which was, after all, impossible to overcome. The more the curious humanists

---

23 Pierre Belon, *Observations de plusieurs singularitez et choses memorables* (Paris: Guillaume Cavellat, 1553), Letter of dedication.
24 For Belon, Bayle and other French authors see Stierle, "Renaissance," 459–461.
25 Giorgio Vasari, *Le vite de' più eccellenti pittori, scultori e architettori nelle redazioni del 1550 e 1568*, ed. Rosanna Bettarini and Paola Barocchi (Florence: Sansoni, 1966–1987), vol. 1, 13, 19, 31; vol. 2, 32; see also Kamp, *Paläolithikum*, 77–87, and Matteo Burioni, "Vasari's rinascita. History, anthropology or art criticism?" in *Renaissance? Perceptions of Continuity and Discontinuity in Europe, ca. 1300–1550*, ed. Harry Schnitker, Pierre Péporte and Alexander C. Lee (Leiden: Brill 2010).
26 Vasari, *Le Vite*, vol. 1, 3: "…discorrer succintamente donde sia nato quel vero buono, che, superato il secolo antico, fa il moderno sì glorioso"; Stierle, "Renaissance," 457.

learned about the admirable but alien ancient world, the more they had to admit that it was indeed gone forever.[27]

Fig. 2 Frontispiece of Giovanni Albino, *Excerpta ex Blondi decadibus*, Naples, 1494.

This experience is made clear in the humanist Flavio Biondo's (1392–1463) *Historiarum ab inclinatione Romanorum Imperii decades* – a history of Western Europe which begins with the fall of the Roman Empire in the fifth century and ends in 1453, when he finished the book. It is the first history of what was simultaneously conceptualized as the Middle Ages – in other words, a history that began after the Roman Empire and not in biblical or Trojan times. An illuminated manuscript (see fig. 2) illustrates the humanists' lamentation: once, in times of concord, the triumphant personification of Roma ruled over the world; but then power without wise guidance collapsed under its own weight, and dole-

---

27 Peter Burke, *The Renaissance Sense of the Past* (London: Edward Arnold, 1969).

ful Roma sheds tears over the fallen symbols of her former rule.[28] This consciousness of a great divide between Antiquity before its decline and the present renewal, a divide made even more deplorable because it was insurmountable, was novel. According to this new view, the Roman Empire had not been transmitted, with its eternal salvific mission, to new dynasties, as in the medieval theory of the *translatio imperii*. Instead, it too was earthly, ephemeral, and transient; it had indeed vanished and no longer existed. This realization constituted a distinct break with medieval understandings of history and remains valid in Europe to this very day.

With this new view of historical evolution, the humanists also fostered a new understanding of themselves: they felt, on the one hand, that they belonged to a period of renewal and rebirth – and on the other, that they could and must actively implement this revival. It was they who realized the epoch in practice which they had conceived as necessary in theory. If one wanted to overcome the distance from Antiquity and reinstall the bemoaned cultural bloom of ancient Greek and Roman *bonae litterae*, it appeared crucial to adopt the intellectual world of these pagan "strangers." To the humanists, the classical authors had more to offer than the few singular maxims that had already been integrated, provided they were found to be compatible with Christian Truth, into the scholastic theology of the Middle Ages. The classical texts made sense as a whole, as a confrontation with a different civilization and with the personalities who had experienced, described, and analyzed it. The humanists wanted to reestablish a complete system of discourse.[29] These texts, but also their genres (dialogues, but also epic poems, orations, letters, historiographical genres) in their perfection helped to understand a world that could no longer be explained sufficiently using Christian concepts and convictions as practiced during the Middle Ages. The latter can be characterized, in a very general way, by elements such as: a monistic vision of the universe (monotheism, one pope, one emperor), rural nobility as ruling elite in a feudal system based on direct personal dependence and interaction, illiteracy as the rule in an agrarian society, communication mostly local and oral, collective memory based on familial and dynastic continuity, literacy as a monopoly of a very small group of clergymen that integrated old

---

28 Bayerische Staatsbibliothek, Munich, Hss Clm 11324, https://bildsuche.digitale-sammlungen.de/index.html?c=band_segmente&bandnummer=bsb00010832&pimage=00005&l=de; Giovanni Marco Cinico from Parma wrote and signed this manuscript with excerpts from Biondo for Alfonso II of Aragon, King of Naples, in 1494.
29 Klaus W. Hempfer, "Probleme traditioneller Bestimmungen des Renaissancebegriffs und die epistemologische 'Wende'," in *Renaissance. Diskursstrukturen und epistemologische Voraussetzungen. Literatur – Philosophie – Bildende Kunst* (Stuttgart: Steiner, 1993), 17.

and recent knowledge into one metaphysically predetermined system combining revealed biblical truth and an encompassing Aristotelian structure of natural philosophy.

This world had changed radically by the fourteenth century. In a very summary way, the following phenomena were characteristic of the new situation in Italy. The universal powers, both the pope (who was exiled to Avignon and in schism with two and sometimes even three competing popes) and the emperors (weak princes who were reduced to their hereditary territories in Germany), lost a considerable part of their political and moral authority. On the other hand, national dynasties arose (especially in France) and provoked a corresponding or opposing national identity (first in Italy, with many references to the glorious Roman times). The rural and feudal world gave way to the predominance of an urban and courtly lay culture in a system of cities with intense economic exchange, urbanized noblemen, burghers and merchants who were accustomed to bookkeeping and to reading texts – which would soon be rapidly multiplied by the printing press – and also to interregional communication by letters. This included diplomacy as a new form of political interaction based on regular reporting and eloquence within a society of petty, but growing states, and an expanding legal culture based on the written Roman law. Quick political change showed little respect for tradition and legitimacy, empowering social climbers such as the Sforza family – descended from rural mercenaries – whose bastard Francesco became Duke of Milan in 1450; or the Medici merchant bankers who came from humble beginnings and whose offspring included grand dukes of Tuscany, popes and Queens of France.

To come to terms with these new realities, the traditional Scholastic system of knowledge revealed itself as insufficient. What was unique in the Italian and European case was the fact that next to the Christian culture that had dominated Europe for a millennium, there were still visible traces of a polytheistic civilization that had only seemingly been overcome. More similar sources could be discovered through systematic, collaborative endeavors. Unlike the monistic hierarchy of the Christian world, the classical world presented a wide range of coequal diversities: many nations and tribes, languages, religions and schools of thought, customs, legal systems, and so on. Pagan antiquity thus offered a matrix and benchmark with which to understand and categorize the varieties of the present which no longer fitted into the Scholastic frameworks of systematization. At the same time, it also helped to understand the shortcomings of the contemporary world in comparison with an idealized, but concrete and tangible, past.

The humanists described their new engagement with Antiquity as a dialogue.³⁰ The form of the dialogue was also known and occasionally used in the Middle Ages, especially in the tradition of Pope Gregory the Great.³¹ However, as a genre it became really dominant only during the Renaissance, which in its undogmatic openness to new and different sources of insight has even been labeled a "dialogic epoch" (Karlheinz Stierle).³² The form and structure of dialogic thought was useful for an "epistemological turn," as it conceded a plurality of possible opinions and hence multiperspectivity; this changed its character from not only Christian, but also the Antique forms of dialogue.³³ In Antiquity,

---

30 What follows owes a lot to the reflections of two rarely quoted authors, Walter Rüegg, *Anstöße. Aufsätze und Vorträge zur dialogischen Lebensform* (Frankfurt am Main: Metzner, 1973), especially 91–111 ("Das antike Vorbild in Mittelalter und Renaissance"), and Leonid Batkin, *Die italienische Renaissance. Versuch der Charakterisierung eines Kulturtyps* (Basel/Frankfurt am Main: Stroemfeld, 1981), especially 265–315. Batkin's work has not been translated into English, but into Italian, see the decisive chapter: "Il dialogo," in *Gli umanisti italiani. Stile di vita e di pensiero* (Rome: Laterza, 1990). See also Eugenio Garin, *Italian Humanism. Philosophy and Civic Life in the Renaissance* (Oxford: Blackwell, 1965), and the works of Klaus W. Hempfer mentioned in the following notes and his project "Performativität und Episteme: Die Dialogisierung des theoretischen Diskurses in der Renaissance (Italien, Frankreich, Spanien)," SFB 447: Kulturen des Performativen (see www.geisteswissenschaften.fu-berlin.de/we07/institut/forschung/sfb447/index.html); and August Buck, *Humanismus: Seine europäische Entwicklung in Dokumenten und Darstellungen* (Freiburg/Munich: Alber, 1987), 136–146. Modern research on the dialogue has been stimulated especially by Mikhail Bakhtin, *The Dialogic Imagination: Four Essays* (Austin and London: University of Texas Press, 1981).
31 Carmen Cardelle de Hartmann, *Lateinische Dialoge 1200–1400. Literaturhistorische Studie und Repertorium* (= Mittellateinische Studien und Texte, vol. 37) (Leiden: Brill 2007).
32 Karlheinz Stierle, "Gespräch und Diskurs. Ein Versuch im Blick auf Montaigne, Descartes und Pascal," in *Das Gespräch*, (= Poetik und Hermeneutik, 11), ed. Karlheinz Stierle and Rainer Warning (Munich: Fink, 1984), 307. For an English introduction, see David Marsh, *The Quattrocento Dialogue. Classical Tradition and Humanist Innovation* (Cambridge Mass.: Harvard University Press, 1980), and the insightful article by Peter Burke, "The Renaissance Dialogue," *Renaissance Studies* 3, no. 1 (1989). An overview on research in Franco Pignatti, "Il dialogo del Rinascimento. Rassegna della critica," *Giornale storico della letteratura italiana* 176 (1999), 417 (on Batkin). In the voluminous miscellany Emannuel Buron, Philippe Guérin and Claire Lesage, eds., *Les états du dialogue à l'âge de l'humanisme* (Rennes: Presses Universitaires de Rennes, 2015) 21–24, a helpful *Orientation bibliographie* complements the introduction. An extensive and commented bibliography can be found in Hans Honnacker, *Der literarische Dialog des Primo Cinquecento. Inszenierungsstrategien und Spielraum* (= Saecula Spiritalia, vol. 40) (Baden-Baden: Verlag Valentin Koerner, 2002); see also Bodo Guthmüller and Wolfgang G. Müller, *Dialog und Gesprächskultur in der Renaissance* (Wiesbaden: Harrassowitz, 2004).
33 Hempfer, "Renaissancebegriff"; id., "Zur Interdependenz und Differenz von 'Dialogisierung' und 'Pluralisierung' in der Renaissance," in *Pluralisierungen. Konzepte zur Erfassung der Frühen*

dialogues were used as a didactical tool, a tutorial ("*Lehrgespräch*") to convince the reader of the one and eventually undeniable Truth. This was the aim, explicitly formulated by Augustine in *Contra Academicos*, not only of the medieval Christian dialogues, but also of Plato's prototypical dialogues, with Socrates demonstrating verity both as a system of proof and as a concrete result. Both resulted in one undeniable truth within one clear system of verity.[34]

By contrast, there is no such thing as a humanist ideology or orthodoxy.[35] Even on the most urgent political and moral issues, humanists would disagree and even diverged within their own writing: one text could be at odds with another. The same was true for their protagonists who could also change their opinions, as in Bruni's *Dialogi ad Petrum Paulum Histrum* or in Lorenzo Valla's *De voluptate*.[36] Humanist dialogue did not develop an idea; the idea appeared as expressed by different and antithetic actors. Humanist dialogue was analytical and not didactic; it thus often left a question unanswered or a problem undecided without a conclusion.[37] Pietro Bembo (1470–1547) stated that truth was hidden and human judgement very limited – there was nothing one could not dispute for or against with verisimilitude.[38] In the same sense, Lodovico Dolce (1508–1568) maintained, in his 1565 dialogue on colors, that there was nothing without its own contradiction; and that anybody could defend his opinion as being probable.[39]

It was not only the practice of dialogue that was popular, but also theories about it. These even spawned a new genre among authors of the time such as Carlo Sigonio, Torquato Tasso, and Sperone Speroni, who were well aware that their models were classical and not Christian. Tasso (1544–1595) distinguished theatre, as a performance of action (*azione*), from dialogue, which reproduced speculative reasoning (*ragionamento*) about conflicting opinions on any issue. What was uttered in a dialogue remained merely opinion, even in the concilia-

---

Neuzeit, ed. Jan D. Müller, Wulf Oesterreicher and Friedrich Vollhardt (Berlin/New York: De Gruyter, 2010).
34 Batkin, *Renaissance*, 311–314.
35 Paul Oskar Kristeller insisted a lot on this fact, see e.g. Kristeller, "The Humanist movement."
36 Batkin, *Renaissance*, 295–302.
37 Batkin, *Renaissance*, 279, 286–87, 305–306.
38 Pietro Bembo, "Gli asolani," III, 1, in *Prose e rime*, ed. Carlo Dionisotti (Turin: Unione Tip.-Ed. Torinese, 1966), 455: "niuna [cosa] pare che se ne veda sì poco dubbiosa, sopra la quale e in pro e in contro disputare non si possa verosimilmente."
39 Lodovico Dolce, *Dialogo … de i colori* (Venice: Giovanni Battista Sessa, 1565), 35: "…non è cosa alcuna, che non habbia la sua contradittione; e ciascuno puo difender la sua ragioine probabilmente," quoted by Hempfer, "Renaissancebegriff," 29.

tory synthesis which was never an end point but rather an initiation for the next dialogue and thus could not and did not want to be Truth.⁴⁰ This explained the humanists' predilection for the paradox, not as an origin for finding Verity but as a format that allowed for the articulation of any kind of opinion.⁴¹ In its intention and composition, the different voices in the dialogues of the Renaissance pluralized possible truths and hence relativized Truth itself, or at least the human capability of genuine knowledge for those questions which could and should be discussed in a dialogue, because they resulted in *opinione* and not in *scienza*.⁴² According to Tasso, this form of speculative, seeking prose was particularly appropriate for moral philosophy – discussing the duties and virtues of the citizen (*all'uomo civile, il qual rationi degli uffici e delle virtù*) – something Hans Baron would have called "civic humanism."⁴³

From Petrarch onwards, the most famous humanists wrote dialogues to structure their thoughts: Leonardo Bruni, Poggio Bracciolini, Lorenzo Valla, Leon Battista Alberti, Baldassare Castiglione, Pietro Aretino, and beyond the Alps, Erasmus in his *Colloquia familiaria* and Thomas More in his *Utopia*. In the *Dialogi ad Petrum Paulum Histrum* (i. e. Pier Paolo Vergerio, the addressee), Bruni begins with a meeting between himself and other young scholars and their admired teacher Coluccio Salutati. He first blames them because they neglect the practice and exercise of disputing (*quod disputandi usum exercitationemque negligitis*), although nothing else would be more helpful for their studies. Discussions, in his view, are most apt to lead to an understanding of subtle problems: the plurality of views among the participants helps avoid that certain phenomena escape from attention, are hidden, or delude the reader. Debates in a group will renew the energy of the individual scholar who may be tired of mere reading, they serve to stimulate his competitiveness, and to make him quicker and more eloquent.⁴⁴

As mentioned, the humanists' dialogue, while sometimes didactic, was characteristically open. Different opinions were presented as equally valid, and it

---

40 Batkin, *Renaissance*, 301.
41 Hempfer, "Renaissancebegriff," 31–32.
42 Klaus W. Hempfer, "Die Poetik des Dialogs im Cinquecento und die neuere Dialogtheorie. Zum historischen Fundament aktueller Theorie," in *Poetik des Dialogs. Aktuelle Theorie und rinascimentales Selbstverständnis* (Stuttgart: Steiner, 2004), especially 79, 85–88.
43 Torquato Tasso, *Dell'arte del dialogo*, ed. Guido Baldassarri (Naples: Liguori, 1998), 44, (§ 13–14); see Hans Baron, *The Crisis of the Early Italian Renaissance: Civic Humanism and Republican Liberty in an Age of Classicism and Tyranny* (Princeton: Princeton University Press, 1955).
44 Leonardo Bruni, *Dialogi ad Petrum Paulum Histrum*, ed. Stefano Ugo Badassari (Florence: Olschi, 1994), 237–238.

was often not obvious which one belonged to the author. Both for the alleged participants and the real readers of the imagined conversation, the dialogue was used as a tool to collectively develop new types and styles of subjectivity through the confrontation with different alterities and their particular perspectives. The interlocutors in a humanist dialogue could be allegories, deities, or fictitious figures with literary names like More's Hythlodaeus, an "expert in trifles." Very often, however, they were famous individuals, known to the author and to his audience, some still alive, others recently deceased or even from the more distant past.[45] With Petrarch's texts, especially the *Secretum*, Saint Augustine became a prominent conversationalist of the humanists. In Antonio Galateas (1444–1517) *Eremita* (1496/98), he appears together with a number of other key figures of salvific history such as Adam, Abraham, Moses, the Evangelists, Peter, Paul, Jerome and Thomas Aquinas. All of whom eventually yield to the convincing arguments of the eremite claiming access to Paradise, which the Virgin finally grants.[46]

Galatea's is an exceptional dialogue. In the Middle Ages, the setting of this dialogue would have been impossible: as would have any a person advancing a very personal view against that of the Church's foremost authorities. In this case, however, the interlocutor is still a Christian eremite, after all. The humanist's dialogue went even further: in the narrow literary sense of the genre, but *a fortiori* also in its passion for Antiquity, it introduced another category of fully entitled discussants: the heathen. This was the first time in world history that, lasting for a period of roughly two centuries, a collective of thinkers (quite an international group, by the end) would style themselves as successors not of *one* great timeless past, but of *two* very different and distinct, historically contextualized and fundamentally incompatible cultural legacies.[47] Since late Antiquity, and in spite of the many and inevitable adaptations of classical traditions in Christian culture, it had always been clear that the latter was superior, the former inferior, especially when it came to the question of verity and truth. A millennium later, however, the humanists emancipated even the heathen and engaged them in conversation, in dialogues, even trialogues among partners who were all equal in their being students, nobody *a priori* the superior: the ancient, the Christian, and the humanist, whose curiosity resurrected the ancient in and through dialogue.

---

45 Burke, "Renaissance Dialogue," 4–5.
46 Hempfer, "Interdependenz," 85–87; see also Bernd Häsner and Angelika Lozar, "Providenz oder Kontingenz? Antonio Galateos Eremita und die 'Lukianisierung' des religiösen Diskurses," in *Grenzen und Entgrenzungen des Renaissancedialogs*, ed. Klaus W. Hempfer (Stuttgart: Steiner 2006).
47 Batkin, *Renaissance*, 314.

In their new dialogic understanding, the humanists saw themselves as not just facing a text, but as taking up a real conversation with some of the old Greek or Roman protagonists, who became tangible through and behind those texts. The humanist attempted to grasp them as singular personalities in all their alterity. The Romans, in turn, would "thank" the humanist for this act of resurrection by sharing his perspectives and insights on life. Practicing this dialogical principle, the humanists hoped to combine the Christian and the classical heritage, as they believed them to be complementary. In contrast to medieval authors, they did not extract only those passages of the classical texts that suited their Christian beliefs. Surviving evidence from Antiquity was no longer denigrated for not being Christian. Even while keenly aware of the fact that theirs was a conversation between fundamentally different cultures and worlds of thought, the humanists felt that they were conducting a dialogue between equal partners.

There is a considerable difference between, on the one hand, reading and using only those sentences from a rather small corpus that Antiquity offered to isolated monks and other clerics who tried, by all possible means, to understand and to interpret the divine Truth in the demanding texts of the Bible and (early) Christian authors and, on the other, systematically reviving, in a translocal and later transnational collective endeavor, an existential curiosity not only for texts which the humanists had systematically retrieved, but for pagan culture as a whole and its representatives as individuals in flesh and blood. This was very different from scholarly practice during the "renaissances" in the Middle Ages.[48]

In Carolingian times, classical heroes and writers had been functional authorities: Charlemagne was a new Augustus, his counselor, the scholar Alcuin, a new Horace. They and their erudite circle modeled themselves on these prototypes without paying attention to their particular historical and biographical context; or rather without being aware of the fundamental differences between Augustan Rome and Aachen (the "new Athens") around 800, except for the one decisive difference: the new Athens surpassed the old because it had been ennobled by Christendom and hence encompassed not just the seven liberal arts of Plato, but the complete secular wisdom as well.[49] In the twelfth century,

---

[48] For the following, I am much obliged to Walter Rüegg, "Das antike Vorbild in Mittelalter und Renaissance," in *Anstöße. Aufsätze und Vorträge zur dialogischen Lebensform* (Frankfurt am Main: Metzner, 1973).

[49] Alcuin, Epistola LXXXVI. "Ad domnum regem" (anno 798), in *Epistolae Karolini aevi* (vol. II) (= Epistolarum vol. 4), ed. Ernst Dümmler (Munich: Monumenta Germaniae Historica, 1895), 279: "forsan Athenae nova perficeretur in Francia, imo multo excellentior, quia haec Christi Domini nobilitata magisterio, omnem Academicae exercitationis superat sapientiam. Illa tantummodo

then, references to the classics were "architectural," so to speak: they belonged to a cathedral of knowledge whose structure God had conceived and which, hence, only a Christian could understand. In his *Anticlaudianus*, Alanus ab Insulis (1120–1202) presented exemplary classical authors in a temple of nature as the imperfect pupils of the perfect Almighty. These figures stand not as historical figures, but merely as allegories of the eternal ideas conceived by God in heaven: Cicero for rhetoric, Virgil for poetry, and so on.[50]

The hierarchy between Christians and heathens is as clear as in Dante's (1265–1321) *Divina Commedia*, where the latter are numerous – but only in hell, where they represent all kind of vices. Even the virtuous pagans are not allowed beyond limbo, and Virgil explains this to Dante: "they did not sin; and yet, though they have merits, that's not enough, because they lacked baptism, the portal of the faith that you embrace. And if they lived before Christianity, they did not worship God in fitting ways; and of such spirits I myself am one. For these defects, and for no other evil, we now are lost and punished just with this: we have no hope and yet we live in longing."[51] While Dante's guide Virgil is still allowed to show him purgatory, for heaven, he must hand over the lead to Beatrice. Virgil is not a person in his own right shaped by a foreign culture; instead, he is a figure in the divine order of time and the universe. He is an admirable poet, but no longer helpful when it comes to the real purpose of human existence: he is a guide through unknown territories, but not towards the good life. Christian revelation has surpassed Antiquity and by extension the outdated recipes Virgil and the classics could offer. They deliver, at best, confirmations of what the Bible teaches: only the afterworld will recompense for the vale of tears.

The humanists of the Renaissance had a more positive understanding of this world and of man-made change in history. Hence their focus on education, pedagogy, moral philosophy, and on language (grammar, rhetoric, poetics) as the decisive tools to discuss and impart relevant knowledge to those who are ready and able to learn. Learning, in turn, was an open process, not limited to the acquisition of canonical knowledge. The production, discovery and selection of relevant information were a joint adventure for the humanists who no longer understood intellectual curiosity as sinful human hubris and who opposed surrendering

---

Platonicis erudita disciplinis, septenis informata claruit artibus; haec etiam insuper septiformi sancti Spiritus plenitudine ditata omnem saecularis sapientiae excellit dignitatem."
50 Alanus ab Insulis (Alain of Lille), *Anticlaudianus* (Paris: J. Vrin, 1955), 1, 130–151; 6, 214–231; see also Ernst Robert Curtius, *Europäische Literatur und lateinisches Mittelalter* (Bern: Francke, 1948), 125–129, and Batkin, *Renaissance*, 312.
51 Dante, *Divina Commedia*, Inferno, 4, 34–42.

themselves trustingly to the omniscience and wisdom of God. The dialogue was the genre that allowed them to bring into consideration (and not into subordination) all possible sources of knowledge and to scrutinize them. The form of the dialogue unavoidably implied multi-perspectivity. It presented different, alternative opinions on conventional topics and introduced new issues that had not been debated before in the Christian world.

The special and very literal character of the dialogue is evident already in Petrarch who, in his *Secretum* (1347–1353), tells us that Cicero serves as his literary model for the genre, and that Cicero learned it from Plato.[52] The dynamics of the dialogical principle was, however, not limited to the genre of the dialogue itself. One can see this in Petrarch's letters to famous men, one of them written in 1345 to Cicero. This is a dialogue reaching across more than a millennium in the classical form of *Familiares*, letters among intimate friends. Consequently, Petrarch describes how he and his friends "rallied around" Cicero. He addresses him as "a man I loved and honored above all others."[53] That does not mean that Petrarch spares him or Seneca from the vigorous critique of their "faults," however: "I have dealt lightly with these great geniuses, perhaps boldly, but lovingly, sorrowfully, and I believe, truthfully, in fact somewhat more truthfully than I wanted to."[54] Deploring Cicero's "inconstancy in friendship" and his "childish mania for wrangling" is a critique Petrarch owes to an intimate friend and feels free to express:

> After a lengthy and extensive search for your letters, I found them where I least expected, and I then read them with great eagerness. I listened to you speak on many subjects, complain about many things, waver in your opinions, O Marcus Tullius, and I who had known the kind of preceptor that you were for others now recognize the kind of guide that you were for yourself. Now it is your turn, wherever you may be, to hearken not to advice but to a lament inspired by true love from one of your descendants who dearly cherishes your name, a lament addressed to you not without tears. O wretched and distressed spirit, or to use your own words, O rash and ill-fated elder, why did you choose to become involved in so many quarrels and utterly useless feuds? ... Oh, how much better it would have been, especially for a philosopher, to have grown old peacefully in the country, meditating, as you write somewhere, on that everlasting life and not on this transitory existence; how much better for you never to have held such offices, never to have yearned for triumphs, never to have had any Catilines to inflate your ego. But these words indeed

---

[52] Francesco Petrarca, "Secretum," in *Prose* (*La letteratura italiana. Storia e testi* 7) (Milan/Naples: Ricciardi, 1955), 26: "Hunc nempe scribendi morem a Cicerone meo didici; at ipse prius a Platone didicerat."

[53] Petrarca, *Letters on Familiar Matters*, vol. 3, 314 (24, 2). See appendix for the full text.

[54] Petrarca, *Letters on Familiar Matters*, vol. 3, 316 (24, 2).

are all in vain. Farewell forever, my Cicero. From the land of the living ... on 16 June in the year 1345 from the birth of that Lord whom your never knew.⁵⁵

Consider the farewell: "aeternum vale, mi Cicero": Petrarch is wishing Cicero to stay well forever, (i.e. in eternity) even though Cicero could never have known the God whose birth explains Petrarch's dating of his letter and his location in the "land of the living" ("apud superos"). It is obvious that the humanist is not blaming Cicero for being pagan and heathen. He acknowledges how much he owes to Cicero's letters and adores them. Cicero has been Petrarch's teacher, and by teaching, he has revealed himself as a human being in flesh and blood, with all his strengths, such as patriotism, and all his weaknesses, such as wrath and inconsistency. Relying on the familiarity they share, Petrarch responds and criticizes his Roman interlocutor in the manner that one might criticize a beloved friend for whom one wishes a fate much different from the dreadful assassination that Cicero finally endured. Petrarch does not refer to the Holy Bible as an authority, but to Cicero's own writings (his letter to Atticus, 10, 8, 8) in order to tell him that he behaved inconsistently; and in order to draw a lesson for his – Petrarch's – own present. A "bad guide for himself," Cicero still turns out to be "a good preceptor for others." By thus studying and critically evaluating the complexity of a rich and peregrine personality – Cicero – Petrarch came to understand his own self better. His individuality did not consist in being just a Christian or in becoming a Roman again, which was impossible; but in becoming a creative selector who was able to choose fitting elements from different civilizations once he has understood them thoroughly through debate with the authors who explained them to him.⁵⁶

In *De vita solitaria* (*On Solitary Life*), Petrarch praises books as his grateful and assiduous friends and companions, always ready to accompany him, discuss with him, and reveal the secrets of the world to him. He mentions especially issues of history and moral philosophy: the way of living, contempt of death, modesty, strength, equability and constancy.⁵⁷ His *Epistolae metricae* (*Letters in Vers-*

---

55 Petrarca, *Letters on Familiar Matters*, vol. 3, (24, 3) (16 june 1345). See appendix for the full text.
56 See Batkin, *Renaissance*, 309–311.
57 Francesco Petrarca, "De vita solitaria," 2, 14, in *Prose*, ed. G. Martellotti (Milan/Naples: R. Ricciardi, 1955), 556–557: "Libros preterea diversi generis et simul per quos aut de quibus scripti sunt comites gratos et assiduos, et promptos vel in publicum prodire vel ad arculam redire cum iusseris, paratosque semper vel tacere vel loqui, et esse domi, et comitari in nemora, et peregrinari, et rusticari, et confabulari, et iocari, et hortari, et solari, et monere, et arguere, et consulere,

es), formally inspired by Horace, in similar manner thank the authors of the books he has read for being illustrious hidden companions from many different times and regions who loyally answer all his questions about the secrets of nature, the best way of living and dying, the deeds of the past and their own personal experiences.[58] In 1353, Petrarch, who lived far from his native Italy in Avignon and stayed in Fontaine de Vaucluse, at the source of the Sorgue, wrote that he had there "established my Rome, my Athens, and my spiritual fatherland."

> Here I gather all the friends I now have or did have, not only those who have proved themselves through intimate contact and who have lived with me, but also those who died many centuries ago, known to me only through their writings wherein I marvel at their accomplishments and their spirits or at their customs and lives or at their eloquence and genius. I gather them from every land and every age in this narrow valley, conversing with them more willingly than with those who think they are alive because they see traces of their stale breath in the frosty air. I thus wander free and unconcerned, alone with such companions, I am where I wish to be.[59]

Reading the classics means conversing with friends: this became a *topos*.[60] Petrarch's correspondent and the leading figure of the following generation of humanists, the Florentine Coluccio Salutati, thanked a friend who sent him a copy of Cicero's *Familiares*, by saying that he could not imagine anything more pleasant than to talk with Cicero ("quid enim michi iocundius esse potest quam cum Cicerone loqui") and to have seen the eloquence, the habits, the virtue, the vicissitudes and the emotions of the many grand and most erudite men who became accessible through Cicero's correspondence.[61] In the 1470s, Ermolao Barbaro (1454–1493) introduced his lectures on Aristotle by recommending that readers should speak to the philosopher himself as if he were alive and pres-

---

et docere secreta rerum, monimenta gestorum, vite regulam mortisque contemptum, modestiam in prosperis, fortitudinem in adversis, equabilitatem in actionibus atque constantiam."

[58] Petrarca, *Epistulae metricae/Briefe in Versen* (Würzburg: Königshausen & Neumann, 2004), 78 (1, 6):
> "comitesque latentes,
> quos mihi de cunctis simul omnia saecula terris
> transmittunt lingua, ingenio, belloque togaque
> illustres ; ...
> Nunc hos, nunc illos percontor, multa vicissim
> respondent et multa canunt et multa loquuntur."

[59] Petrarca, *Familiares*, 15,3 = *Letters on Familiar Matters*, vol. 2, 256–257. See appendix for the full text.

[60] Christian Bec, "De Pétrarque à Machiavel. À propos d'un 'topos' humaniste (le dialogue lecteur/livre)," *Rinascimento* 16 (1976).

[61] Coluccio Salutati, *Epistolario*, ed. Francesco Novati (Rome: Tipografi del Senato, 1893), 389.

ent.⁶² When in 1416, Poggio Bracciolini (1380–1459) discovered the manuscript of Quintilian's *Institutio oratoria* (*Institutes of Oratory*) in the monastic library of St. Gallen, he wrote to his fellow collector Guarino Veronese (1374–1460) not about finding a book, but about how he had saved a man who had come back "from a lengthy and cruel prison sentence among the barbarians" to delight the erudite of the present, just as Cicero had rejoiced when Marcus Marcellus had returned from exile.

> By Heaven, if we had not brought help, he would surely have perished the very next day. There is no question that this glorious man, so elegant, so pure, so full of morals and of wit, could not much longer have endured the filth of that prison, the squalor of the place, and the savage cruelty of his keepers. He was sad and dressed in mourning, as people are when doomed to death; his beard was dirty and his hair caked with mud, so that by his expression and appearance it was clear that he had been summoned to an undeserved punishment. He seemed to stretch out his hands and beg for the loyalty of the Roman people, to demand that he be saved from an unjust sentence. ... There amid a tremendous quantity of books which it would take too long to describe, we found Quintilian still safe and sound, though filthy with mold and dust. For these books were not in the Library, as befitted their worth, but in a sort of foul and gloomy dungeon at the bottom of one of the towers, where not even men convicted of a capital offense would have been stuck away.⁶³

The ancient authors, according to the addressee Guarino Veronese, "are alive and converse with us in a familiar way. The humans who have remained silent to us for such a long time, have found back to our familiarity."⁶⁴ The idea of a Renaissance was thus linked to the dialogue as its precondition and its consequence. In his *Theogenius* (*The Origin of the Gods*, about 1440), Leon Battista Alberti (1404–1472) maintained, quite paradoxically, that he never felt less lonely than when he was in fact alone, "because I am always accompanied by experienced and most eloquent men" with whom he could spend long evenings reasoning. Some of those would make him laugh, others provide him with helpful advice, and teach him about agriculture, children's education, on how to handle family and friendship, or how to administer politics, on how to know the causes of natural phenomena, how to distinguish right from wrong, and how to know

---

62 Ermolao Barbaro: "ut cum ipso vivo et praesente loqui videamur," quoted by Garin, *Italian Humanism*, 14.
63 Phyllis Walter Goodhart Gordan, ed., *Two Renaissance Book Hunters: the letters of Poggius Bracciolini to Nicolaus de Niccolis* (New York: Columbia University Press, 1974), 193–196; see appendix for the full text.
64 *Guarino Veronese, Epistolario*, vol. 1, ed. Remigio Sabbadini (Venice: A spese della Società, 1915), 124 (no. 58).

himself. Being able to understand all these phenomena made him recognize and revere God as their origin. At the same time, he is most indebted to all those (pagan) philosophers who are welcome or agreeable to God. This is probably the best way to translate "santissimi filosofi," which obviously cannot mean holy in the sense of canonized philosophers, but rather thinkers who have their share in the divine order of knowledge. Ultimately, then, reasoning and arguing with these heathens enabled the humanist to understand the world as it was created by God.[65]

In the preface to his 1523 edition of Cicero's didactic dialogue *Tusculanae disputationes* (*Disputations in Tusculum*), Erasmus of Rotterdam, the most famous humanist north of the Alps, defended Cicero against the "blockheads who are always repeating that there is nothing notable in Cicero except the splendour of his language." Against them, Erasmus raises the richness of sources Cicero quotes, his truly moral precepts, his range of knowledge, his memory for ancient and modern history, his profound reflections on the true felicity of man: "the clarity, the openness of mind, the easy movement, the ready flow of words, and last but not least the lightness of touch!" There seems to be no topic for which it would not be useful to read the heathen Cicero, who, in the mind of Erasmus, must have "something divine" in his bosom, since Cicero believed in the existence of some supreme power and in the immortality of the soul. "The present dwelling-place of Cicero's soul is not perhaps a subject for human judgment to pronounce on. I at least shall not be found actively in opposition, as they count the votes, by those who hope that he lives peacefully among the heavenly beings." Erasmus then praises the invention of the printing press for expanding the humanist dialogue with authors whom he quasi-canonizes:

> Who went to him in a time of mourning and was not more cheerful when he came away? What you read seems to be happening, and your mind feels the breath of a kind of enthusiasm in the style, exactly as though you had heard it coming from the heart and the eloquent lips of the living man. This is why I often think that among all the discoveries that enterprise has made for the profit of mortal life, nothing is more profitable than the use of writing, and no art more valuable than the craft of printers. What blessing can be greater than to converse at will with the most eloquent and the most saintly of men, and to have as

---

[65] Leon Battista Alberti, "Theogenius," in: *Opere volgari* (Bari: Laterza, 1966), 74: "io mai men solo che quando me truovo in solitudine. Sempre meco stanno uomini periti, eloquentissimi, apresso di quali io posso tradurmi a sera e occuparmi a molta notte ragionando; ... non a me mancano i santissimi filosofi, apresso de' quali io d'ora in ora a me stessi satisfacendo me senta divenire più dotto anche e migliore."

clear a view of their gifts and character and thoughts and ambitions and actions as if you had lived in their company for many years?[66]

In a letter to his friend Francesco Vettori, Niccolò Machiavelli, a contemporary of Erasmus, describes in 1513 his everyday life in involuntary exile in a Tuscan village after he lost his position as chancellor of the Florentine Republic when the Medici princes had regained power a year before. Machiavelli who remained very ambitious, politically, deplored his "latest disasters" and the "malice of my fate" among unrefined and common peasants. His daily routine included quarrelling with them while playing cards, catching thrushes, and reading the love poetry of Dante, Petrarch, Tibullus, or Ovid outside, work that he considered entertaining, though relatively lowbrow fare: "I read about their amorous passions and their loves, remember my own, and these reflections make me happy for a while." Of quite a different quality is Machiavelli's dialogue with dead authors once he returns home:

> When evening comes, I return home and enter my study; on the threshold I take off my workday clothes, covered with mud and dirt, and put on the garments of court and palace. Fitted out appropriately, I step inside the venerable courts of the ancients, where, solicitously received by them, I nourish myself on that food that alone is mine and for which I was born; where I am unashamed to converse with them and to question them about the motives for their actions, and they, out of their human kindness, answer me. And for four hours at a time I feel no boredom, I forget all my troubles, I do not dread poverty, and I am not terrified by death. I absorb myself into them completely. And because Dante says that no one understands anything unless he retains what he has understood, I have jotted down what I have profited from in their conversation and composed a short study, *De principatibus*, in which I delve as deeply as I can into the ideas concerning this topic, discussing the definition of a princedom, the categories of princedoms, how they are acquired, how they are retained, and why they are lost.[67]

The answers Machiavelli receives by way of human kindness from his interlocutors form one of the two pillars of one of the most famous books of political thought, his *Principe* (*The Prince*), which he mentions in the same letter. In the dedication to the book – to a leading member of the Medici family –Machiavelli claims that the most valuable gift he can offer is "the knowledge of the ac-

---

[66] R.A.B. Mynors and James M. Estes, eds., *The Correspondence of Erasmus*, vol. 10: *Letters 1356 to 1534, 1523 to 1524* (Toronto: University of Toronto Press, 1992), 97–101 (no. 1390, to Johann van Vlatten, October 1523). See appendix for the full text.
[67] James B. Atkinson and David Sices, eds., *Machiavelli and his Friends. Their Personal Correspondence* (DeKalb: Northern Illinois University Press, 1996), 262–265, here 264. See appendix for the full text. For the possible influence of Petrarca see Bec, "De Pétrarque à Machiavel."

tions of great men, acquired by long experiences in contemporary affairs, and a continual study of antiquity."[68] The dialogue with classical authors, also in his *Discorsi*, the *Discourses on the First Ten Books of Titus Livy*, absorb Machiavelli completely and reveal the "motives for their actions." Together with a second pillar – his personal experience as a politician – this enables Machiavelli not only to understand his own times, but to give timeless advice to his addressee and all his readers over the centuries. More explicit than other humanists, Machiavelli invites his readers to really imitate the classics not only in letters, but also in the practice of politics.[69]

It was, however, a humanist topos that one should learn from examples how to perform "worthy deeds and virtuous actions," as Palmieri would put it in *Civil life*. He insisted that there was not just one model (as Jesus Christ could have been) and that one could not ape it. Instead, one should combine "many excellences" of several "great thinkers": "We must not adhere so closely to one model, even one of excellent learning and morals, that we cannot strive to adopt what is best in someone else who surpasses our model. ... Imitating many people, each the best in respect to one quality, we shall strive to become as perfect as we can in every virtue."[70] The humanist dialogue was an open-ended conversation with many eminent partners who contributed different elements from their own personal experience to the eternal question of how the citizen should live a good life.

Many Renaissance artists also took up the subject and show how humanist readers brought different sources into dialogic contact. Study cabinets, especially, which were embellished with portraits of scholars, are vivid illustrations of the new dialogic perspective that they both advocated and lived. A famous example is the tiny *Studiolo* that Federigo of Montefeltro, the Duke of Urbino (1422–1482), had made for himself in the 1470s. Federigo, sitting in his small cabinet room, reading, must be imagined as a participant conversing with the scholars whose portraits surrounded him on the walls (see fig. 3). Originally, the cabinet contained 28 images of distinguished men from the past and the present, Christians and heathen, clergymen and laymen alike. Unfortunately, only half of these are still in Urbino, the other half were moved to the Louvre

---

[68] Niccolò Machiavelli, Dedication to *The Prince*, trans. W.K. Marriott (London: J.M. Dent & Sons, 1958), https://www.gutenberg.org/files/1232/1232-h/1232-h.htm.
[69] Niccolò Machiavelli, *Discourses on Livy*, trans. Harvey C. Mansfield and Nathan Tarcov (Chicago: Chicago University Press, 1995), p. 5–6. See appendix for the full text.
[70] Matteo Palmieri, "Civil Life," in *Cambridge Translations of Renaissance Philosophical Texts*, vol. 2: *Political Philosophy*, ed. Jill Kraye, trans. David Marsh (Cambridge: Cambridge University Press, 1997), 166. See appendix for full text.

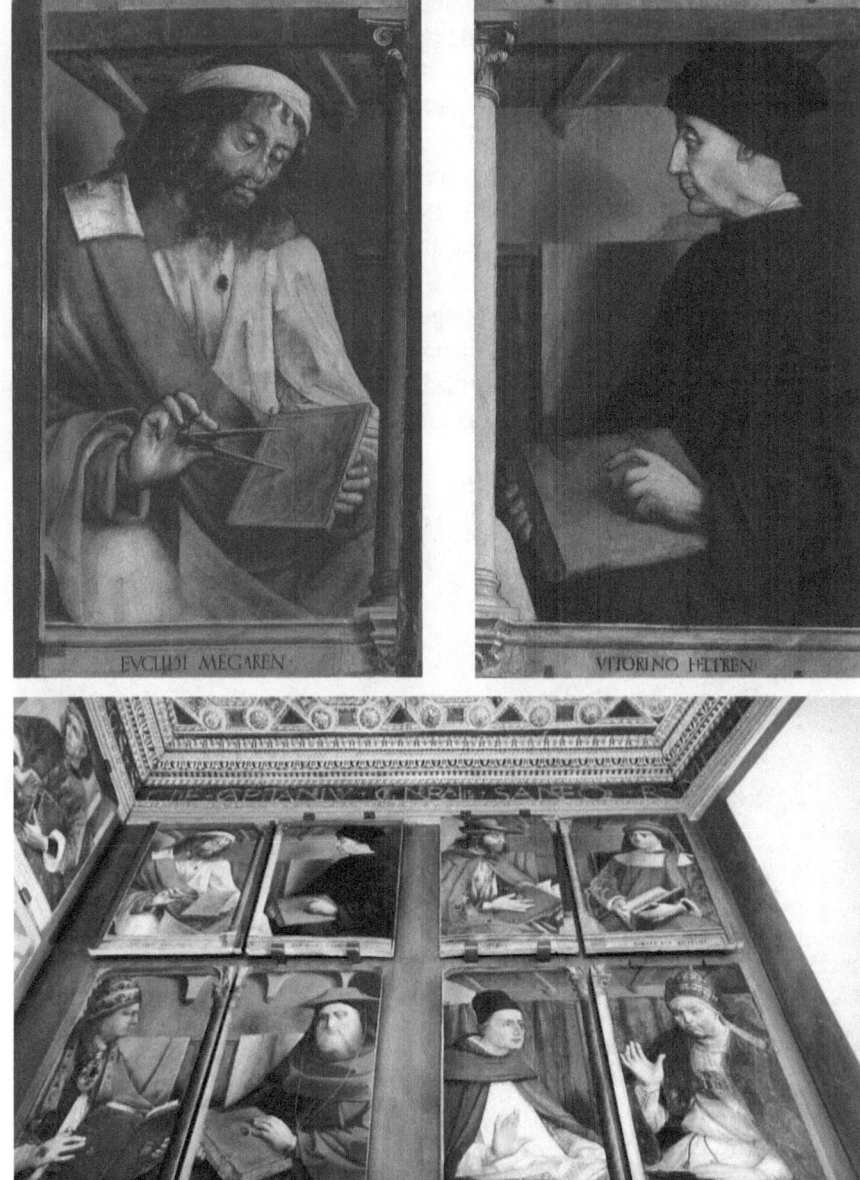

Fig. 3 Justus of Ghent, *Euclid* and *Vittorino da Feltre*, ca. 1474, Studiolo, Palazzo Ducale, Urbino.

in Paris. The portraits face each other and show the discussion between, for example, the Greek mathematician Euclid (from the third century BCE) and the humanist pedagogue Vittorino da Feltre (1378–1446) or the Greek legislator Solon (around 600 BCE) and the Italian lawyer Bartolo from the fourteenth century, all of whom are gesticulating and engaged in conversation.

Such a conversation is actually depicted in *The Three Philosophers* (see fig. 4), a painting by Giorgione (1478–1510), which was finished in 1509 for a Venetian merchant. While these three have been identified differently in the long history of the canvas' interpretation, for example as the three epochs of European civilization (Antiquity, Middle Age, Renaissance) or, alternatively, as the three Abrahamic religions, the three figures of the old man, the Arab figure, and the young man, whoever they are, are clearly engaged in a peaceful dialogue that occurs across space and time and has an open outcome.

Fig. 4 Giorgione, *The Three Philosophers*, 1508/09, Kunsthistorisches Museum Wien, Gemäldegalerie.

Raphael (1483–1520), too, has depicted a kind of transtemporal and translocal dialogue with the "pagans," in his famous *School of Athens* (see fig. 5) from around 1510, which was painted, somewhat paradoxically, for the most "Christian" place imaginable: the Apostolic Palace of the Popes in Rome.[71] The fresco in the *Sala della Segnatura*, which was designed to house the private library of the commissioner, Pope Julius II, is facing and complementing Raphael's *Adoration of the Holy Sacrament*, an image of the Church and its "*disputa*," or theological discussions. The two shorter walls show Jurisprudence and Arts (Parnassus), so that with Theology (entitled DIVINARUM RERUM NOTITIA, knowledge about divine matters) and Philosophy (entitled COGNITIO CAUSARUM, understanding of the causes) the room as a whole presents the world of knowledge as a series of intellectual exchanges occurring between the different frescoes. When describing the *Sala*, Giorgio Vasari went so far as to speak about "the theologians reconciling philosophy and astrology with theology," a notion that was probably building on Marsilio Ficino's humanist syncretism of "prisca theologia," a special revelation to some pagans about Christian doctrine.[72]

The *School of Athens* expresses the all-encompassing dialogic principle in the central "Concordia Platonis et Aristotelis," a theme that was dear to humanists, including Ficino's most original pupil Pico della Mirandola.[73] Concord here characterizes the discussion between the two philosophers who traditionally represented irreconcilable methods and interests: Plato, the metaphysician who holds his cosmological dialogue *Timaeus* in one hand while pointing with the other to the divine skies and the spiritual beyond, and Aristotle, the writer on morals (the *Etica* which he holds in his left hand) and natural sciences, who holds his right hand horizontally, referring to the here and now, the secular and the natural world. Many other philosophers of the past – as well as contemporaries – can be identified among the 59 figures in this painting. They are ar-

---

71 Batkin, *Renaissance*, 483–490; for recent interpretations Marcia Hall, ed., *Raphael's 'School of Athens'* (Cambridge: Cambridge University Press, 1997), especially her introduction, 1–47.
72 For the problems of interpreting Vasari's text, see Timothy Verdon, "Pagans in the Church. The *School of Athen* in Religious Context," in Hall, *Raphael's 'School of Athens'*, 114–130; on p. 117, Verdon compares viewing the Stanza to an "insider" dialogue and visiting acquaintances "expecting to understand the conversation and to take part in it, on the basis of shared experience and interests." However, Verdon insists maybe too much on the pagans being led by their quest for wisdom and their natural knowledge and thus moving toward Christ.
73 Edgar Wind, "The Fear of Knowledge," in *Art and Anarchy* (London: Faber & Faber, 1963), 62–63; also Eugenio Garin, "Raffaello e la 'pace filosofica'," in *Umanisti artisti scienziati. Studi sul Rinascimento italiano* (Rome: Editori Riuniti, 1989); and Ingrid Rowland, "The Intellectual Background of the School of Athens: Tracking Divine Wisdom in the Rome of Julius II," in Hall, *Raphael's 'School of Athens'*.

ranged into two groups on the respective sides of the two leaders who seem to agree to disagree in an open dialogue in which no human can claim to possess complete knowledge and unquestionable Truth. Apart from shameless Diogenes, who slouches leisurely on the stairs, almost all of them are seen participating in different conversations, as seen, for example, in the group around Socrates and Alcibiades. On the far right, the painters Sodoma (or Perugino) and, next to him, Raphael himself are depicted chatting with Zoroaster and Ptolemy, probably about astronomy since they are holding globes of the earth and the skies.

It was this type of dialogue, as depicted here, which enabled the humanists to combine their own Christian traditions and the pagan classical heritage – a corpus whose contents had seemed completely outdated until their own time. Now Aristotle, Plato, Socrates and other pagan philosophers as well as the "splendid school" of classical poets no longer dwelled in limbo, the first circle of the *Inferno* – as Dante had it.[74] Now the text corpus of these same heathens formed the basis for confronting the world and the future, and not with systematized holistic convictions but as an alternative sphere where humankind had to find its way through conflicting truths and values. It needs to be stressed here how extraordinary and extremely improbable it was in the fourteenth and fifteenth centuries, that over several generations hundreds of Christian authors in a growing number of autonomous states would refer to the ancient authors as their equals. For centuries, the latter had been despised as pagan heathen. The radicalism of the humanist attempt in resurrecting these "heathen" may best be understood by analogy: imagine that in today's schools and universities, Christian mystics and apocalyptics of the twelfth century were introduced as valuable sources with which to study and find out about scientific truth – to be read not only by a few eccentric scholars, but indeed by every single student in school and university in order to explain the world and how best to master it.

The humanists, then, were not primarily interested in drawing attention, in an antiquarian way, to a past that had been lost. Rather, their goal was to produce a new understanding of this very past, its re-evaluation and its complete adaptation as a source of true knowledge about how to cope with the present. In this new perception, it was no longer the point that Christianity had prevailed over heathendom. Both made up a part of one human legacy that humanists wanted to recover and – at least some, such as Marsilio Ficino in his *Theologia platonica* (*Platonic Theology*, 1482) – hoped to integrate or synthesize through dialogue. This explains why the humanists were so successful during their own times: with the help of the ancient classics, they were capable of providing

---

[74] See p. 69 above, which already discusses Dante.

better – that is, more appropriate – answers to the most pressing questions in a time of rapid political, social, and cultural change than their competing antagonists, the Scholastics. Accordingly, their skills and interpretations sold well among the princes, noblemen, and citizens of the Renaissance.

Fig. 5 Raphael, *The School of Athens*, around 1510, Stanza della Segnatura, Vatican.

Barbara Mittler
The view from China: r/Renaissances

"Renaissance" has been used, in some of the interpretations discussed by Thomas Maissen, to refer to a cultural movement which did not actually aim to lead back to Antiquity. The humanists were very conscious about the irremediable divide between their present and ancient times but still, they felt that to enter into a dialogue with classical authors would enable them to provide better – that is, more appropriate – answers to the most pressing questions of the day.[1] Since the nineteenth century, "Renaissance" came to be seen as an epoch that was responsible for rapid political, social, and cultural change. It formed part of the European "path toward modernity" and the "rise of the West"[2] by engaging in a revitalization and systematic adaptation of forgotten texts as a source for discovering the individual and the world (to use Burckhardt's phrase). The fact that these interpretations were possible was the reason why the term "Renaissance" was also used by Chinese protagonists in the first decades of the twentieth century to describe what was happening in their country. What they did was thus to engage with *the* Renaissance, in a dialogue across time and space, to benefit, precisely, from what they saw as one of its most salient characteristics: a critical spirit (which, as we have seen amply illustrated above, can best be called dialogic).

I have already discussed how taken with European periodization schemes Chinese intellectuals and scholars were (although some of them explained the newly adopted linearity by referring back to Chinese models such as the "three stages" theory from the *Gongyang* commentary to the *Spring and Autumn Annuals*). The chronotypical idea of a period of degeneration, of darkness and stagnation (like the European Middle Ages, *media aetas*), followed by a period of political, social and cultural reawakening (like the European Renaissance), including the retrieval – and the beginning of a serious dialogue with – a long-forgotten (or, better, long misinterpreted) cultural heritage crowned by the successful arrival of a new age (global modernity), fit their purposes and their analysis of China's contemporary predicament, perfectly.

In China, the traditions to be retrieved were not those of Antiquity, however – an unbroken dialogue had already been established across space and times and lasting for millennia (and into the very recent past, since the last Chinese dynas-

---

1 See Maissen on p. 81 for "appropriate answers."
2 See Maissen on pages 26–30 (where he says that the Renaissance contributed to the "rise of the West and modernity").

tic emperor resigned in 1911). Instead, the Chinese who referred to themselves as the protagonists of the "Chinese Renaissance" (a term that they used in its original French, not in Chinese)[3] would take up a dialogue with, not pagan or heathen, but equally "wild" *ye* 野, and, in Chinese terms, "heretic/heterodox" *xie* 邪, as well as long-neglected traditions: the age-old vernaculars, both oral and written.[4] These had been denigrated throughout China's history as "low," or "small" *xiao* 小 traditions, and thus as insignificant, vulgar, and crude practices that were produced by menial, lesser educated authors, storytellers and actors or poor teachers who had not passed the civil service examinations to reach the high status of officials; this category also included women.[5] Just like Europe's humanists, the Chinese protagonists of the New Culture Movement 新文化運動 *Xin wenhua yundong*, were not only "drawing attention to a past that had been lost."[6] Their goal was also to create a new culture by producing a dialogue with and a "new understanding of this past"[7] as a source of knowledge and a new kind of alternative T/truth, thus ushering in (in true Burckhardtian fashion) a period of modernity for China.

With the events of May 1919, when student protests arose over China's treatment in the Treaty of Versailles, the New Culture Movement (also called the May Fourth Movement 五四運動 *Wusi yundong* because of the involvement of many protagonists in the political demonstrations around that date in 1919) became even more widespread and politicized.[8] As an openly nationalist movement, the New Culture Movement would also become an integral part in the foundational myth of the Chinese Communist Party (founded in 1921). In this myth, the New Culture Movement is seen as a liberating and democratizing movement, one that pushed new truths and new ("scientific") understandings of the individual and the world. This included the use of a new (but old) language – the vernacular – which, in the newly established ideology by and for the masses, and

---

[3] See Hu Shi's several English-language publications already cited above, first and foremost his *Chinese Renaissance*. For a more thorough discussion of these terminologies, see p. 100 below.
[4] See, for example, Lu Xun, *A Brief History of Chinese Fiction* 中國小說史略 *Zhongguo xiaoshuo shilue*, trans. Gladys Yang and Yang Xianyi (Beijing: Foreign Languages Press, 1959), one of the first histories of vernacular literature, based on lectures given in 1923–24.
[5] See Lu Xun, *Chinese Fiction*.
[6] See Thomas Maissen on p. 80.
[7] See Thomas Maissen on p. 80.
[8] The May Fourth demonstrations were a reaction to the Versailles Treaty: China had been convinced, that it would be able to reclaim the territories occupied by the Germans in present-day Shandong Province, since it had, after all, fought in the World War alongside the Allies. But this was not to be, due to a secret deal that was brokered between the British and the Japanese.

later advocated by the Chinese Communist Party, was the long-neglected language of the people.

One important protagonist in the movement was Hu Shi 胡適 (1891–1962) who, in July 1933, was invited as a "Haskell Lecturer" to discuss "Cultural Trends in Present-Day China" at the University of Chicago. A year later, in 1934, these lectures were published in English as a book, with the title *The Chinese Renaissance*. In the book, Hu compares the European Renaissance and the Chinese New Culture Movement as follows: according to him (1) both set out to replace classical literature with a new literature in the living language of the people – the vernacular; (2) both were movements of deliberate protest against established cultural ideas and institutions, and of conscious emancipation of the individual from the bondage of tradition; (3) both were "humanist" movements.[9]

How did Hu develop these particular ideas about "*the* Renaissance"? He had spent the years between 1910 to 1917 as a student in the United States and had received his Bachelor's Degree in philosophy from Cornell University in 1914. He then went on to study at Columbia University under the guidance of John Dewey. His understanding of "*the* Renaissance" would undoubtedly have been influenced by these years of formal education in the United States. Although it may be impossible to reconstruct this exactly, his ideas have been traced back to perceptions of the European Renaissance in the scholarship and in the American popular imagination at the time, both of which were dominated by Burckhardt[10] who, together with Michelet, as we have already learned, brought about a paradigm shift in the use of "Renaissance" as a term. Once confined to describing the rebirth of the arts and the revival of the ancient *bonae litterae*, by the humanists themselves, the concept had been broadened by Burckhardt and Michelet to include what would later be regarded as the defining "essence" of the period: individualism and the "discovery of world and man."[11] Thomas Maissen has illustrated how for both, *the* Renaissance was not only about the rediscovery of the ancient world and its subsequent effects on Western civilization: it was also a monumental leap in the development of the individual and the discovery of subjectivity.[12] Burckhardt writes:

> In the Middle Ages both sides of human consciousness – that which was turned within as that which was turned without – lay dreaming or half awake beneath a common veil. The

---

9 Hu, *Chinese Renaissance*, 44.
10 See Zhou, *Modern Chinese Vernacular*, chapter 2.
11 For a discussion of this title from Burckhardt, *Die Cultur der Renaissance in Italien*, chapter 4, see Thomas Maissen's description above on p. 55.
12 See Maissen on p. 67 above and Anderson, "Promises," 60–61.

veil was woven of faith, illusion, and childish prepossession, through which the world and history were seen clad in strange hues. Man was conscious of himself only as a member of a race, people, party, family, or corporation – only through some general category. In Italy this veil first melted into air; an objective treatment and consideration of the State and of all the things of this world became possible. The subjective side at the same time asserted itself with corresponding emphasis; man became a spiritual individual, and recognized himself as such.[13]

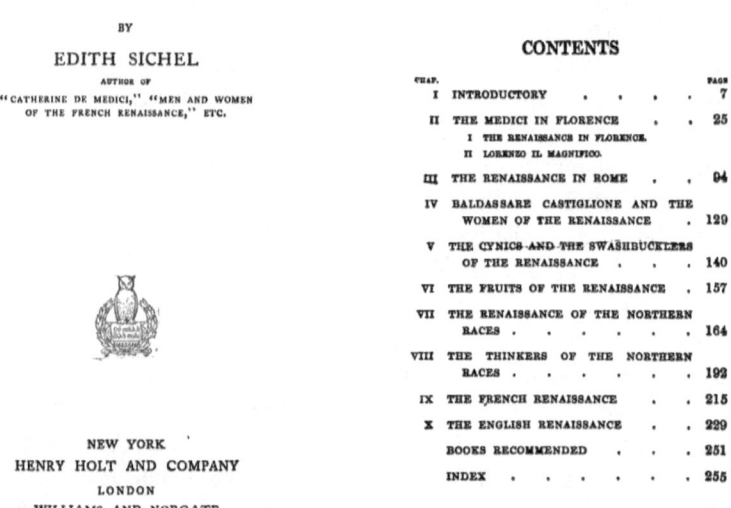

Fig. 6 Edith Sichel, *The Renaissance* (London: Williams & Norgate, 1914), Cover Page and Table of Contents.

There is no conclusive evidence that Hu Shi actually read Burckhardt during his years of study in the United States, but what he certainly did read on his travels back to China in June 1917, was a small popular history called *The Renaissance*, by English author Edith Helen Sichel (1862–1914), a publication clearly based on Burckhardt's premises (see figs. 6 and 7). It defined the Renaissance as "two main things: it signified Emancipation and (individual) Expression."[14]

---

13 Jacob Burckhardt, *The Civilization of the Renaissance in Italy*, trans. S. G. C. Middlemore (London: C. K. Paul & Co., 1878), 129 ("The Italian State and the Individual").
14 Edith Sichel, *The Renaissance* (London: Williams & Norgate, 1914), 8. The text of her introductory chapter is excerpted in the Appendix below.

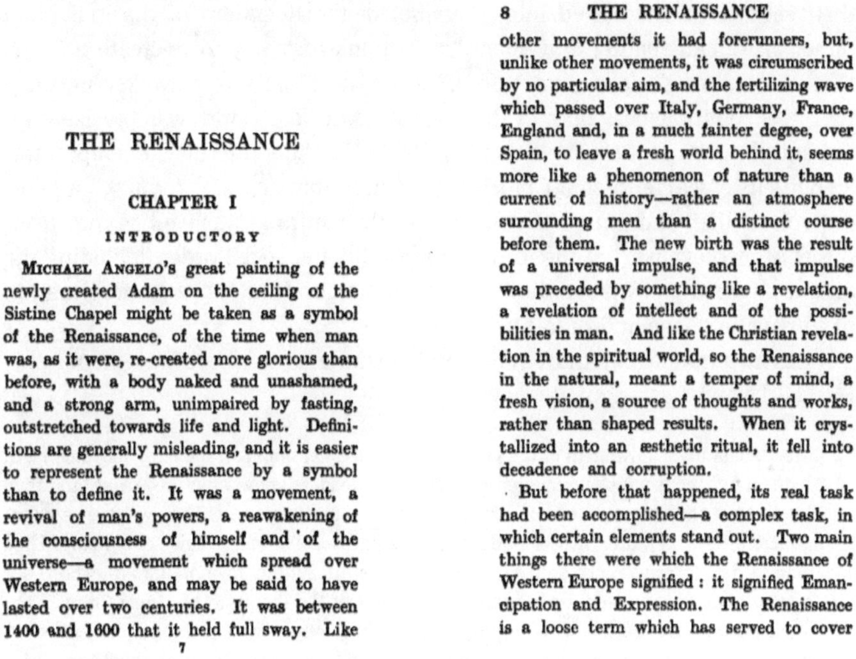

> ### THE RENAISSANCE
>
> #### CHAPTER I
>
> ##### INTRODUCTORY
>
> MICHAEL ANGELO's great painting of the newly created Adam on the ceiling of the Sistine Chapel might be taken as a symbol of the Renaissance, of the time when man was, as it were, re-created more glorious than before, with a body naked and unashamed, and a strong arm, unimpaired by fasting, outstretched towards life and light. Definitions are generally misleading, and it is easier to represent the Renaissance by a symbol than to define it. It was a movement, a revival of man's powers, a reawakening of the consciousness of himself and of the universe—a movement which spread over Western Europe, and may be said to have lasted over two centuries. It was between 1400 and 1600 that it held full sway. Like other movements it had forerunners, but, unlike other movements, it was circumscribed by no particular aim, and the fertilizing wave which passed over Italy, Germany, France, England and, in a much fainter degree, over Spain, to leave a fresh world behind it, seems more like a phenomenon of nature than a current of history—rather an atmosphere surrounding men than a distinct course before them. The new birth was the result of a universal impulse, and that impulse was preceded by something like a revelation, a revelation of intellect and of the possibilities in man. And like the Christian revelation in the spiritual world, so the Renaissance in the natural, meant a temper of mind, a fresh vision, a source of thoughts and works, rather than shaped results. When it crystallized into an æsthetic ritual, it fell into decadence and corruption.
>
> But before that happened, its real task had been accomplished—a complex task, in which certain elements stand out. Two main things there were which the Renaissance of Western Europe signified : it signified Emancipation and Expression. The Renaissance is a loose term which has served to cover

Fig. 7 Edith Sichel, *The Renaissance* (London: Williams & Norgate, 1914), introductory pages (7–8).

Already in the very first sentence (and the Table of Contents) of Sichel's book (see figs. 6 and 7), it is easy to imagine why her reading of "The Renaissance" must have appealed to Hu: Sichel begins with a description of Michelangelo's painting of Adam on the ceiling of the Sistine Chapel, which she takes as "a symbol of the Renaissance, of the time when man was, as it were, re-created more glorious than before, with a body naked and unashamed, and a strong arm ... outstretched towards life and light."[15] According to Sichel, the Renaissance was "a revival of man's powers, a reawakening of the consciousness of himself and of the universe."[16] The value that Burckhardt and Sichel thus placed on this ascendance of the individual had a profound effect on the young Chinese man whose country's recent tragedies were often blamed on its reluctance to break with a past that had enslaved its citizens for millennia.[17] *The* Renaissance, in

---

15 Sichel, *Renaissance*, 7.
16 Sichel, *Renaissance*, 7.
17 Anderson, "Promises," 60–61.

this reading, transmorphed into a symbol of the liberation of the individual mind, an "emancipating movement."[18] To think of a way to re-create a China that was "more glorious than before," to revive its people, reawakening them to a new consciousness both of themselves and of the world, was precisely Hu Shi and the New Culture Movement's mission. To Hu and to his contemporaries "renaissance" came to stand precisely for "free thinking and inquiry," a "new outlook on life" and thus a "change in people's attitude," as well as the "overthrow of medievalism" in the form of the traditional social order, including the all-encompassing powers of the Chinese Classics, and the subsequent formation of a "new language and literature."[19]

It is no surprise then that Hu Shi explained the New Culture Movement in his Haskell Lectures as a Renaissance:

> The Renaissance movement of the last two decades differs from all the early movements in being a fully conscious and studied movement. Its leaders know what they want, and they know what they must destroy in order to achieve what they want. They want a new language, a new literature, a new outlook on life and society, and a new scholarship. They want a new language, not only as an effective instrumentality for popular education, but also as the effective medium for the development of the literature of a new China. They want a literature that shall be written in the living tongue of a living people and shall be capable of expressing the real feelings, thoughts, inspirations, and aspirations of a growing nation. They want to instill into the people a new outlook on life which shall free them from the shackles of tradition and make them feel at home in the new world and its new civilization.[20]

Hu's idea of reviving China, of "making her more glorious than before," hinged upon (1) vernacularization: replacing the old (classical) literature with a new literature in the living language of the people; which would lead to (2) emancipation: enabling everyone's liberation from traditionally established institutional, cultural and social bonds; and finally also to (3) scientification: the possibility for an open and critical spirit, of "humanist scrutiny," in knowledge production.[21] Both emancipation and scientification hinged on the first, vernaculariza-

---

18 Eber, "Thoughts on Renaissance," 216: "it was synonymous to free thinking and inquiry; renaissance was change in people's attitude; renaissance was overthrow of medievalism; and renaissance was new language and literature."
19 Eber, "Thoughts on Renaissance," 216.
20 Hu, *Chinese Renaissance*, 44–46.
21 Hu, *Chinese Renaissance*, 44; over twenty years later, Hu would reinforce and extend the significance of the notion in his 1956 lectures at Berkeley. China's Renaissance, the New Culture Movement, was elevated above all other global iterations of rebirth, including Italy's, for having been built upon a well-laid foundation of centuries of critical thought and scholarship. See Hu

tion, which was also something he found evidence for in Sichel.²² It was his conviction that both the European and the Chinese Renaissance (in the form of the New Culture Movement) must be viewed primarily as ages of rebirth, due to their appreciation and support for vernacular literature, and thus, using Renaissance as a chronotype, he provided the perfect model for a movement that looked to the future while at the same time harking back to the (European) past.²³

These ideas had been developed for many years. Already in 1915, Hu had been exchanging letters with his friend Huang Yuanyong who would write:

> Politics is in such confusion that I am at a loss to know what to talk about. Ideal schemes will have to be buried for future generations to unearth.... As to fundamental salvation, I believe its beginning must be sought in the promotion of a new literature. In short, we must endeavor to bring Chinese thought into direct contact with the contemporary thought of the world, thereby to accelerate its radical awakening. And we must see to it that the basic ideals of world thought will be related to the life of the average man. The method seems to consist in using simple and simplified language and literature for wide dissemination of ideas among the people.²⁴

While none of the protagonists of the New Culture Movement were sure that they would be able to reach a final victory of vernacular (白話 *baihua*) over classical Chinese as a literary language, their particular interpretation of the European Renaissance was key to their belief that such a change could be successful and that it would be helpful in effecting more encompassing changes in China's social and political orders. In his diary entry of 19 June 1917, Hu wrote: "we can see from Sichel's book that the national languages in Renaissance Europe all started as very small forces but ended up having a wide-reaching and powerful influence. Hence, we who advocate vernacular literature today, ought to be confident about a promising future."²⁵

When Hu encountered Sichel's text, it functioned as a "contact zone," a space where what would usually be separated, geographically, and/or culturally engages in co-creative meaning-making.²⁶ In Hu Shi, the text meets a reader entirely unanticipated by its producer. While we might begin to deliberate about whether the new possibilities of interpretation that Hu Shi opens up in his read-

---

Shi, "39th May Fourth Celebration in 1958," *The Chinese Renaissance Movement* 中國文藝復興運動 *Zhongguo wenyi fuxing yundong* (Taipei: Wentan, 1961).
22 Sichel, *Renaissance*, 12–13. See the excerpt in the Appendix.
23 See Zhou, "The Chinese Renaissance, a Transcultural Reading," *PMLA* 120, no. 3 (May 2005).
24 The letter is cited in translation by Hu Shi in his "The Literary Renaissance," 129.
25 Zhou, "Other Asias, Other Renaissances," *Concentric: Literary and Cultural Studies* 34, no. 2 (September 2008), 94. See Sichel, *Renaissance*, 12–13 in the Appendix.
26 See Zhou, *Modern Chinese Vernacular*, chapter 2.

ing of "Renaissance" on Chinese terms, make the concept itself vulnerable, we could also argue the opposite: it reveals, instead, the very vitality of the idea itself and the importance of actors such as Hu Shi in its making.[27] Here, we see how "Renaissance" – not unlike other vocabularies and patterns of periodization – is reconfigured in the hands of actors around the world, who would invoke "the term, and what they saw as its most important claims, for their own specific purposes."[28] Hu's (and others) creative uses of the "European Renaissance" (the regional variation it becomes by virtue of being compared to other Renaissances) and his passionate promotion of a "Chinese Renaissance" reveal some of the "performative magic" of the concept itself.[29]

And indeed, the "European connection," the example of the successful and epoch-making resurrection of the vernacular during the Renaissance in Europe (even though this had not been at all central to the actors of the European Renaissance, who were primarily interested in reviving Ciceronian Latin), is constantly, consciously, and deliberately cultivated by New Culture intellectuals. The two seminal articles that successfully launched the so-called literary revolution in 1917, one by Hu Shi, the other by Chen Duxiu 陳獨秀 (1879–1942) and published in the New Culture Movement's flagship journal *New Youth* 新青年 *Xin Qingnian*, both used the European Renaissance as their most important reference point. In the concluding eighth point "Do not avoid vulgar diction" from his essay "Some Modest Suggestions for Literary Reform" 文學改良芻議 *Wenxue gailiang chuyi* which raves about the faults of traditional Chinese literature in the classical language and its devastating effects on China, Hu makes a case for vernacularism as a means of reviving China's "dead" literary language. He does so by drawing extensively on Renaissance examples and turning Dante and Luther – advocates first and foremost of the vernacular, in his interpretation – into formidable heroes of this movement:

> Looking back from our contemporary perspective, the Yuan [the Mongolian Dynasty that reigned China between 1271–1368] should, without doubt be seen as the most vigorous period of Chinese literature, producing the greatest number of immortal works. At that time, Chinese literature came closest to a union of spoken and written languages, and the vernacular itself had nearly become a literary language. If this tendency had not been arrested, then a "living literature" might have appeared in China and the great endeavor of Dante and Luther might have developed in old Cathay. (In the Middle Ages in Europe, each country had its own vulgar spoken language and Latin was the literary language. All written works used Latin, just as the classical language was used in China. Later, in Italy appeared

---

27 See Zhou, "The Chinese Renaissance, a Transcultural Reading," 783.
28 Conrad, "Enlightenment in Global History," 1001.
29 Zhou, "The Chinese Renaissance, a Transcultural Reading," 783.

Dante and other literary giants who first used their own vulgar language to write. Other countries followed suit, and national languages began to replace Latin. When Luther created Protestantism, he began by translating the *Old Testament* and the *New Testament* into German, which ushered in German literature. England, France, and other countries followed this pattern. Today the most widely circulated English Bible is a translation dating from 1611, only 300 years ago. Hence, all contemporary literature in the various European nations developed from the vulgar languages of that time. The rise of literary giants began with a "living literature" replacing a dead literature in Latin. When there is a living literature, there will be a national language based on the unity of the spoken and written languages.) [But in China and quite] unexpectedly, this tendency was suddenly arrested during the Ming [the Han-reigned dynasty following the Mongolian Yuan, which reigned 1368–1644]. The government had already been using the "eight-legged essay" to select its civil servants, and scholars ... [it] raised "archaism" [returning to the old 復古 fugu] as the most lofty of literary goals. So the once-in-a-millennium opportunity to affect the unity of the spoken and written languages died a premature death, midway in the process. Yet, from today's perspective of historical evolution, we can say with complete certainty that vernacular literature is really the canonical and will be a useful tool for developing future literature. (My "certainty" is only my opinion, one shared by few of my contemporaries.) For this reason, I propose the appropriate use of vulgar diction in the writing of prose and poetry. It is preferable to use the living words of the twentieth century than the dead words of three millennia past ...; it is preferable to use the language of *The Water Margin* and *The Journey to the West* [two Ming novels originating from oral story-telling traditions and written in the vernacular], known in every household, than the language of the Qin [221–207 BCE], Han [206 BCE–220 CE], and Six Dynasties [220–589], which is limited and not universally understood.[30]

The text clearly betrays a hesitation (e. g. when Hu writes "my certainty is only my opinion") and a sense of crisis that was typical of the early efforts of the New Culture Movement, which was by no means building on majority opinions and which was seeing China at a threshold, an abyss, a turning-point, if not a point of no return. Their rhetorics are accordingly rather sharp and radicalizing (speaking of dead languages and cultures) as well as pompous and self-aggrandizing, when they take the European Renaissance (as they view and interpret it) as a parallel case for what a future for China could (and, in their view, should) look like.

Chen Duxiu's "On Literary Revolution" 文學革命論 *Wenxue geming lun*, in similar, but perhaps even more spectacular manner, emphasizes the overall importance of the Renaissance for the development of European civilization and its

---

30 Hu Shi, *Wenxue gailiang chuyi* 文學改良芻議 XQN 2.5 (January 1, 1917); translation follows Kirk A. Denton, trans., *Modern Chinese Literary Thought: Writings on Literature, 1893–1945* (Stanford: Stanford University Press), 123–139; additions by this author are added [in square brackets].

"modernization." According to him, the Renaissance had changed all aspects of life, the political, the social, the religious, the cultural (again, the Burckhardtian frame is clearly echoed, here), and this was what he also hoped for in China. Chen's text begins quite aptly – in grandiose but revolutionary fashion – in the emotional and personalized new style (*xin wenti* 新文體) that had only recently been established by the likes of Liang Qichao.[31] He argues as follows:

> From whence arose the awesome and brilliant Europe of today? I say from the legacy of revolution. In European languages, "revolution" means the elimination of the old and the change over to the new, not at all the same as the so-called dynastic cycles of our Middle Kingdom. Since the artistic renaissance, therefore, there have [sic] been a revolution in politics, a revolution in religion, and a revolution in morality and ethics. Literary art as well has not been without revolution: there is no literary art that does not renew itself and advance itself with revolution. The history of contemporary European modernization can simply be called the history of revolutions. So I say that the awesome and brilliant Europe of today is the legacy of revolution.[32]

Both Hu and Chen declared that the literary revolution they called for in China was a parallel development to the one that had taken place since the European (artistic) Renaissance and thus they marked and gave authority to their declaration of a new age, a new nation, a new China that, accordingly and inevitably, would someday be as awe-inspiring and brilliant as Europe. This appraisal of the Renaissance as an enabling, revitalizing chronotype appeared everywhere in the publications of the New Culture Movement. It picks up on some of the discourses of vitality, strength, speed, etc., that were circulating globally at the time to reflect modernity's vibrancy (and thus to create its dynamic self-fulfilling prophecy). According to them, the vitality that characterized modernity had originated with the Renaissance: another prominent article appeared in 1916 entitled "Youth" and was published in the journal *New Youth* (青春 *Qingchun*); it was authored by journal editor Li Dazhao 李大釗 (1881–1927) who would become one of the founding members of the Chinese Communist Party in 1921.[33] In it Li argues that just as the organic world is self-regenerating, so too would China come to life and bloom again: "Old China is the fruit from which young

---

[31] On the making of this new style of writing in newspaper language, see Barbara Mittler, *A Newspaper for China? Power, Identity, and Change in Shanghai's News Media, 1872–1912* (Cambridge: Harvard University Press, Asia Center Series, 2004), 108–113.
[32] Chen Duxiu 文學革命輪 XQN 2, no. 6 (1.2.1917); the translation follows Denton, *Modern Chinese Literary Thought*, 140–145, here 140.
[33] Anderson, "Promises," 51–52.

China is born; young China is the rebirth/renaissance (再生) resulting from old China's passing."[34]

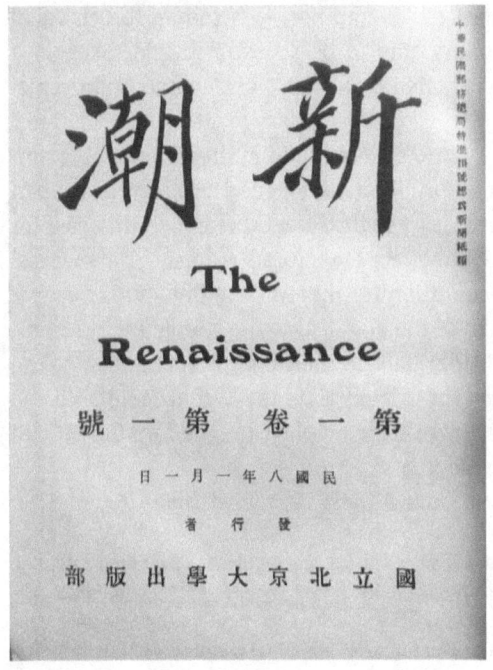

Fig. 8 Bilingual cover page of a journal edited by Fu Sinian 傅斯年 (1896–1950), entitled *Xinchao* 新潮 (New Tide) and *The Renaissance*, 3.2.1919.

Everywhere in the discourse of the New Culture Movement, youth and revolution, rebirth and, ultimately, renaissance is invoked: in the winter of 1918, when the group of intellectuals around linguist Fu Sinian 傅斯年 (1896–1950) began editing the journal *Xinchao* 新潮 (New Tide) at Beijing University, they gave it the English title *The Renaissance* (see fig. 8).[35] The most important aspect of their renaissance, or *xinchao* (new tide), as they explained, was its being a *xinchan* 新產 – that is, technically, a new production and biologically, a new birth. China's more recent tragedies and losses (in the opium wars, the war against Japan and the ensuing territorial losses, among them, Taiwan etc.) were often

---

34 Li Dazhao, "Youth," *Qingchun* in XQN 2, no. 1 (1916).
35 Hu, *Chinese Renaissance*, 44.

blamed on the country's reluctance to break with the past,³⁶ and thus, for Hu, Fu, Li and others active in the New Culture Movement, Renaissance became tantamount to the end of this old life and a new birth through the liberation of the individual and society from all bondages of tradition – including the classical heritage. This was a truly revolutionary step to be proclaimed and taken in a country that had for so long been sustained by a homogenized and homogenizing literary tradition.

To its Chinese mediators, then – quite differently from their European counterparts – "Renaissance" was not at all primarily understood as a recuperation of the classical past, rather, it was a necessary and strategic break with the past (or at least, specific aspects of it) in order to effect the reforms requisite to a successful rebirth into modernity. The pre-condition for this was the final and irreversible change in the written language from the classical to the vernacular.³⁷ Appropriating the idea of a linguistic shift that had, in their interpretation, also taken place in the European Renaissance, Hu formed a narrative that facilitated the transformation of the vernacular in China from a vulgar tongue into the official language of the nation and the language of the future.³⁸

Naturally, this was not an easy task and thus, Hu reflects in 1926:

> We want to be modernised, and we are expected to become modern. But at the same time we are requested not to lose what we have. We are expected to perform a miraculous task – to change and to remain the same. There is little wonder then that the Chinese have continued to live in comfortable dreams of compromise, accepting certain externals from the Western Barbarians whilst preserving the restrictions and negations of the past. But a new age has dawned. We have realised at last that certain things must be given up if China is to live. If we really want education, general and universal education, we must first have a new language, a language which can be used and understood by tongue and ear and pen, and which will be a living language for the people. For years and years we tried to have education, but we feared to use the spoken language. We tried to compromise in various ways, but we clung as scholars to the scholarly language. This Literary Revolution formed the first phase of the Chinese Renaissance. It marked a new phase, a new life.³⁹

The ultimate aim of the New Culture Movement – and here they felt themselves very much akin to the Renaissance in Europe – was to foster and engage a critical spirit which would, in the case of the Chinese Renaissance, however, be built primarily upon a broadening, a democratization, so to speak, of education that

---

36 Anderson, "Promises," 61.
37 Anderson, "Promises," 58.
38 See Zhou, "The Chinese Renaissance, a Transcultural Reading."
39 Hu Shi, "The Renaissance in China," *Journal of the Royal Institute of International Affairs* 5 (1926), 271–272.

would be "related to the life of the average man" as Huang Yuanyong had argued, or a "popular" or "general and universal education" as Hu Shi put it.[40] This would have to occur through vernacularization and not through a creative dialogue with China's ancient Classics, however. Indeed, as we have seen, a dialogue with that "dead past" was explicitly rejected by the Chinese New Culture Movement. They wanted to get rid of their classical heritage and instead revive the vernacular as a "living language." Although the unbroken, once venerated and orthodox classical tradition that, according to them, had put China "in shackles" for so many years was a parallel to the unbroken Christian traditions in Europe, the neglected and (from the point of view of classical orthodoxy) "heretic/heterodox" vernacular traditions in China, which are in turn taken up – in dialogue – and thus revalorized by the "Chinese Renaissance," (as in Hu Shi's elaborate description of lost vernacular literatures above) were a parallel to lost heathen or pagan Antiquity in Europe.[41]

And while they would surely admit that the European Renaissance, as a humanist movement, was a movement of the elites, in their minds this same Renaissance had inbuilt democratizing ideas and effects which were evident to them in Luther's or Dante's vernacularisms (or the ramifications of developing the printing press, an endeavor which all of the New Culture Movement protagonists were involved in China, too). By their own interpretation, Hu and his Chinese Renaissance obviously felt that they matched the European model.[42]

Theorized as a progressivist force, the renaissance as chronotype thus became a tool by which Chinese culture and its cosmopolitan representatives felt they could be ushered into the modern world.[43] And therefore, the idea found many followers: the general appreciation of the Renaissance's significance in world history was shared by Chinese modernists who believed that all of modernity's characteristic traits, ranging from economic expansion, political centralization, and secularization, to philological precision based on a new type of in-

---

[40] Quotations here are taken from the passages by contemporaries of the New Culture Movement, cited at length in the previous pages.
[41] See also the argumentation by Zhu Jinpan, "The Chinese Renaissance" in *Taizhong* 台中18 (1930), 56 as provided in full in the Appendix who speaks of a "transvaeuation (sic) of uolues (sic)" (transevaluation of values) and argues: "Nothing is too sacred to be submitted to the scrutiny of intelligent criticism." See also the discussion by Zhou Zuoren who recognizes that the Renaissance, disrupting a thousand-year trend, resurrected Socrates and Plato who had been "censored as heterodox... their books banned." See Luo Zhitian, *Inheritance within Rupture. Culture and Scholarship in Early Twentieth Century China*, trans. Lane J. Harris and Mei Chun, (Leiden: Brill 2015), 80.
[42] Hu, *Chinese Renaissance*, 44.
[43] Anderson, "Promises," 40–41.

tellectual and scientific curiosity, could be linked to *the* Renaissance. In the process, "Renaissance" was reduced to a rather more superficially sweeping concept of a particular revolutionary spirit and a period of cultural florescence that had severed its old ties with a repressive dark age of tradition, an idea which, as we will see below, was wholly advantageous to modernist schemes in China.[44] Renaissance in China thus came to stand for the revitalization of some of the forgotten glories of the past through the advancement of a new (vernacular) national culture, by way of which that which was understood as China's authenticity and sovereignty was to be asserted within the modern world system. The pursuit of her own Renaissance promised to liberate China from foreign perceptions of her historical stagnation, and instead catapulted China into the forward thrust of modernity.[45] Accordingly, "Renaissance" became the battle call for the protagonists of the New Culture Movement, and it was used internally as well as externally on the international stage to indicate that China was on the rise again, that she had overcome stagnation (in parallel to the Middle Ages), that the old "stationary" China (which Hegel had condemned in his *Philosophy of History*),[46] the "sleeping dragon" (of which Napoleon had allegedly warned), was finally waking.[47]

What Hu and his contemporaries did was what Prasenjit Duara has recently called an act of "national naturalization through resignification."[48] Hu's use of "Chinese Renaissance" aimed to redefine his own country's history while propelling it into a modern, progressive, global order which, at that point in time, naturally included the Renaissance as an indispensable stage on a necessary path toward modernity. From a rather low-profile debut to this glorious staging, which, as already mentioned, foreshadowed the Chinese Communist revolution to come, the European Renaissance was firmly established as a blueprint for China's nationalist moves. To speak of China's "Renaissance" was to "think globally"[49] – to position China within a larger, world system, one that was connected, inevitably, with evolution and modernity. At the same time, the urgency with

---

[44] See a very elaborate and illuminating description of the phenomenon in Anderson, "Promises," 2.
[45] Anderson, "Promises," 60.
[46] Georg Wilhelm Friedrich Hegel, "China," in *The Philosophy of History*, trans. John Sibree (New York: American Home Library, 1902).
[47] Rudolf G. Wagner, "China 'Asleep' and 'Awakening.' A Study in Conceptualizing Asymmetry and Coping with It," *Transcultural Studies* 1 (2011). Open access: archiv.ub.uni-heidelberg.de/ojs/index.php/transcultural/index.
[48] Prasenjit Duara, *The Global and Regional in China's Nation-Formation* (London: Routledge, 2009).
[49] Conrad, "Enlightenment in Global History," 1019.

which such rhetoric was invoked as a mighty tool was a response to obvious "differentials of power."⁵⁰ The idea of a Chinese Renaissance, inspired by the European model, was used, somewhat paradoxically, to create parity with this model, and, eventually, to rid China of European domination. China's use of "Renaissance" as an epochal marker, was at the same time a symbol of the uneven power relations between China and Europe, and a way of registering uniqueness and asserting agency through active cultural negotiation.⁵¹ The act of appropriating Renaissance in China thus reveals itself as a "going-out into the world of global ideas informed by the centripetal pull of national introspection."⁵² As Zhu Jinpan 朱錦盤 would put it in 1930: "The Literary Revolution has succeeded in revolutionizing the whole language of China, has succeeded in writing over all the textbooks in the schools, has succeeded in producing a literature capable of being understood by the vast majority of the people." He continues: "The Youth Movement of 1919, which arose as a protest against the action of Paris Convention on German possessions in China, found expression in this new language, and in 1920 the government was persuade [sic] to require its use in all newly printed textbooks. The developmnt [sic] of this new language is but one phase of the Chinese Renaissance, which is the *conscious development* of an unconscious movement that has been gathering force for two thousand [sic] years."⁵³

Thomas Maissen has already questioned whether and to what extent proclaiming "we had one, too"⁵⁴ could ever be a successful antidote to cultural and political superiority, and this is precisely the question one might pose here. At the time and for the protagonists of the New Culture Movement, however, the answer was clear. In using Renaissance as "their" special chronotype, Hu Shi and the New Culture Movement were not primarily interested in searching for universally valid patterns or principles of human activity – epochal frames. Their aim was to assert their national identity.⁵⁵ Ultimately, what was important to Hu and his contemporaries was not any *de facto* coherence between Chinese, European, or, more specifically, any distinct Italian understandings of Renaissance, but the way in which the idea and the name of Renaissance enabled a refashioning of China's history and identity and the possibility of building the prospects

---

50 Conrad, "Enlightenment in Global History," 1019.
51 Anderson, "Promises," 7.
52 Anderson, "Promises," 72, see also ibid. 12.
53 See the complete quote from the journal *Taizhong* as cited in the Appendix below: Zhu, "The Chinese Renaissance."
54 See Maissen on p. 26 where he talks of this type of "retaliation-act" for political superiority.
55 Anderson, "Promises," 72.

for its glorious future.⁵⁶ Accordingly, Hu Shi begins the publication of his Haskell lectures as follows (a passage which I have already briefly discussed in my introduction):

> I want my readers to understand that cultural changes of tremendous significance have taken place and are taking place in China.... Slowly, quietly, but unmistakably, the Chinese Renaissance is becoming a reality. The product of this rebirth looks suspiciously occidental. But, scratch its surface and you will find that the stuff of which it is made is essentially the Chinese bedrock which much weathering and corrosion have only made stand out more clearly, the humanistic and rationalistic China resurrected by the touch of the scientific and democratic civilization of the new world.⁵⁷

Making a concept such as renaissance "organically Chinese" through abstraction, and the possibility for thus engaging in the resignification of the term in early twentieth-century China shows how fluid and mobile the idea – or chronotype – of Renaissance was or could become. While I am not questioning that power structures direct the traffic of such a chronotype, I would hold – against the postcolonial stance – that this is not most important in such covers or resignifications. Indeed, as the example of the New Culture Movement shows, resignifications such as Chinese Renaissance illustrate the potency and the agency in transcultural imagination that is exercised by those who participate in the complex culminations of cultural contacts that are – more often than not, and certainly in this case – instigated and consciously manipulated by those inspired and not at all by those who serve as inspiration.⁵⁸ The particular discursive mechanisms and structures that allowed for the Renaissance's translatability to China in the early twentieth century privileged particular "local positions,"⁵⁹ those which the mediators chose to enjoy. The broker of words, much more than the originator of words (the author is, after all, dead), occupies a position of considerable power. Accordingly, Hu and his contemporaries were using the conceptual term "Renaissance" as a powerful slogan for their own very personal cause, fighting for a new and Chinese modernity. Hu's position and his intellectual influence, along with the "natural authority" and the "symbolic value attributed to

---

56 See Anderson, "Promises," 65.
57 Hu, preface to *Chinese Renaissance*, no page. Some of the responding prefaces are cited in the Appendix below.
58 Taking out the unncessary postcolonial edge, I am playing here with a formulation in Zhou, "Chinese Renaissance: A Transcultural Reading," 793–94.
59 Chen Xiaomei, *Occidentalism: A Theory of Counter-Discourse in Post-Maoist China*, 2nd rev. ed. 2002 (Lanham: Rowman and Littlefield, 1995), 167.

any idea from the West," made Renaissance an almost "indispensable term"⁶⁰ for him and one with which he was able to "invoke modernity."⁶¹

As mentioned, Giorgio Vasari is credited with coining the term *rinascita* in his long introduction to the *Lives of the Great Painters, Sculptors and Architects* (1550).⁶² His "naming" would shape the ways in which later generations viewed his time. As a chronotype, "Renaissance" is continuously re-born through similar acts of "naming" and with it, "claiming," in China and elsewhere, and it is precisely these acts that excited and empowered (non-European) intellectuals like Hu Shi and his contemporaries, who thus set out to change their worlds through words and who thus continued to promote their particular and distinctive Renaissances, to refine and improve their own status in their own history and on the world stage.⁶³

While the final goal was often the same, the way and manner in which it was reached was quite variable. The volatility of a term such as "r/Renaissance," as it moves across linguistic, cultural, and also political borders, is significant. Indeed, Chinese claims to "r/Renaissance" throughout the first half of the twentieth century took many forms. Even in his own writings, Hu Shi offered several different options for reading r/Renaissance heuristically. In his Haskell Lectures, he enumerates several Chinese renaissances:⁶⁴ first, the Tang Dynasty (seventh–tenth centuries) rise of the great poets and of a new prose literature that was modeled on the classical style; second, the development of a secular neo-Confucianist philosophy in the Song Dynasty (960–1279); third, the rise of drama and the great novels under the Yuan in the thirteenth century; fourth, the development since the seventeenth century of Qing classical scholarship with its particular critical philological and evidential approach; and fifth, the literary revolution of his own present – that is, the turn to vernacularism which the New Culture Movement advocated.⁶⁵ And he was not the only (or even the first) to bring variety to the term: r/Renaissances had multiplied in China long before Hu Shi claimed the term, donning ever new meanings and shedding old ones. In a speech given in 1906 at a welcome party organized by Chinese overseas students in Tokyo, a cultural conservatist and supporter of the so-called *Guocui yundong* 國粹運動 or National Essence Movement, Zhang Taiyan 章太炎 (1868–1936), had already paired the revival of Han learning (*wenxue fugu* 文學復古 "re-

---

60 Zhou, *Modern Chinese Vernacular*, 60.
61 Anderson, "Promises," 27.
62 Vasari, *Le vite*, vol. 1, 13, 19, 31; vol. 2, 32. See the discussion above p. 60.
63 See Zhou, "Other Asias, Other Renaissances," 92; Anderson, "Promises," 13.
64 See Hu, *Chinese Renaissance*, 45.
65 Hu, *Chinese Renaissance*.

turning to the old in literature") with the recovery and restoration of Antiquity that had taken place in Europe during *the* Renaissance. Zhang was convinced that to revive this movement once more in his own present – a renaissance of the previous renaissance – would help "preserve the nation and the Han Chinese."[66] He was basing his definition on Ma Junwu 馬君武 (1881–1940) who, in a dialogue with Liang Qichao had argued in 1903 that "the key to the richness of Western scholarship was the revival of ancient studies or 'the Renaissance' – the literal meaning of Renaissance is ' A second birth time of the race'."[67] Similarly, Liang Qichao's use of the term "renaissance" for Qing evidential scholarship (engaged in, among others, by his teacher Kang Youwei, the advocate of a "Chinese linear history" and the author of the *Book of Unity* discussed earlier).[68] Liang implied that these Qing scholars had a vital role to play in reviving the past by infusing it with new life to "rejuvenate" and improve the present (*fuxing* 復興 revival/rejuvenation).[69]

By the 1910s, then, while Renaissance as an epoch in European history was well known and widely discussed, renaissance as a generic concept, a metaphorical paradigm or analogy had emerged as well, and it was used to name and claim and thus to give form and force to the promotion of progressive ideas inspired by the past. A number of different translations circulated for both renaissance as generic concept and Renaissance as the particular chronotype from Europe. Each of these terms used to translate r/Renaissance also conveys its own particular analytical and semantic emphasis: 新潮 *xinchao* (new tide) and 新產 *xinchan* (new production/new birth) were the terms used in one of the early journals of the New Culture Movement, already mentioned above, with

---

[66] Zhang Taiyuan is cited in Chen Pingyuan, *Zhongguo xiandia xueshu de jianli* 中國現代學術的建立 (The Establishment of Modern Chinese Scholarship) (Beijing: Beijing University Press, 1998), 336.

[67] Ma Junwu *Xin xueshu yu qunzhi zhi guanxi* 新學術與群治之關係 (The Relationship between new scholarship and governing the people) In *Ma Junwu ji* 馬君武集 (Collected Works of Ma Junwu), Mo Shixiang (ed.). (Wuhan: Huazhong shifan daxue chubanshe 1991), 187. For the general discussion between many different advocates of Renaissance, see Luo, *Inheritance within Rupture*, chapter 3 "The Dream of a Chinese Renaissance: From the Late Qing 'Revival of Ancient Studies' to the Republican 'New Tide'."

[68] See above, p. 46, for Kang's *Datongshu*.

[69] For Liang's uses of the Renaissance, see Anderson, "Promises," chapter 2. For Hu Shi's criticisms of Liang, see Luo, *Inheritance within Rupture*, chapter 3 "The Dream of a Chinese Renaissance: From the Late Qing 'Revival of Ancient Studies' to the Republican 'New Tide'," especially 60–61. See also Elisabeth Kaske, *The Politics of Language in Chinese Education, 1895–1919* (Leiden: Brill, 2008), chap. 5, who elaborates on the inspiration drawn from "the European Renaissance" by conservative Chinese philologists in the 1900s.

the English title *The Renaissance*.⁷⁰ (文藝)復興 (*wenyi*) *fuxing* (artistic) revival/rejuvenation, was one of the Japanese reverse loan translation terms for *the* Renaissance in its more restricted sense, as an artistic movement.⁷¹ 再生 *zaisheng* (rebirth), 復活 *fuhuo* (resurrection), 再造 *zaizao* (re-creation), and 啟蒙 *qimeng* (enlightenment) would also be used in the early twentieth-century discourse on China's need for renewal and change.⁷² On the other hand, these and related terms such as 'rejuvenation' (復興 *fuxing*), 'returning to the old' (復古 *fugu*), or (in a transitive sense) 'recovery' (光復 *guangfu*, literally, 'return of the light'), were also alternatively used as translations for "The Renaissance" or renaissance more generally. Most of these terms carried meanings from prior usage (in a Chinese setting), dating to a time before the foreign terminology ever entered China – and thus, before there was a need to translate it. Significantly, Hu Shi, who often wrote in English, would use the French term "Renaissance," but both Zhang and Liang, for example, would speak of *the* Renaissance as well as other Chinese r/Renaissances using some of the Chinese expressions mentioned above. While it may be clear in most instances when these terms actually refer to *the* Renaissance and when they are used to translate a term employed figuratively for some moment in the past that the respective authors wished to qualify, metaphorically or generically as a renascence, a revival of sorts, either in a more Chinese or European sense, nevertheless, these prior (or multiple) usages (in Chinese) would always resonate. Accordingly, when *the* Renaissance as an emblematic movement from the European past was appropriated in China in the late nineteenth and early twentieth centuries,⁷³ its meanings would be identified with, and at the same time augmented by, the many possible conceptual and semantic constellations emerging around r/Renaissance and its Chinese cognates, and these in turn would continue to reshape (and, indeed, make fuzzier, as Thomas Maissen puts it) its message.⁷⁴

While the sheer range of connotations and significations between the general and the historically specific senses of the term allows for quite a few nuances, the indisputable frequency of its occurrence, especially in Republican China –

---

70 See above, p. 93.
71 See Luo, *Inheritance within Rupture*, 80.
72 For further discussion, see Anderson, "Promises," 51.
73 See Gamsa, "Uses and Misuses of a Chinese Renaissance," 642; Kiyama Hideo, "The 'Literary Renaissance' and the 'Literary Revolution'," *Acta Asiatica* 72 (March 1997): 30 points out that when Zhang Taiyan used the term *wenxue fugu*, it was most likely applicable to both "the Italian renaissance and . . . the current movement in China to revive ancient learning."
74 See Kurtz/Fisac/Jenco/Dusinberre *East Asian Uses of the European Past: Tracing Braided Chronotypes*.

that is, during the first half of the twentieth century – but also to the present day, is significant, as are the rhetorical practices (of naming and claiming) by respective historical actors.[75] And as we have seen already, these could (and can) be found on all sides of the political spectrum: it was not only the rather more leftist writers of the journal *New Youth* that drew on the Renaissance as model, those on the opposite side of the political spectrum, "cultural conservatives" such as Zhang Taiyan and his supporters writing for the *Scholarly Journal on National Essence* (*Guocui xuebao* 國粹學報), did the same.[76]

By the 1930s, the Chinese State Socialist Party (*Zhongguo guojia shehuidang* 中國國家社會黨), founded in 1932, under the leadership of Zhang Junmai 张君勱 (Carsun Chang, 1887–1969), published a journal *Zaisheng* 再生 (rebirth), with the English title *The National Renaissance* (see fig. 9).[77] At the time, many in China considered the "rebirth" of Germany after the First World War and its humiliation at Versailles an impressive example for the glorious "regeneration of an oppressed nation." Germany, like China (as the May Fourth protests had shown), had been offended by the terms of the peace treaty of 1919. Accordingly, in 1932 the Chinese Nationalist Party 國民黨 (*Guomindang/Kuomintang*) in the first issue of its journal entitled in English, the *Renaissance Monthly* (復興月刊 *Fuxing yuekan*) discussed the "German example" and lauded Germany's "renaissance" under Hitler.[78] Chiang Kai-shek followed up with the founding of the *Blue Shirt Society* 藍衣社 (1932–38), which was modeled after the German *Braunhemden* and would alternatively style itself – quite fittingly – as the *Chinese Renais-*

---

75 Gamsa, "Uses and Misuses of a Chinese Renaissance," 642.
76 See Zhu Weizheng, "China's Lost Renaissance," in *Coming Out of the Middle Ages: Comparative Reflections on China and the West*, trans. and ed. Ruth Hayhoe (Armonk, NY: Sharpe, 1990), 190–92; and, more recently Tze-ki Hon, *Revolution as Restoration:* Guocui xuebao *and China's Path to Modernity, 1905–1911* (Leiden: Brill, 2013).
77 Gamsa, "Uses and Misuses of a Chinese Renaissance," 643–644 explains that a few years later (in 1935), Zhang also published a book he called *The Academic Basis of National Renaissance*, which was presented as a Chinese parallel to Johann Gottlieb Fichte's early nineteenth-century *Addresses to the German Nation*, a book which Zhang himself had previously translated into Chinese in 1932. In both the journal and the book, he set forth a political program that emphasized the attainment of national consciousness through education. See Roger B. Jeans, *Democracy and Socialism in Republican China: The Politics of Zhang Junmai (Carsun Chang), 1906–1941* (Lanham, MD: Rowman & Littlefield, 1997), 203.
78 For more details, see Gamsa, "Uses and Misuses of a Chinese Renaissance," 643. For the significance of the German example, see William C. Kirby, *Germany and Republican China* (Stanford: Stanford University Press, 1984), 151, 165.

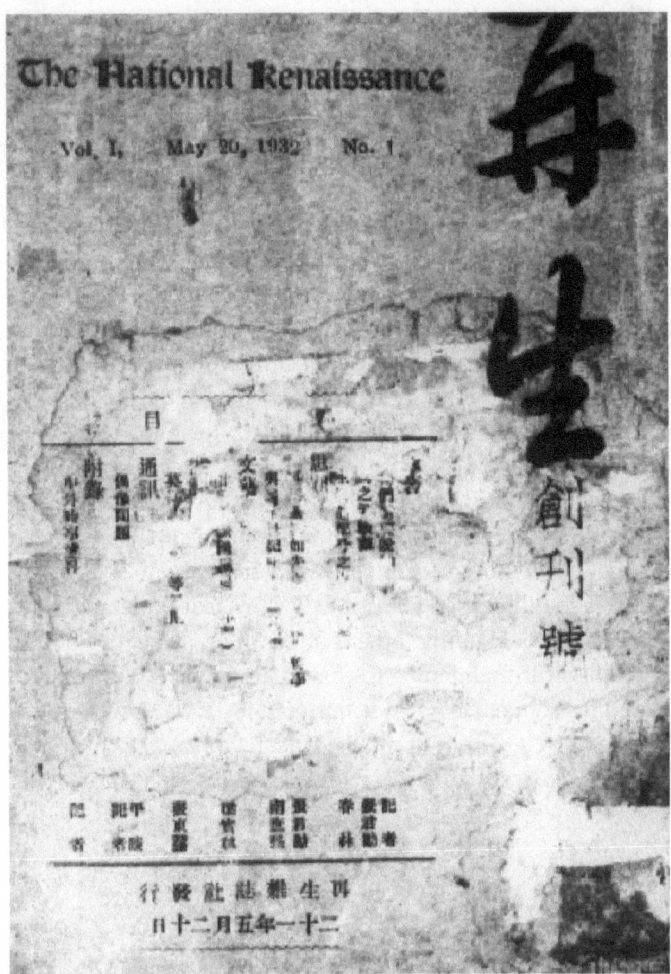

Fig. 9 Bilingual cover page of a journal published by Zhang Junmai 张君劢 (Carsun Chang, 1887–1969), 20.5.1932.

sance Society 中華復興社 *Zhonghua fuxingshe*.⁷⁹ At the same time, Mussolini's speeches describing the history of Italy's oppression by foreigners as a succession of slurs to the national pride that needed redeeming through the re-creation

---

79 See Maria Hsia Chang, *The Chinese Blue Shirt Society. Fascism and Developmental Nationalism* (Berkeley: Center for East Asian Studies, 1985) and, more recently Frederic Wakeman, *Spymaster: Dai Li and the Chinese Secret Service* (Berkeley: University of California Press, 2003).

(or rebirth) of a new Roman Empire (a *translatio imperii?*), also found sympathetic Chinese audiences and were mirrored in a rhetoric, this time of Confucian "revival/renaissance," in Chiang Kai-shek's *New Life Movement* 新生活運動 *xin shenghuo yundong*.[80] The year 1937 saw the publication of *Italy's Way to Revival* 義大利復興之道 *Yidali fuxing zhi dao* by a Guomindang official Xue Guangqian 薛光前 (alias Paul K. T. Sih, 1910–78), and it was clear that the publication was meant to inspire China on its way to rejuvenation/revival, and R/renaissance, too.[81] At the same time, as the term was thus used extensively by those on the far right of the political spectrum, a liberal literary monthly named *Wenyi fuxing* 文藝復興, e.g. *Artistic Revival/Renaissance* (the translation terminology referring to the European Renaissance in its restricted sense of an artistic revival), was published in Shanghai between 1946 and 1947.[82]

The tide turned a bit between the 1950s to 1970s when r/Renaissances receded from view on the China mainland. The "Father of China's Renaissance,"[83] Hu Shi, "defected" to Taiwan and, accordingly, the New Culture Movement was thereafter associated in official parlance more with the politicized May Fourth demonstrations (as May Fourth Movement) than with European ideas of emancipation and liberation of self (Chinese Renaissance). The Great Proletarian Cultural Revolution in the mid-1960s, on the other hand (which picked up on the idea of destroying the classical traditions once formulated by the New Culture intellectuals but never did so "in name"),[84] was mirrored in Taiwan by a "Cultural Renaissance Movement" 文化復興運動 *wenhua fuxing yundong* which was committed, somewhat paradoxically in view of Hu Shi's contrary ideals, to pre-

---

80 For more details, see Gamsa, "Uses and Misuses of a Chinese Renaissance," 643; for the *New Life Movement*, see Airif Dirlik, "The Ideological Foundations of the New Life Movement: a Study in Counter-Revolution," *Journal of Asian Studies* 34, no. 4 (August 1975); see also Sakai Tadao, "The New Life Movement with Relation to the Neo-Confucian Culture in Modernizing China," *Proceedings of Conference on Chiang Kai-shek and Modern China*, vol. 3 (Taipei: China Cultural Service, 1987).
81 An elaborate discussion of more recent examples of usage of renaissance can be found in Gamsa, "Uses and Misuses of a Chinese Renaissance," 645–46.
82 See Gamsa, "Uses and Misuses of a Chinese Renaissance," 644.
83 The epithet was given Hu during a lecture tour in Britain in 1926. It appeared on the posters advertising his lectures on the Chinese Renaissance. Cf. Yu, "Neither Renaissance nor Enlightenment," 300.
84 For the importance of iconoclastic and anti-Confucian ideas derived from the New Culture heritage during the Cultural Revolution, see Barbara Mittler, *A Continuous Revolution. Making Sense of Cultural Revolution Culture* (Cambridge: Harvard University Press, Asia Center Series, 2012), passim and especially chapter 3.

serving China's classical traditions which were seen to be destroyed in Communist China.[85]

More recently, the r/Renaissance has enjoyed a massive comeback on the mainland, and is employed once more by protagonists at opposite ends of the ideological spectrum: in 2001 President Jiang Zemin 江泽民 (1926–) was the first Chinese politician since 1949 to declare that the Chinese Communist Party was leading the nation towards a great *fuxing* 復興 (revival), a terminology which had been used so frequently to mean r/Renaissance. His message fell on fertile ground during the increasingly nationalist atmosphere in the 1990s (following along with patriotic education since 1989) and abounded in publications such as He Xin's 何新 (1949–) two-volume collection of essays published in 1996 as *China's Renaissance and the World's Future* 中华复兴与世界未来 *Zhonghua fuxing yu shijie weilai*.[86] On the other hand, a liberal academic and philosopher like Liu Junning 刘军宁 (1961–), who has been periodically criticized by the Chinese government (for signing *Charter 08* which calls for 19 changes in China's political system, including an independent legal system, freedom of association and the elimination of one-party rule),[87] published an essay in December 2006 entitled "China, You Need a Renaissance! *Zhongguo ni xuyao yige wenyi fuxing* 中国你需要一个文艺复兴!" (here going back to one of the first translation terms of "Renaissance" which emphasizes it as a revival *fuxing* 复兴 of literature and the arts *wenyi* 文艺) in the popular Guangzhou weekly *Southern Weekend* 南方周末 *Nanfang Zhoumo*. The article sparked a lively debate on the topic.[88] The Chinese Communist Party in turn continued to claim the powerful terminology: a

---

[85] See Allen Chun, "From Nationalism to Nationalizing: Cultural Imagination and State Formation in Postwar Taiwan," *Australian Journal of Chinese Affairs* 31 (January 1994); Wang Shou-nan, "Chiang Kai-shek and the Promotion of the Chinese Cultural Renaissance Movement," *Chinese Studies in History* 21, no. 2 (Winter 1987–1988); Barbara Mittler, *Dangerous Tunes. The Politics of Chinese Music in Hong Kong, Taiwan and the People's Republic of China since 1949* (Wiesbaden: Harrassowitz, 1997).

[86] The book was published in Chengdu in 1996, see Gamsa, "Uses and Misuses of a Chinese Renaissance," 645. On He Xin, see the biography by Geremie R. Barmé in Edward L. Davis, ed., *Encyclopedia of Contemporary Chinese Culture* (London and New York: Routledge Taylor & Francis Group, 2005), 344.

[87] *Charter 08* was a manifesto initially signed by over 350 Chinese intellectuals and human rights activitists. It was published on 10 December 2008, the sixtieth anniversary of the Universal Declaration of Human Rights, and adopted its name and style from the anti-Soviet *Charter 77* issued in Czechoslovakia. Liu Xiaobo 刘晓波 (1955–2017) who was awarded the 2010 Nobel Peace Prize, was one of the authors of the charter.

[88] Liu Junning, "*Zhongguo, ni xuyao yige wenyi fuxing!*" 中国你需要一个文艺复兴 (China, You Need a Renaissance!), 南方週末 *Nanfang zhoumo*, December 7, 2006. See also the discussion forum in the Beijing monthly *Yishu pinglun* 艺术评论 *Arts Criticism* 5 (2007).

six-part TV series with the official translation title "The Road to Revival" 复兴之路 *Fuxing zhi lu*[89] was produced in conjunction with the 17th Party Congress in December 2007 and in preparation for the Olympics in 2008. It recounts the history of China since 1840 from the perspective of its "revival," allowing China to be tied with the history of the great nations and entering the world, while setting itself apart through its regained glory and power.[90] Indeed, during the staging of the Beijing Olympics, which formed one of China's most forceful recent bids for international recognition, China's "road to revival," *fuxing zhi lu* became a key term and was repeated incessantly with every gold medal that went to the Chinese team. This trend has continued: when the new National Museum of China reopened in spring 2011 (the result of a merger between the former *Museum of the Chinese Revolution* and the *National Museum of Chinese History*), *Fuxing zhi lu* (this time officially translated into English as "The Road of Rejuvenation") was used as the title for its permanent exhibition, beginning with the "national humiliation" 国耻 *guochi* in the Opium Wars and ending with the confident announcement of breathtaking achievements in the Chinese space program.[91] Quite fittingly, the museum also devoted its first international exhibition to the European Enlightenment which, in Chinese parlance, is indeed often used synonymously with Renaissance, a point that we shall return to later. That same year, the ninetieth anniversary of the Chinese Communist Party in July 2011 would be celebrated with the release of a propaganda film on the decade between 1911 and 1921. The film was marketed to international audiences as the *Beginning of the Great Revival* (while its Chinese title 建黨偉業 *Jiandang weiye* actually says nothing of revival or renaissance, but must be translated as "The founding of the Party, a great undertaking").[92] The film takes the 1911 revolution and, following this, the Chinese Renaissance or New Culture Movement (but here, politically correctly, termed the May Fourth Movement) as significant movements that pre-

---

89 Gamsa, "Uses and Misuses of a Chinese Renaissance," 645–46 points to the somewhat ironic parallel of this title to the fascist publication *Italy's Way to Revival* 義大利復興之道 *Yidali fuxing zhi dao* by the Guomindang mentioned above. It went unnoticed, however.
90 For a discussion of the TV series and its background see Gotelind Müller, *Documentary, World History, and National Power in the PRC: Global Rise in Chinese Eyes* (London: Routledge, 2013).
91 See Anne Hennings, "The National Museum of China. Building Memory, Shaping History, Presenting Identity" (PhD diss., Universität Heidelberg, 2012).
92 Gamsa, "Uses and Misuses of a Chinese Renaissance," 646 remarks that this, in turn, alludes to the title of a previous self-congratulatory production, Jianguo daye (literally "The Founding of the Republic, a Great Enterprise of State-Building"; English title: *The Founding of a Republic*), a film covering the years from 1945 to 1949, which was released for the sixtieth anniversary of the PRC in 2009.

pared the path for today's Chinese Communist government.⁹³ Later that year, as President Hu Jintao 胡锦涛 (1942-) addressed the nation in the autumn, on the 100th anniversary of the 1911 revolution, he would once again drive home his point on China's revival with the help of twenty-three repetitions of the "magic" term *fuxing* – rejuvenation/revival/r/Renaissance.⁹⁴

r/Renaissance as both chronotype and generic terminology has thus been employed extensively in recent state propaganda, and therefore in 2010, when China's most popular and outspoken blogger, Han Han 韩寒 (1982–), planned to found a magazine with the English title *Renaissance* and the Chinese title *Wenyi fuxing* 文艺复兴 (*Wenyi fuxing* – again using the terminology "Revival of literature and the arts"), the state censors refused to license it: clearly, the Communist Party now seeks to monopolize the term or at least its "proper use." This has been quite unsuccessful, however, as demonstrated by the example of an anti-government internet blog operating from abroad and associated with the banned *Falungong* 法轮功 (Dharma Wheel Practice) movement, which, through its English URL-name "atruechineserenaissance.blogspot.com" seeks to inaugurate a "True Chinese Renaissance."⁹⁵

Evidently, throughout the long twentieth century, Chinese uses of "r/Renaissance" as the term for contemporary or historical mo(ve)ments in history are both supremely nationalist and also constitute a manner of speaking and positioning on the global stage – that is, speaking to the world at large, not just to China.⁹⁶ This is evident from the fact that in these texts, renaissance appears not just in its several Chinese translations but often also (exclusively!) in its English/French variations (sometimes, as the *Beginning of the Great Revival*, mentioned above shows, in deliberate mistranslation of the original). The use of references to r/Renaissance in products that openly cater to a foreign audience (such as Hu Shi's lectures, Chiang Kai-shek's personal support troupe, Jiang Zemin's political speeches, Chinese state anniversary films, or National Museum exhibits etc.) have to do with the assumption that a familiar term helps both to bring events in China closer to a foreign audience and to highlight – in a way that this par-

---

93 See Gamsa, "Uses and Misuses of a Chinese Renaissance," 646.
94 See Mark Elliott, "The Historical Vision of the Prosperous Age (shengshi)," *China Heritage Quarterly* 29 (March 2012) and Gamsa, "Uses and Misuses of a Chinese Renaissance," 646.
95 The *Falungong* website is atruechineserenaissance.blogspot.com. For this and Han Han, see Gamsa, "Uses and Misuses of a Chinese Renaissance," 646–647.
96 Anderson, "Promises," 40–41. See Conrad "Enlightenment in Global History," 1019: "The equivalence of civilization and Enlightenment points to the degree to which the latter had changed meaning; it was now primarily a gauge for the relative geopolitical position of a given nation in the global arena."

ticular audience might find flattering – the positive contribution of the West/Europe to China's development. Yet at the same time, Hu Shi's discursive choices (many of his speeches and publications on the "Chinese Renaissance" were published in English) and those by Chinese governments on both sides of the Taiwan straits (in the English translations given for political speeches, movements, films, exhibitions) as well as the *Falungong* movement (on its English-language website), all still reflect the assumed imbalances of power between East and West in the manner of "we have it, too" even while attempting to redress them.[97]

Hu's English-language book on the *Chinese Renaissance*, for example, is carefully formulated for his foreign audience, but this will not prevent the foreign reader from being bewildered by the set of images and ideas that a concept as profoundly familiar to a European or North American audience as r/Renaissance will conjure up in this new context. Clearly, over the course of its multifaceted Chinese career, the label "r/Renaissance" is more or less uncoupled from the ideas with which it was once associated elsewhere.[98] Just like Chiang Kaishek with his Blue Shirt Society, or the makers of the exhibit in the National Museum in Beijing, or those in charge of an officially endorsed film like *Beginning of the Great Revival*, Hu substantially revised and reimagined the term to serve his own purposes. This often occurred in ways and manners that may or may not resemble those of Michelet, Burckhardt, and the medievalists claiming – or women not claiming – "their" Renaissance. Hu's *Haskell Lectures* as well as some of the more recent examples mentioned here thus provide us with perfect cases to examine how *the* Renaissance travels back and forth geographically while semantically moving away from (and sometimes closer to) what it may once have meant to those who lived *the* Renaissance in Italy. Moreover, it was not only in China that those who transformed it, claiming "r/Renaissance" as a useful and strategic label for themselves and thus "doing things with words,"[99] firmly re-rooted the terminology in new grounds. And, indeed, their particular performative utterances would have consequences.

Jiang Fangzhen 蔣方震 (1882–1936), who in 1921, published a history of the European Renaissance,[100] compares it to "light" *guang* 光 travelling through the "air" *kongqi* 空氣, thus echoing Voltaire who had spoken of the Renaissance as "that same genius which made the fine arts flourish at Rome, Naples, Florence,

---

[97] See Gamsa, "Uses and Misuses of a Chinese Renaissance," 641.
[98] See Anderson, "Promises," 2 and Conrad "Enlightenment in Global History," 1016 who uses a similar formulation for the Enlightenment in its global transformation.
[99] John L. Austin, *How to Do Things with Words* (Oxford: Clarendon Press, 1962).
[100] Jiang Fangzhen, *European Renaissance*. The following passage is indebted to Anderson, "Promises," 68–70.

Venice, Ferrara, and brought their light from Italy to Europe."[101] Linking the constituent ideas of the Renaissance to the rays of the sun instantly justifies its accessibility to all possible worlds of thought and civilization in Jiang's mind:

> Waves of light travelling through different substances account for changes in light's color and luminosity. The development of thought in different environments explains differences in tendencies. By an understanding of history and place, we can approach an understanding of these flows of differences. At the same time, we'll also be able to discover the origins of their similarities.[102]

The use of the light metaphor also stresses the boundless circulation of universal ideas through space while at the same time neglecting the conception of time. Although, strictly speaking, light travels at a certain speed, and nothing can match or rival it, it becomes, quite literally, the standard for time itself. Perceiving light in this way, Jiang subtly shifts a diachronic concept of history, as events occurring in temporal units of measurement, to a more synchronic model that marks the circulation of thought through space as history's true "metronome." History is no longer what occurs in reference to time, but what occurs in reference to place. As an essential and universal measure of history in modernity, he argues, China was an heir to the European Renaissance's light, irrespective of the clock.[103] After all, Jiang points out, that light had already passed through Florence, Venice, France, Germany, Holland, and Northern Europe. To him, the Italian Renaissance's evident fitness for European translatability justified and assured its passage through China, too, as a transformative force for modernization.[104] It was also always discussed in terms of a *desideratum*, as something China should have, and this turned r/Renaissance into a "thing" that could be possessed and that conveyed particular expectations about the *future:* the essayist Zhou Zuoren 周作人 (1885–1967), once called the "Chinese Renaissance" – modeled after the European Renaissance – "a dream" that his generation bequeathed to the next. It appears to have remained an "unfulfilled promise," as most recent government moves under Xi Jinping 习近平 (1953-), foremost

---

[101] Voltaire, *Essay on Manners*, 1756, is discussed in greater detail above.
[102] Jiang Fangzhen, *European Renaissance*, 3. The translation follows Anderson, "Promises," 68–69.
[103] Jiang Fangzhen, *European Renaissance*, 2. The translation and argument is indebted to Anderson, "Promises," 68–69.
[104] Anderson, "Promises," 70.

among them his "Chinese dream" 中國夢 *Zhongguo meng*, illustrate quite aptly.¹⁰⁵

Chinese players are not using the term r/Renaissance simply as a neologism, adapting wholesale what may be attached to it. Instead, in all of these cases – Jiang's history, Hu's lectures, as well as Chiang Kai-shek's or Jiang Zemin's political speeches or the revelations of *Falungong* – the term takes on a great many new dimensions, indeed, it may become a creation beyond any correspondence with *the* Renaissance that is familiar to European audiences.¹⁰⁶ Accordingly, such texts are inviting foreign audiences to ask: What do these other renaissances allow me to see and understand about or question in "our" Renaissance. Why, for example, did Chinese women have a renaissance, while European women did not? Studying Renaissance as a chronotype encompasses these readings that are remote in space and time from its first 'privileged' usage. The "translated" Chinese renaissances introduced here intimate that questions of authenticity and realness, and the distinctions between "ours" and "theirs" should probably be replaced with questions about circulation and appropriation, about performativity and a/effect. Thus privileging processuality and agency and studying renaissance from a global perspective as part of a History-in-common, has fundamental consequences for understanding the term.¹⁰⁷

The global perspective allows us to see that chronotypes such as "Renaissance" can no longer be considered the "exclusive property" of those who once allegedly "produced" them: these terms enter into a pool in which "global co-production," as Conrad calls it, or, continuous re-interpretation, as one could also term it, is taking place and by which they are enriched, they grow and develop.¹⁰⁸ To use Renaissance as a chronotype in China, then, is not tantamount to a wholesale adaptation of a foreign system of periodization into a foreign cul-

---

105 Zhou Zuoren, *Kukou gankou wenyi fuxing zhi meng* 苦口甘口文藝復興之夢 (The bittersweat Dream of a Renaissance), (Shanghai: Taiping shuju 1944), 12. Gamsa, "Uses and Misuses of a Chinese Renaissance," 648, shows that the latest addition to the stream of historical analogies was mobilized to lend lustre to the Party's achievements, the notion of the "prosperous age" *shengshi* 盛世 to come has the advantage over the foreign "renaissance," of evoking the glory of imperial China, with such ages" in mind as the high Ming and the early to mid-dynasty Qing.⁴ It is thus able to appeal to an alternative vision of a Chinese modernity that preceded the country's traumatic confrontation with the West in the nineteenth century. See Elliott, "Prosperous Age (*shengshi*)."
106 Gamsa, "Uses and Misuses of a Chinese Renaissance," 641.
107 This passage borrows from Conrad, "Enlightenment in Global History," 1008.
108 Conrad, "Enlightenment in Global History," 1022: "Rather than a process of diffusion, the longer history of Enlightenment was the result of its constant reinvention. We may speak thus of the global co-production of Enlightenment knowledge."

ture. It does not mean that everyone who is inspired by it, complies, at the same time, with a particular "*Weltanschauung* which they saw as a key element of the European success and its success story" as Thomas Maissen puts it.[109] Instead, r/Renaissance is continually reinvented as a critical category that is used to legitimize and glorify an ever-changing set of very particular cultural values and practices all over the world. Maissen also mentions that every transfer and adaptation has its "unique and particular historical and cultural context that allowed for the invention of such terminologies."[110] Indeed, and as this happens, Renaissance can no longer be understood as the sovereign and autonomous accomplishment of European intellectuals alone: it develops in response to cultural flows and global integration, it is the work of historical actors all around the world.[111] Hu's Chinese Renaissance (and the many more r/Renaissances to precede and follow in his course) and the fact that various non-European countries have declared and promoted their own Renaissances, each invite scholarly reconsideration of r/Renaissance as a transcultural term rather than as a linguistic and conceptual category "originating in" and therefore "owned by" a certain culture. As Edward Said comments, "Culture [and by implication a particular cultural vocabulary] is never a matter of ownership, of borrowing and lending with absolute debtors and creditors, but rather of appropriations [I would call them variations], common [if always already specific] experiences, and interdependencies of all kinds among different cultures."[112]

Indeed, the very resilience and mobility of r/Renaissance shows that the term must be understood as a translatable, transcultural phenomenon, not a historical ontology. Taking a global perspective decenters the debate on universalism that is so crucially linked to notions of *the* Renaissance as one element in a particular periodization scheme. Indeed, it is less the inbuilt universality of renaissance as a particularist generic structure than the global history of references to and creative borrowings of Renaissance as an idea, or chronotype (i.e. its constant re-articulation) that transforms it into one ubiquitous – perhaps even universal – presence.[113] According to Reinhart Koselleck, "every reading by later generations of past conceptualizations alters the spectrum of possible transmitted meanings. The original contexts of concepts change; so, too, do

---

109 See Maissen above on p. 33.
110 See Maissen above on p. 27.
111 This passage is indebted to Conrad, "Enlightenment in Global history," 1001.
112 Edward Said, *Culture and Imperialism* (New York: Vintage Books, 1993), 217. Passages added in [square brackets] have been added by the author of this section, Barbara Mittler.
113 See Conrad, "Enlightenment in Global History," 1008.

the original or subsequent meanings carried by concepts."[114] Accepting this, we are able to stress r/Renaissance's plural (and even its contested) character, and we are no longer able to insist on the "uniqueness" of *the* Renaissance and its meanings: *the* Renaissance thus becomes simply a regional variation, and r/Renaissance in turn changes into a generalized rather than a specific term – an analytical term (renaissance/renascence) or a chronotype (Renaissance) rather than a strictly fixed periodization scheme attached. So, indeed, there is a lot to be learned about *the* (European) r/Renaissance by following the history of its dissemination and reception. This history, however, need no longer consider who "had it first" or who "came delayed."[115] This kind of argumentation ensues from an acceptance of Eurocentric chronology and periodization schemes instead of seriously tracing the vibrant fabrication of renaissance/renascence as an analytical term or the notion of Renaissance as chronotype that contests periodization schemes as strictly ordered and delimiting the temporal *imaginaire* or the chronologics for the rest of the world. Indeed, it is crucial not to see the repercussions of r/Renaissance as merely the after-effects of a singular foundational moment. They are part of a continuous and unceasingly processual Renaissance-in-common that is determined by coincidence and simultaneity but never by identity or mere reproduction of thoughts and ideas.[116]

In this context, it is not just time, but also space which needs to be reconsidered: r/Renaissance as a concept is not an "intellectual monopoly of Europe."[117] Instead r/Renaissance has created an intellectual dynamic as well as having a revolutionary impact in many places of the world and on a global scale, both by diffusion and by permanent reinvention. [118] r/Renaissance is an experience that women may not have had in sixteenth-century Europe, but one women had in twentieth-century China. r/Renaissance is part of Indian, Irish and American history. Its very globality cannot be explained simply as emanating from a single and identifiable center, however. Only when the various ways in which Renaissance as a chronotype or renaissance as a generic, analytical term have been used in different parts of the world are understood not as

---

114 Reinhart Koselleck, "A Response to Comments on the Geschichtliche Grundbegriffe," in *The Meaning of Historical Terms and Concepts: New Studies on Begriffsgeschichte*, eds. Hartmut Lehmann and Melvin Richter (Washington D.C.: German Historical Institute, 1996), 62.
115 See Conrad, "Enlightenment in Global History," 1015.
116 Conrad, "Enlightenment in Global History," 1015.
117 Conrad, "Enlightenment in Global History," 1026.
118 Taking this seriously, I am at variance, with Conrad who instead of highlighting, as I would do, the ever-shifting nature of cultural flows and transmissions, denies, a bit too categorically, the importance of diffusion.

mis-readings, abuses, misapprehensions, misunderstandings or even, aberrations,[119] but rather as part of *the* Renaissance's continuous history and its conceptual development,[120] including some naturally developing shifts in contents and meaning, have we finally been able to rid ourselves of the potential *Denkzwang* caused by a stiff "cookie-cutter" use of such terminologies.[121]

Embracing rather than discarding "misrepresentation" as an integral part of Chinese (and by analogy, world) history, is a route that was suggested in Chen Xiaomei's seminal book *Occidentalism: A Theory of Counter-Discourse in Post-Mao China* (1995).[122] It was her aim to show – through a critique of Edward Said's exclusively negatively perceived model of Orientalism and the practice of Occidentalism, which she constructed in parallel (standing for the "willful misrepresentation of things Western") – that both Orientalisms and Occidentalisms reveal themselves as well-traveled and versatile practices whose significance and impact can be captured as "strategies of bondage" just as much as, or perhaps even more than, as "strategies of liberation."[123] Taking this perspective, in contrast to the traditional quest for the "correct" reading and the commonplace privileging and positive view of "understanding," "misunderstanding" no longer seems a symptom of confusion but a legitimate and necessary factor in the making and the complexities of Renaissance-in-common-in-the-making. "Misunderstanding" or "misapprehension" is thus transformed: no longer a target, it becomes the very object in a new way of writing global history. As Kyle Anderson, in his stupendous dissertation on Chinese uses of the Italian Renaissance, puts it:

> a historical quest to dispel myth leaves untouched the reverse exposure of the historically paramount role that fantasies and misunderstandings have played in intercultural exchange. In other words, in trying only to make "right" what is historically askew, the very nature of world history as we know it – a boundless volume of mutual imaginations and misprisions – awaits analysis. Instead of regarding this intercultural distance as something to be correctly bridged, the present study treats "misrepresentations" as crucial ingredients in the historical development of modern Chinese culture. The misunderstandings of Chinese intellectuals with regard to Italian culture and literature constituted precisely the

---

119 See Chen, *Occidentalism*, Gamsa (who provocatively calls his essay "Uses and Misuses of a Chinese Renaissance"), the writings on China's transcultural Renaissance by Zhou, and Anderson, "Promises."
120 Conrad, "Enlightenment in Global History," 1022.
121 See my discussion of Keazor and Fleck above, p. 48–49.
122 Chen, *Occidentalism*. For a very good summary of her impact on the field, from which the following is also informed, see Anderson, "Promises," 42–44.
123 Chen, *Occidentalism*, 167.

"right" understandings for the development of a national culture in Chinese modernity. Misrecognition has always been an important ideological device and cultural resource.[124]

What he describes very aptly here is the heuristic use of particular terminologies, such as the chronotype Renaissance, that I have attempted to illustrate so far. This heuristic use of particular vocabularies – practiced by historical actors all over the world – allows for shifts in the meaning of previously firmly defined notions. Ludwik Fleck in his work on the *Entstehung und Entwicklung einer wissenschaftlichen Tatsache*[125] (and similarly, Thomas Kuhn in his *The Structure of Scientific Revolutions*)[126] see precisely this option of shifting meanings in the paradigmatic readings of certain vocabularies as responsible for every significant change in scientific thinking. Thus, to Fleck, it is precisely this which enables progress: new discoveries are, according to him, only possible when the *Denkzwang*, exerted in every (scientific) community and dictated by their particular usage of certain vocabularies, is lessened and only when the meaning of once fixed terminologies begins to change and new possibilities of interpretation become visible.[127]

So if China has a Renaissance after all – a "Chinese Renaissance" (or even several) – how far can we go in broadening our vocabularies? By the mid-1930s, an alternative term, "Enlightenment" (or *qimeng* 啟蒙, which means "to break open what had once been obscure"), was offered in China for naming *the* Chinese Renaissance or New Culture Movement. Why? In the face of local, regional, and global challenges, and in an attempt to make a complex world legible to themselves and others, China's intellectuals in the long twentieth century were constantly on the lookout for new ideas. When Hu and his contemporaries had developed their New Culture discourse, they began combining Renaissance and Enlightenment not only because these two terms were part of a *lingua franca* that promised to endow Chinese ideas with a "universal" validity, but also because the terms themselves had already been transformed, not least through their own efforts.[128]

---

124 Anderson, "Promises," 42.
125 Fleck, *Entstehung und Entwicklung einer wissenschaftlichen Tatsache*.
126 Thomas S. Kuhn, *The Structure of Scientific Revolutions*, 2. ed., enlarged (Chicago: University of Chicago Press, 1970).
127 Fleck, *Entstehung und Entwicklung einer wissenschaftlichen Tatsache*, see especially 85–86.
128 Conrad, "Enlightenment in Global history," 1022. Kurtz/Fisac/Jenco/Dusinberre *East Asian Uses of the European Past: Tracing Braided Chronotypes* describe that, as was the case with "Renaissance" before, translations of the word "Enlightenment" were grafted onto a previously exist-

So why move to the Enlightenment? There are, of course, certain characteristics which *the* Enlightenment may be said to share with *the* Renaissance. Indeed, in a master narrative in which the Renaissance, humanism, and the Reformation "gave a new impetus to intellectual and scientific development that, a little more than three and a half centuries later, flowered in the scientific revolution and then in the Enlightenment of the eighteenth century" the latter (Enlightenment) appears to be at least a logical continuation of the former (Renaissance).[129] There are important differences, however, in the European context and within a European periodization scheme, or within an order of historical evolution and change, between Renaissance and Enlightenment. To name just one: while the (European) Renaissance was closely related to a search for the accumulation of past knowledge, the (European) Enlightenment involved a conscious and rational critical testing of the past, its privileges and their legitimacy – Chinese New Culture practice, as we have seen, actually made use of both.

The convergence between the two terminologies did not just occur in China, but also in many other parts of the world.[130] Accordingly, the metaphorical terminology and dyadic combination of the "Renaissance/Enlightenment"– as opposed to the preceding "Middle Ages," a period of darkness and stagnation – leading straight into "Modernity," was willingly adopted in many Asian countries, including Turkey and India. The period they would describe as "their" "Renaissance" and "Enlightenment" was often dated to the times when these empires with millennial traditions of civilization were confronted with the military superiority of the Western powers. Ever since, concepts and terminology such as "Renaissance" have been used, not only by Chinese actors living their Chinese r/Renaissances, but also in the writing of Asian histories within disciplines including Sinology, Japanology, or Indology, thus invoking a myriad of different historical and cultural phenomena.

Thus far, we have accepted the historical actors' perspective, and granted that, in their eyes, China *did* have a Renaissance. We realize, however, that concepts and terminologies such as r/Renaissance have not only been used by Chinese actors experiencing Chinese r/Renaissances. Many sinologists, and historians of China, too, have declared the New Culture Movement either "China's Renaissance" or, alternatively, "China's Enlightenment," and these two categories are not only used as a reflection of "indigenous terminology" but as part of these scholars' analytical vocabularies. Vera Schwarcz, for example, one of

---

ing lexicon with similar connotations but now, the terms were redefined to build expectations for the emergence of a national awakening and no longer an individual one.
129 Conrad, "Enlightenment in Global history," 999.
130 See Conrad, "Enlightenment in Global History," 1016, 1026.

the most influential students of the New Culture Movement, has in fact wavered between the two terms. Her dissertation was titled "From Renaissance to Revolution. An Internal History of the May Fourth Movement and the Birth of the Chinese Intelligentsia,"[131] whereas her later book on the same topic was named *The Chinese Enlightenment: Intellectuals and the Legacy of the May Fourth Movement of 1919*.[132]

What do we make of this? Yu Yingshi, in an essay provocatively called "Neither Renaissance nor Enlightenment: a historian's reflections on the May Fourth movement" argues that the very multidimensionality of the Chinese New Culture (or May Fourth) Movement – Renaissance, Enlightenment, Modernity – should preclude the use of such allusionary terms, which bring in more levels of possible understanding and thus obscure more than they illuminate in analytical writing.[133] It is questionable, indeed, if what I have so far called the "generic" use of periodizations by analogy actually helps or rather hinders our analytical understanding of a particular historical movement. In Goody's study *Renaissances: The One or the Many*, to be sure, the danger of this approach can be seen. In his chapter on China alone, he quotes scholar after scholar, sinologist after sinologist, defining and describing one and then another, period in Chinese history as a "renaissance/renascence" so that in the end, even the smallest common denominator between all of these different renaissances is entirely unclear – fuzzy, as Thomas Maissen would call it.[134] To use "renaissance" for any period or any phenomenon that somehow engaged in "something new" by reviving "something old," as is illustrated in some of the work Goody cites, appears to me to go too far – indeed, it no longer allows us to use these terms as usefully "discrete patterns of continuity or distinction" in the sense that Bentley suggests.[135]

This is even more significant since sometimes these attempts by scholars – nervously looking for parallels, so it seems in non-European histories for what happened in Europe (building upon the retaliatory idea of "we have had it first") – come across as either apologetic or, quite the opposite, needlessly glee-

---

[131] Vera Schwarcz, "From Renaissance to Revolution: An Internal History of the May Fourth Movement and the Birth of the Chinese Intelligentsia" (PhD diss., Stanford University, 1978).
[132] Vera Schwarcz, *The Chinese Enlightenment: Intellectuals and the Legacy of the May Fourth Movement of 1919* (Berkeley: University of California Press, 1986).
[133] Yu, "Neither Renaissance nor Enlightenment."
[134] Goody, *Renaissances*, chapter 7 (with S. Fennell). For a useful critique of Goody's approach, see Gamsa, "Uses and Misuses of a Chinese Renaissance" and, even more harshly, Burke, "Jack Goody and the Comparative History of Renaissances," 24–25. For "fuzzy," which Maissen associates with "enriching vocabularies," which, however, is conceived by myself on the level of the actors' and not the historian's analytical vocabularies, see p. 162.
[135] See our discussion of Bentley in the prologue above.

ful, and indeed, they simply reaffirm the absence of something like Renaissance or Enlightenment outside of Europe as one of their axiomatic tenets. While European claims to originality and to exclusive authorship of Renaissance must be called into question, it is not very fruitful to begin looking for parallels, comparisons, or analogies elsewhere, or for autochthonous processes that did not depend upon developments in Europe but led to similar results and thus could be considered the "origins of Renaissance/Enlightenment/Modernity" in another country.[136] The result of such an "archaeological" endeavor, searching for "independent seeds" of "the modern," even when it is connected to the larger (postcolonial) project of revising modernization theory, is not what I would strive for. Indeed, the usage of such highly specialized (or should we say, cookie-cutting?) vocabulary – not unlike the Weberian ideal types already evoked by Thomas Maissen[137]– is not very helpful, as these terms themselves, as used by historical actors, are never generic types but very specific and distinct moving targets that are variously specified, locally as well as temporally, by the actors at hand. In a discussion of the term Modernity, Frederick Cooper once questioned why scholars always want to "try for a slightly better definition" instead of simply mediating the terms of their historical actors. In his view, and I share his position, historians should do no more than "listen to what is being said in the world," they should trust and relate "what they hear, they should ask how it is being used and why."[138] Accordingly, I would also suggest that we pay attention to our historical actors' claims and names, and shift our attention to Asian (as well as European) reformulations of chronotypes such as "Renaissance" rather than defining a fixed meaning for "Renaissance" that will never hold. I would suggest that we must always maintain a clear distinction between what a historical event or discourse *was*, generically (in analytical terms – a renaissance, a rebirth, a renewal),[139] and the forms (unexpected, interesting and hence undoubtedly important) in which it is *presented* or claimed and named (i.e. the vocabularies used by the agents involved).[140] My own take on this matter would be, therefore, to keep to a strong separation between the concepts found in the sources (something Koselleck calls "quellengebundene Begriffe") and our own categories of analytical

---

136 Conrad, "Enlightenment in Global History," 1007.
137 See p. 31.
138 Frederick Cooper, "Modernity," in *Colonialism in Question: Theory, Knowledge, History* (Berkeley: University of California Press, 2005), 115.
139 For Thomas Maissen's take on these terms, see below on p. 126.
140 Gamsa, "Uses and Misuses of a Chinese Renaissance," 652, comes to a similar conclusion.

knowledge acquisition (his "Erkenntniskategorien").[141] I would resort, therefore, to using Renaissance – and other such epochal names that are part of the self-fashioning of a particular period – only as source-based terminology, but never as an analytical category.

One could, of course, argue that even those scholarly uses of loaded terminologies as analytical terminology or repertoire constitute new and creative or variable (and exchangeable) enrichments of a particular concept – and they may well be – especially for the history of science. It is true, no matter whether it is contemporary actors debating, or later scholars reflecting (as we have seen in the case of Burckhardt or Sichel or as we can observe in medievalists' claims to "r/Renaissance"), that uses of a particular terminology of periodization are indeed never innocent, never an act of simple imitation or transfer, but always a creative (or manipulative) act of variation which may well make eclectic use of periodization concepts that do not follow in a particular order – even among scholars. This, in turn, of course also means that these periodization systems are neither universal, nor are they ever taken over lock, stock and barrel. But if used as an analytical category, and by a European scholar, this may not be immediately evident, and thus confusion is almost inevitable. Therefore, I would contend, again, they are best avoided.[142] In spirited words, Yu Yingshi, one of the most important scholars of intellectual history around the time of the New Culture Movement maintains that this movement should not be addressed as either *the* Renaissance or *the* Enlightenment (both in analytical terms and as a chronotype – no identical copies).[143]

I suggest, therefore, that we must clearly distinguish between the voices of the actors who might adapt an epochal name, a periodization scheme or chronotype for good reason – that is, to name and claim and make themselves interesting or powerful, and to raise their status by doing so – and those who describe and analyze what these actors do – the scholars and historians. If we do so, we may be able to avoid several traps at the same time. First, we avoid fuzziness in our terminologies. The terms do not mean what we make them to mean but what the actors suggest they mean. This helps us avoid, second, the faulty insistence on the universality of the European path,[144] as there have been numerous ways of reading r/Renaissance and these must be acknowledged. At the same time, we

---

[141] Reinhart Koselleck, "Begriffsgeschichtliche Probleme der Verfassungsgeschichtsschreibung." In *Der Staat* Beiheft 6 (1983), 12–13, 13.
[142] See Gamsa, "Uses and Misuses of a Chinese Renaissance."
[143] Yu, "Neither Renaissance nor Enlightenment," 311, is quoted more extensively in the epilogue below, p. 162–163.
[144] See Gamsa, "Uses and Misuses of a Chinese Renaissance," 654.

also avoid applying the deeply flawed logic of "we/they had (or are having) a Renaissance, too (or even, first)." This framing – making use of typical late twentieth-century "entitlement discourse" – represents no advance on Eurocentrism in its earlier, justly discarded guises. Indeed, as Mark Gamsa aptly puts it: "the urge to prove such a thesis vitiates the claims of comparison while leaving unexplored the potential of studying forms of appropriation and cross-continental contact."[145] So this is a third trap to be avoided: not to retaliate but instead, to acknowledge the other, in order to become, ultimately, enriched oneself; to show and tell, and to see and understand what is going on elsewhere and what to learn from it, not because the other is "striking back" but simply to enhance one's own historical consciousness. This is what I envisage when I talk about History-in-common. The point of allowing for multiple r/Renaissances is precisely not to give "subalterns" a voice (that would be accepting superiority on the other side). The point is not that "We" "give permission" to "them" for the usage of "Our" i.e. *the* Renaissance, either, but instead that seeing multiple r/Renaissances allows everyone to learn more about the versatilities of the chronotype itself and its applicability in everyone's multiple presents and futures. And thus, we can think of the history of *the* Renaissance in terms of History-in-common.

---

[145] Gamsa, "Uses and Misuses of a Chinese Renaissance," 654.

Conclusion

Thomas Maissen
The Renaissance and the rise of the West

The aim of this dialogue was to understand and question historical periodization as a cultural practice and to test the possibilities of using periodization schemes in a transcultural perspective. Focusing on the particularities of the humanist dialogue which informed the making of the European "Renaissance" as a historical epoch, my discussion has underlined those elements that distinguish the Italian and then, more broadly, the European Renaissance from other movements that involved reinterpretations and rediscoveries of neglected elements of the past elsewhere. It is clear, be it just in the impossibility of imposing a copyright, that nobody can be kept from using such terminologies at will. Somebody may call his pet Renaissance, with a capital R, without creating a scandal. The question is, however, whether such naming and claiming could become a contribution to historiographical research. The point is not whether Hu Shi and his followers used the word "renaissance" (they did and were free to do so), but whether "enriching" our occidental concept of "Renaissance" by experiences of Chinese or other actors can render this and similar concepts of epochs appropriate for use in global history. While Barbara Mittler has shown that it is interesting and rewarding to study why and how a group of Chinese reformers in the early twentieth century used the Italian Renaissance as an explanatory model for their own project of modernization, I am still not convinced that we can understand the Italian or European Renaissance, prerevolutionary China or global history better, if we make their self-fashioning choice of a name into a global or a particular, Chinese epoch called "renaissance."

I am aware that this conviction may look like wanting to monopolize, in a traditional Eurocentric manner, the term for the one and only Renaissance as "ours," or even like ontologizing an epoch. This is, however, not what I am doing when I take seriously the self-fashioning of the humanists and their metaphorical language of rebirth. Unlike the self-stylization of the New Culture or May Fourth Movement, humanist self-fashioning creates an epistemological link to our modern, Burckhardtian concept of *the* Renaissance, one that scholars can and that I would still use today, both for historiographical description and as an analytical tool. What can the claims for "renaissances" in distant cultures really contribute to a better understanding of their own or the European past, for instance about the changing role of women?[1] Their destiny is one of many issues that must be tackled by research in social, economic or intellectual histo-

---

[1] See Barbara Mittler on p. 112.

ry. "Enriching" and thus blurring the concept of an epoch does not further such research; it is misleading or, at best, irrelevant.

Therefore, and for the following reasons, I argue that it is not only fair but indeed important to say that China did not have, and indeed does not need a "Renaissance" or a "renaissance," even though some historical actors have used the term to describe their ambitions.

1. *Like other historiographical concepts, periodization schemes are but constructions. They are only helpful as long as they are clearly defined and fit the concrete cultural phenomena that they are supposed to explain.* Periodizations are always problematic in the first place, and they are arbitrary, to a considerable extent, as they transport preconceptions about historical change, even about an unknown future (paradise, progress, classless society). The periodizations developed and currently used in the West systematize European experiences since Antiquity and order them in a teleological narrative of progress towards Modernity, which can be seen as a secularized version of Christian salvific history. Renaissance with a capital R only makes sense when situated within these specific experiences of Europe. It is attractive for nations elsewhere, however, because of the positive connotations of individualism and emancipation associated with the concept. If other civilizations begin to use such terms, they must inevitably also comply with the *Weltanschauung* of the "occidental imperialist" and subordinate their national or cultural narratives to a foreign model. Discovering antiquities, middle ages, and renaissances in other areas of the world distorts their own particular historical experiences. It is well known, for example, that the core ambition of the elitist Renaissance humanists was to reestablish classical, Ciceronian Latin – a dead and exigent language that was difficult to master, especially for the common people, because the Italian vernacular had long since become a very different language. This was exactly the case with vernacular and classical Chinese in the early twentieth century, too. Therefore, in order to democratize society and make it less elitist, the New Culture Movement promoted the vernacular instead of the classical language, which they considered to be dead and exigent and difficult to master. If, in their core intentions, the two movements proclaimed completely contrary goals, why should they receive the same name as a historical epoch?

Furthermore, the occidental narrative of progress towards modernity, with Renaissance as one key element, has become ambivalent again today – as was already the case with Jacob Burckhardt, but much less among succeeding vulgarizers such as Edith Sichel. If one insists on using "Renaissance" for non-European civilizations, one must also adopt the negative elements of the plot. One should not forget that Burckhardt's book introduces individualism and "the modern political spirit of Europe" by discussing despots and despotism. In the German version this is even stronger, he uses the term "tyrants" ("Tyrannen") and argues that they often displayed "the worst features of an unbridled egotism, outraging every right, and killing every germ of a healthier culture."[2] Was that what the New Culture Movement aspired to?

And did China also have a "Confessional age" (with its Wars of Religion, such as the Thirty Years war) or experience "Absolutism" (with its endemic wars and political oppression)? When it comes to the twentieth century the similarities are more obvious. But does China want to extend its contributions to the "Age of Extremes" (Eric Hobsbawm) to include "genocide" and other accompanying concepts that, for obvious reasons, are less attractive than terms such as Renaissance or Enlightenment? I am aware that some people would talk about the Cultural Revolution as a "holocaust," and others likewise adopt the victim's stance to baptize the Nanjing massacre a "Chinese holocaust." I believe that such terminological transfer is not only inappropriate, but useless and confusing. This is not a moral judgment, but the conviction of the historian that we should distinguish the particularities of the phenomena we are studying and that we should not subordinate too big a variety of these phenomena to one concept. If we use periodization schemes without distinction, we do not explain anything. We will find phenomena which may be baptized with the same names all over the world without understanding what is special and particular about them. Furthermore, we will not understand the rationale behind periodization – the Renaissance does not make sense without corresponding epochs such as Antiquity, Middle Ages and Modernity. It is not enough to say "we had this, too"– meaning, by "this," for example, individuals and beautiful works of art, a renewed interest in the past, or wars and genocides. Periodization schemes not only categorize, they also explain the past by squeezing an immense multitude of historical phenomena into a rather simple scheme of advancement –and that is both their advantage (clear and illustrative structure, conventional understanding) and their risk (reductionism, simplification, teleology).

2. The period of the Renaissance means more than a fascination with millennia-old authors and artists: it encompasses crucial changes in different fields not just for one nation or one region, but eventually for the history of humanity. In the European experience, the triad Antiquity-Middle Ages-Modernity is fundamental, and so is the Renaissance as a turning point. "Renaissance" in the comprehensive sense ascribed to it by Jacob Burckhardt hence comprises much more than a re-

---

[2] Burckhardt, *Civilization*, 4 (Part 1, Introduction).

newed interest in forgotten authors and artists, texts and antiques (one may recall that this is only the third and a rather shorter chapter of his book). Such an interest, alone, may indeed be a common human practice in moments when, due to linguistic change or historical rupture, a collective realizes that its cultural heritage, its sacred texts, for example, are no longer understandable by themselves and thus need commentary and exegesis, but also reconstitution, selection, and canonization. The simple glance backwards does actually amount to a cyclical understanding of history, which then appears similar to nature: blossoming, fall, new blossoming. To describe such moments of looking backward in other civilizations, one could easily use terms such as "renewal," "revival" or – why not? – "rebirth." These terms capture cultural rediscoveries or regenerations without the subtext of the particular experience that Italians and other humanists already described in the fourteenth to sixteenth centuries. When they spoke about "*rinascere*," they did not mean that they would return to an idealized model in the past, nor did they want to become pagans again in a cyclical understanding of historical time. They were well aware of the fundamental rupture that separated them, definitely, from Antiquity. But they looked for and found a procedure – the dialogue – to self-consciously evaluate, select, and combine the many different sources they studied. The effects of this encounter with a neglected other went far beyond scholarship and erudition, literature and the arts.

Therefore, when nineteenth-century historians took up the humanist metaphors of reawakening and rebirth to baptize "Renaissance" an epoch – first Italian and later on European – they took it to mean decisively more than just a prolonged moment of looking back or a very richly documented cultural epoch, even less a politico-cultural initiative with clearly defined aims in one particular state, such as the New Culture or May Fourth Movement in China. The latter is much better understood if compared not to the Renaissance, but to the innumerous self-proclaimed "renewal movements" in the religious and the political realm, especially in the time when the construction of nation-states, not only in China, was romanticized as a return to the roots. Unlike such particular national movements, historians described and describe the epoch of the Renaissance as a pivotal process lasting some 200 years, and comprising the introduction of a large number of fundamental changes in many important fields of politics and society all over Europe (and beyond).[3] It is the characteristic of any a concept of epoch that the changes it encompasses are more important in some areas than in others: the Renaissance did not instigate spectacular transformations

---

3 See p. 63.

(e. g. in medicine or in gender relations), and in spite of Copernicus, the scientific revolution only happened in the seventeenth century. Economic growth actually predated the Renaissance which turned out to be, after the Black Death of 1348, rather more an epoch of demographic decline and stagnation. However, the emergence, since the twelfth century, of long-distance trade using the Italian cities as hubs between the Levant and Europe beyond the Alps not only generated the wealth that could then be spent on the artistic production of the Renaissance; it also contributed to the increasing recognition of difference and alterity that demanded explanation. Owing to the recent invention of the printing press, a growing number of humanist lawyers, diplomats, historians, and geographers were engaged in coping with the pluralization and diversification of phenomena in all fields. Often, they also contributed to creating and legitimizing these pluralities: discoveries of and in other continents, three popes instead of one, a dismembered empire in the West and a vanishing empire in Byzantium, the rise of national dynasties and national narratives (France, Spain, England), and of counter-narratives where political unity was missing (Italy, Germany), all contributing to the rise of the system of states.

To avoid the wrath of medievalists, sinologists and others: this is not to say that there was no plurality in the Middle Ages or in China at a given time. But both the Middle Ages and China conceived the world in a monistic conceptual framework: one God, one Church, one Empire or one Emperor, one Mandate of Heaven. The humanists found a way to integrate plurality into their *Weltanschauung*, not as a flaw within a dichotomous order (opposing for example forces of good and evil, such as the Muslims), but in a positive way, by way of the dialogue between complimentary yet not self-sufficient worlds. They left this heritage to the early modern republic of letters that was interconnected all over Europe thanks to letter writing and printed books – while in the Ottoman Empire it would be forbidden to print Islamic texts until 1803, and East Asians, who invented moveable types around 1000 CE, only began to use them when they imported the printing press at the end of the nineteenth century, to engender modern mass-communication. Likewise, it cannot be excluded that Chinese sailors landed in America before Columbus, as probably the Vikings had done in the tenth century. Still, theirs did not become "discoveries" that changed anything for their own polity and even less beyond. After 1494, however, a fundamental change occurred which opposed a known old world to a possible new world, accessible thanks to the combination of ancient authorities such as Ptolemy on the one hand, and recent sailing experiences on the other. Both Columbus and his European audience were mentally ready to cope with the alterity and plurality of civilizations, which he related in his *Epistola de insulis nuper inventis* (*Letter on the recently discovered islands*), immediately printed in 1493 and often reprinted and translated thanks to competitive communication and dialogue in the system of states that emerged in Europe. These states eventually became so powerful that for some time they conquered almost the whole globe and imposed the political structure of the modern state onto all these territories, too.

3. *The humanists' approach to rediscovered alterity in the unique form of an open dialogue was a necessary precondition for the rise of the West.* What happened in Italy was different from what other erudite rediscoveries produced, both in the European past and on other continents. The dialogic principle became an important element in the rise of the West in the centuries following the Renaissance. Dialogic humanism meant juxtaposing different sources of truth, which fundamentally contradicted and even excluded each other: divine revelation and pagan immanence. We must recall that this juxtaposition – which relativized religious Truth – was a highly improbable event in a society of true believers. Nevertheless, dialogue became a widespread practice among scholars. Their openness toward an entirely new type of critical dialogue created an awareness that, in order to handle the earthly issues of this world, the Christian religious explanations and their commentaries were no longer complete or sufficient. Ever since that fascinating other world, pagan Antiquity, appeared to them – a world that was much easier to understand than many more recent, Christian centuries, with their uninteresting and inaccessible sources – the Christian world was no longer just taken for granted. The classical texts, on the other hand, appeared to offer not only comprehensive descriptions of and deep insights into the alterity of antique men, but also into their psychology: Machiavelli would begin to understand the reasons for the ancients' military bravery, but also compared his sentimental feelings with those described by Ovid and Tibullus. A wide range of historical behaviors was presented and readers were invited to choose among them and to fashion themselves in a competition with other individuals making other choices in the same situation. The individual of the Renaissance became a "homo eligens," a man who knew how to choose autonomously in the sense that, after engaging in a dialogue with the dead but reanimated pagan and Christian experts, he selected the best aspects of these different, yet commensurate models – if only commensurate in their imperfection.

Such relativism could not convince, however, those who were in search of an absolute Truth, for example, about the preconditions for God's grace. The Reformation established a new plurality of competing fundamental verities, adding a series of discordant Protestant denominations to a reconfirmed Catholic tradition. Martin Luther's unconditional and systematic theology of salvation found more followers than the elitist erudition of Erasmus, who did not pretend to know all the answers to the metaphysical questions that went beyond human reasoning. But even during the wars of religion in the sixteenth and seventeenth centuries, the Dutch authors in the Erasmian tradition especially, such as Justus Lipsius (1547–1606) and Hugo Grotius (1583–1645), showed that undogmatic philological humanism, and later on skepticism, remained legitimate options. Also in the Netherlands, Pierre Bayle (1647–1706), a founding father of the Enlightenment, poured his skepticism for all kinds of dogma, traditional authority, and superstition into his *Dictionnaire historique et critique* (1695–97). This biobibliographical *Historical and Critical Dictionary* offered often controversial sources and interpretations of the learned traditions and left it to the eclectic reader to make up his mind, perhaps in a spirit of tolerance similar to Bayle's. Thus, the dialogic principle became the basis of the knowledge society that would eventually combine Enlightenment rationality and economic pragmatism in the industrial revolution. There is neither a direct nor an inevitable line of development leading from the Renaissance to the industrialized societies that, in the long run, completely and irreversibly changed life for all humans in a globalized world. But the conflicting pluralities within the common classical-Christian tradition of Western Europe were the decisive precondition for a sometimes peaceful and often martial competition between states, religions, economies and ideas that engendered the modern world. With the system of states, the democratization of knowledge thanks to the printing press, the discoveries, colonies and other phenomena, the Renaissance contributed humanist dialogue as an appropriate procedure to evaluate conflicting heritages that they had begun to collect and comment on systematically.

This conclusion may sound rather like a conventional narrative about the rise of the West, and this remains a legitimate historiographical concern for me. But this narrative is, very probably, no longer sufficient as a structure for global history. It matters, therefore, to examine alternative narratives, problems, approaches and concepts. The test of historiographical theory, however, is in the writing. I admit that so far, the proposed "History-in-common" or "Renaissance-in-common" remain well-intentioned but empty words to me. I still wonder how they really could influence and even change the concrete practice of writing (global) history. I do not agree that "misunderstanding" should become its "very object," nor that its "guiding principle" should be a syncretism that juxtaposes "totally different" ways of addressing the same topic and combines "radically different interpretations" – without weighing which one of the "different perspectives" might be "more or less truthful than the other."[4]

---

4 See p. 27 and 113.

On the contrary, I am convinced that historiography (and scholarship) must integrate the variety of phenomena it studies into one overarching narrative that is as true and as clear as possible. Barbara Mittler's postulate that we researchers must "open ourselves to the logic of others"[5] is a precondition of such a narrative and the hermeneutic basis of all scholarship in the humanities and of interdisciplinary work in particular. But it is not sufficient by itself for defining a research question, an appropriate terminology, and a historical narrative. It is one – rewarding – issue to compare, on a global level, movements of renewal; it is something different to transfer established categories and concepts, of epochs, for example, to fields or areas for which they were not developed originally. This can be done and often is done. We do not hesitate to speak about the "state" or the "society" in China or elsewhere, although these concepts were developed first in a European context. It is essentially a matter of definition: does a concept fit the phenomena it wants to describe? Consequently, depending on the definition of "renaissance," there will be different answers to the question of whether China experienced one or not.

If one thinks that China *did* indeed have *a* Renaissance, as Barbara Mittler asserts,[6] there is no reason why one should not use "renaissance" also as a descriptive and analytical category. If this creates "confusion," the term should not be avoided for the sake of European scholars but to actually avoid confusion – which is one of the major tasks of scholarship. Hence, I cannot follow Mittler's distinction between a legitimate use of "renaissance" by the historical actors and an inappropriate use of "renaissance" if sinologists and historians of our own time use it for the New Culture or May Fourth Movement.[7] The latter seems to me to be the question that is at stake in this book, since no historian would tell his sources in hindsight what words they should have used. If Mittler explains that the New Culture Movement itself not only promoted a "Renaissance," but that, for exactly that reason, China *did have* a Renaissance,[8] why then should Vera Schwarcz and other modern scholars not be equally entitled to "various readings and appropriations" of a Chinese Renaissance (or renaissance)? In the European case, it is precisely one advantage of the concept "Renaissance" that the later, Burckhardtian denomination of the epoch and our current usage coincide with the experience and self-definition of a considerable group of historical actors.

---

5 See p. 156.
6 See p. 115 and 147.
7 See p. 115.
8 See p. 115, 137, 147 and 161.

The self-stylization of contemporaries is not, however, a sufficient criterion for establishing an epoch, and not only because there are far too many competing self-designations at a given time. We would not today talk about colonialism as an "epoch of the civilizing mission," although historical actors did. Defining and selecting epochs is not a continuous series of voluntarist acts of "naming and claiming,"[9] and even less a game of naming in which everybody can participate at his will. The historical actor's naming and claiming does not constitute by itself a historiographical object, let alone an epoch. On the contrary, periodization results from the naming and claiming – or rather from the hypotheses and interpretations – of the historian, and it displays his definitions, selections, and hierarchizations of possible historiographical objects. Periodization is a problematic and difficult challenge for historians who definitely would have to do more than "listen to what is being said in the world,"[10] since it needs methodological awareness and theoretical reflection about precisely these problems. Periodization schemes as ways of structuring the past then impose themselves if they are successful and functional – that is, if they explain the past by reducing it into a convincing historiographical narrative. It is obvious that the occidental master narrative that leads from Mediterranean Antiquity to Atlantic Modernity cannot be convincing for nations all over the world the way it has been for those who wanted to explain the rise of the West. Global history, therefore, must develop multi-perspectival narratives which combine core elements of both the isolated and the shared histories of various regions of this world. This awareness, after all, is indispensable for any good historian's daily work; global history only makes its linguistic prerequisites more exigent.

To select such core elements and to build up a corresponding narrative structure, interdisciplinary research needs to discuss which concepts are appropriate and which are not. Can it be helpful to transfer into such a global narrative a concept, an epoch "Renaissance" or several "renaissances" that go beyond the European experience of the fourteenth to sixteenth centuries? It has become clear that I do not think so. It is not at all about posthumously stripping Hu Shi and other sources from the early twentieth century of a model they admired. It is not so much about criticizing a metaphorical language used, often unconsciously, by scholars today – although I would not recommend doing so. It is about using Renaissance as an epoch of global history that describes and analyzes not only the European case, but also others. The only way to do this is precisely "enriching" the concept to encompass historical experiences of different

---

9 See p. 99.
10 Frederick Cooper as quoted by Barbara Mittler, see p. 117.

regions worldwide – which is nothing if not defining it very broadly. I doubt that our historical understanding is sharpened if our heuristic tools are blurred in such a way.

Barbara Mittler
Renaissance-in-common?
History-as-dialogue

This book asks why China did not have a Renaissance – and why that matters. Thomas Maissen holds staunchly to his claim that China did not have a Renaissance, not even a renaissance, and that that, indeed, matters. For a historian like him, to study the Renaissance with a capital R means something very particular: it means to study a period pivotal in European history, one which encompassed crucial changes in many different fields not just for one nation or one region, but for humanity at large, since the humanists' approach to rediscovered alterity in the unique form of an open dialogue became a necessary precondition for the rise of the West. While he considers the global impact of the Renaissance with a capital R, he holds that it was and remains unique to Western Europe which is why, according to him, China cannot and will not have a Renaissance.

While I agree that indeed, as historians we should not use periodization schemes arbitrarily and we should thus not be using an epistemological category of a generic period type "renaissance" or "renascence" and that indeed, therefore, periodization schemes are only adequate if they are clearly defined and fit the concrete cultural phenomena that they are supposed to describe, if at all – my position in this dialogue is to present the voice of the historical actor. Chinese intellectuals from the New Culture Movement would insist that they had *a* Renaissance with a capital R. They would claim "Renaissance" to be the perfect fit for a concrete set of cultural phenomena in early twentieth-century China. Accordingly, they would claim, that there was not just *one* Renaissance (*the* Renaissance) but that Renaissance was an experience they shared, that there was something they would be able to experience as Renaissance-in-common; not a shared past, but a shared present in a global context. They would conceive their Chinese Renaissance as an inspired adaptation and co-creation of the chronotype that *the* Renaissance was. They would also consider some qualities of Renaissance-as-chronotype that may not have actually been of great import in fifteenth-century Europe – vernacularism, among them – to be extremely significant, while overlooking others that would have been considered crucial to its success in Europe – the dialogical humanist spirit, for example.

Following from this – the actor's position – what I have suggested in my contribution to our dialogue is that studying the morphologies of Renaissances such as the New Culture Movement, experienced by the historical actors as Renaissances-in-common – i.e. as commensurate co-creations of Renaissance, that must be considered on the same matrix as *the* Renaissance, since they also became pivotal to their nation, their region and (not just in the case of China) to humanity at large (by way of being adopted as part of the foundational myth for and the sustainable success of the Chinese Communist Party, for example) – may also allow historians to sharpen their understanding of the possibilities and limitations of *the* Renaissance. Studying Renaissances-in-common as they have been lived and experienced by historical actors, allows us as historians to pose new questions to *the* Renaissance, as well: why did women and democratic ideas, for example, not play a role in *the* Renaissance at all, while they obviously could have, as rethinking *the* Renaissance on Chinese terms shows? What is the function of the vernacular and the dialogue after all, in China and in Europe? Questions like these enable us to begin enriching and expanding our possibilities for understanding the term and its specific meaning in particular historical circumstances and contingencies.

Thus, to approach multiple Renaissances (with a capital R), I suggested History-in-common as an appropriate analytical approach, and critical dialogue as a befitting medium. History-in-common is a History not of a shared past that we all have "in common," but one of shared "presents." History-in-common is based on joint and dialogical readings of what historical actors, each for their own and individual reasons, have seen to be inspiring thoughts, technologies, or, in the case of the Renaissance, chronotypes in the global context. My suggestion in this dialogue amounted to saying that if historical actors chose to use and adopt certain periodization schemes, we must take them seriously. History-in-common allows us to study these historical adaptations in a way that will refine our understanding of how different periodization schemes have been understood and used under particular circumstances by historical actors. History-in-common does not valorize or judge, but simply tells and shows the actors' stories from multiple perspectives. The choice of critical dialogue as medium and form for this endeavor, a form which does not lead to consensus automatically, and which has an "infinity of possible endings," culminating not in a set of clear-cut conclusions but open questions,[1] is deliberate and apt: this kind of dialogue is a form that sensitizes us to the cultural imprint of the hermeneutic tools we often use without enough reflection.

In the following, I will engage, therefore – in a last installment of this antithetical dialogue – the concluding arguments made by Thomas Maissen just now, offering some modifications and alternative perspectives to these state-

---

[1] Raqs Media Collective, "On Curatorial Responsibility," *The Biennial Reader: An Anthology on Large-Scale Perennial Exhibitions of Contemporary Art*, eds. Elena Filipovic, Marieke Van Hal, and Solveig Øvstebø (Bergen: Bergen Kunstahll, 2010), 276–289, 287–288.

ments as read from my very different disciplinary stance – that of a sinologist. Maissen begins his conclusion with this statement: "1. Like other historiographical concepts, periodization schemes are but constructions. They are only helpful as long as they are clearly defined and fit the concrete cultural phenomena that they are supposed to explain." He argues further that if periodization schemes are adapted elsewhere, this is, more often than not, piecemeal adaptation: only the positive parts of the story are adapted. And indeed, it is not the Renaissance-tyrants but the Renaissance-individualists that play a role for those claiming Renaissance in China. I would go even further, though, by saying, that

(1) *precisely because adaptation of periodization schemes follows a particular purpose and is bound by a particular contingent set of circumstances, China's historical actors took great freedom in constructing their Chinese Renaissance and liberated themselves, therefore, from established European practice, by following their very own particular needs*. This is why the vernacular begins to play a key role in China's Renaissance, for example. These very changes in the semantics of "Renaissance" are a sign, in turn, that and how the chronotype is made to fit concrete cultural phenomena and circumstances, and it thus negates the fact that whoever takes over Renaissance as periodization scheme must "inevitably comply with the *Weltanschauung* of the 'occidental imperialist'."[2] On the contrary, the very act of re-constructing Renaissance for their own purposes is a sign of their independence from this *Weltanschauung*. Sure enough, their Renaissance is not *the* European Renaissance. But their particular terminological transfer need not be confusing either, if they are studied through a close look at the sources – both European and Chinese – as suggested here: knowing that China's Renaissance also had many other (Chinese) names and understanding what connotations these names brought and added to the European chronotype (which in itself had, as Maissen shows, a number of names in different languages, from *rinascita* to Renaissance) is an important way of rethinking Renaissance, not with the aim of "squeezing a multitude of phenomena into one category,"[3] as Maissen contends, but of increasing our knowledge about how differently this very category has been used by historical actors and why, and accordingly, what its potentials really are.

What does this mean for Renaissance elsewhere? My plea for "enriching" vocabularies such as Renaissance is not one that amounts to, in the end, using periodization schemes such as Renaissance without distinction for any phenome-

---

2 Maissen, p. 33 and p. 124.
3 See Maissen, p. 125.

non that offers itself to such purpose, quite the opposite. I advocate using them *only* in accordance with the sources. I am interested in considering how the category "Renaissance" has been used by historical actors in a global context, but not to impose one particular type of variation of "r/Renaissance" as an analytical term or a chronotype on others. I heartily agree that the arbitrary use of periodization schemes is always already problematic, and accordingly, the globalization of the European past and its periodization schemes has rightly been the object of multiple discussions. Many scholars have studied how European pasts have been invoked in the non-European world as a means of self-deprecation or self-assertion, as a (counter-)model for social and intellectual change, or as an ethnocentric trope that reified their alleged universality. For all their merits, these studies share a narrow focus on tracing the global careers of a modern "regime of historicity"[4] whose key features include a teleological emphasis on progress, linear development, and the superiority of the rising West. Obstacles to the adoption of certain regimes of historicity are often related in comparative fashion evoking circular notions of temporality (of which we have seen examples in Part I of this dialogue). The Chinese example, moving on to linear models at the beginning of the twentieth century, however, was not an act of "aping," instead, it signified considerable willingness and creative abilities for adaptation. At the same time, we have seen that circular notions of time are not exclusive to Asia but have dominated in Europe as well. This dialogue intended to go further than simply exposing the self-serving motivation of such attempts at "othering" non-European perceptions of time[5] by looking beyond mere comparative concerns and by exposing how seeing transformations in periodization schemes here and there can help us understand more about them, both there and here, and to begin to build a theory "from Asia and Europe" on this common matrix.[6]

Thomas Maissen's insistence on the uniqueness of the European Renaissance granted, he obviously also concedes that the Chinese New Culture Movement is unique in its own particular way. Still, he insists that it must not be called a Renaissance.[7] Why not? It is true that when Chinese actors are using the term Renaissance for the New Culture Movement, they are inspired by a Eu-

---

4 See Hartog, *Régimes d'historicité*.
5 Gayatri C. Spivak, *Other Asias* (Oxford: Blackwell, 2008).
6 See Sanjay Subrahmanyam, "Connected Histories: Notes towards a Reconfiguration of Early Modern Eurasia," *Modern Asian Studies* 31, no. 3 (1997); Susan R. Suleiman, ed., *The Idea of Europe*, Special issue of *Comparative Literature* 58, no. 4 (2006); Schildgen, Zhou and Gilman, *Other Renaissances*; Davis and Altschul, *Medievalisms in the Postcolonial World*; Kurtz/Fisac/Jenco/Dusinberre *East Asian Uses of the European Past: Tracing Braided Chronotypes*.
7 See Maissen, on p. 30 and 124.

ropean model, inclusive of (carefully selected parts of) its *Weltanschauung*. Indeed, the Chinese agents involved in this process are often even more eager than foreigners would ever be, to impose specific foreign values on themselves and their fellow countrymen.[8] Instead of condemning these actions as "self-orientalist," however, I would suggest approaching them as instances of Occidentalism, which is explained by Xiaomei Chen as "a discursive practice that has allowed the Orient to participate actively and with indigenous creativity in the process of self-appropriation."[9] Adopting a foreign *Weltanschauung*, then, has become part of the established episteme in the modern history of China. To try and "apologize" for it, or worse, to say "you cannot have that" does not change the fact that this kind of adoption has taken place: periodization schemes echoing European conceptions of time – certain chronotypes which became known in Asia a good century ago – while being constantly reworked in creative fashion, have now become "theirs" as well as "ours" in acts of continuous "global co-production."[10] So, of course, why should they *not* have, claim, and name these movements "Renaissance," in their *unique* way…? There is no need, therefore, to discard periodization altogether,[11] but it turns out that periodization schemes are, indeed, much more flexible than we may be willing to admit, they are constantly *made to fit* the particularist history of the places adapting them, and this is perhaps the very process which we have not acknowledged enough to be able to accept them as "commensurate and equal" (in the manner that the humanist accepted the heathen from Rome as his "commensurate and equal").

---

[8] Lu Xun, one of the May Fourth Movement's greatest writers is a good example for this. One of his novellas deals with a Chinese "Everyman" *AhQ*. It turns out that this novella translates into fiction what an American missionary, Arthur Smith, wrote about "the Chinese" in his book *Chinese Characteristics* (see Lydia He Liu, *Translingual Practice. Literature, National Culture and Translated Modernity. China, 1900–1937* (Stanford: Stanford University Press, 1995)). In another short story, *Diary of a Madman*, Lu Xun's madman accuses the Chinese of being cannibals and thus, is even more self-critical than foreigners had ever been (see Barbara Mittler, "'My brother is a man-eater': Cannibalism before and after May Fourth," in *Zurück zur Freude. Studien zur chinesischen Literatur und Lebenswelt und ihrer Rezeption in Ost und West. Festschrift für Wolfgang Kubin*, eds. Marc Hermann and Christian Schwermann (Sankt Augustin: Steyler Verlag, 2007)).
[9] Chen, *Occidentalism*, 2.
[10] Conrad, "Enlightenment in Global History," 1022: "Rather than a process of diffusion, the longer history of Enlightenment was the result of its constant reinvention. We may speak thus of the global co-production of Enlightenment knowledge."
[11] On the dispensability of periodization, see Gamsa, "Uses and Misuses of a Chinese Renaissance," 648–651. See also Arthur F. Wright, "On the Uses of Generalization in the Study of Chinese History," in *Generalization in the Writing of History*, ed. Louis Gottschalk (Chicago: University of Chicago Press, 1963), 46–47.

As Thomas Maissen has also put it,[12] there is no European property or copyright to *the* Renaissance or "the big One" as Peter Burke calls it.[13] The Chinese Renaissance, as I have attempted to show, was democratic in outlook and due to its success, with the takeover by the Chinese Communist Party, it eventually involved many more people than the European Renaissance ever did. It also helped retrieve a culture – that of the vernacular – that had, for many centuries, even millennia, been lost and forgotten because it had been considered "heretic/heterodox." This culture became incredibly influential, with repercussions that are felt to this day, as I have attempted to show. Accordingly, to me it makes more sense to "show and tell" what historical actors did (and continue to do) with a concept such as "Renaissance" elsewhere, than to insist on a periodization scheme's imperialist or oppressive qualities and ultimately to take away the right of naming from these actors by not including their own terminologies in our analytical narratives (which is why I would reject the use of renaissance in lowercase, for these inspired movements).

This is precisely not to say that such Renaissances are the same as *the* (European) Renaissance with a capital R – of course it is different – and this uniqueness is acknowledged. Take the case of Angelo Paratico, an Italian novelist and historian based in Hong Kong who wrote a biography of the man who has been described as the emblematic "Renaissance man," the "mind of the Renaissance," the "Renaissance Genius" – Leonardo da Vinci.[14] Paratico calls his

---

12 See Maissen above on p. 29.
13 Burke, "Jack Goody and the Comparative History of Renaissances," 27, after spending ten pages explaining alternative ways of thinking about Renaissance, at the end suddenly falls back into familiar patterns by arguing for the European Renaissance as "the big One." He writes: "More important, to return to Goody's central theme, there remains a case for regarding the Italian Renaissance as 'the big One', for several reasons: in the first place, in the sense that it involved so many people. There is an important contrast, for instance, between the relatively small numbers of critical philologists in China and their numerous equivalents in Europe. At least by the 16th century. [...] In the second place, the Italian movement to recover and revive the culture of Greek and especially Roman antiquity was of peculiar importance because so much of that culture – though not all of it – had been lost in the period that the humanists were the first to call the 'Dark' or the 'Middle' Ages. There was therefore more need for a renaissance in the case of Europe than in the case of China. In the third place, we might reasonably call the Italian movement the 'Big One' because it was unusually influential. The moment lasted from about 1320 to about 1630 but it has continued to attract interest ever since."
14 Barbara O' Connor, *Leonardo Da Vinci: Renaissance Genius* (Minneapolis: Carolrhoda Books, 2003); Allessandro Vezzosi, *Leonardo Da Vinci: The Mind of the Renaissance* (New York: Harry N. Abrams, 1997); Rachel Koestler-Grack, *Leonardo da Vinci: Artist, Inventor and Renaissance Man* (New York: Chelsea House Publishers, 2003).

study *Leonardo da Vinci: A Chinese Scholar Lost in Renaissance Italy*.[15] He suggests not only that Mona Lisa's face, incidentally, is the face of Leonardo's mother, but also that this face looks distinctly Chinese and that, indeed, the painting's background is a Chinese landscape.[16] He then explains that da Vinci's mother was one of many oriental slaves in Renaissance Italy.

So one of the most important Renaissance figures is half-Chinese? Paratico's theories are being rejected worldwide as "far-fetched." They but evoked outright ridicule among Chinese netizens: "I now understand why her smile looks so mysterious," joked one, "It's so typically Chinese."[17] Evidently, there is no claim, on the part of China, to *the* Renaissance in its "European" guise: Sinocentrism is not the answer to European claims.[18] This, however, does not preclude the possibility of providing Renaissance, with a capital R, with a different color cloak from time to time.

And sure enough, works have appeared on an Arab Renaissance, the Maori Renaissance, the Hebrew Renaissance, the Irish and the Harlem Renaissance, a Black Renaissance in colonial Africa, on the Turkish Renaissance, the Bengal Renaissance and the Renaissance in India: in making claims to European periodization schemes, the Chinese are obviously not alone; there is an established transcultural practice of engaging Renaissance.[19] Calls for Renaissance-like revivals, supported by some general comparison with the emergence of Europe from the darkness of the Middle Ages, have been issued widely in the twentieth

---

15 Angelo Paratico, *Leonardo Da Vinci: A Chinese Scholar Lost in Renaissance Italy* (Hong Kong: Lascar Publishing, 2015), www.lascarpublishing.com/leonardo/ (archived in DACHS: www.zo.uni-heidelberg.de/boa/digital_resources/dachs/).
16 Angelo Paratico, *Leonardo Da Vinci: A Chinese Scholar Lost in Renaissance Italy* (Hong Kong: Lascar Publishing, 2015), www.lascarpublishing.com/leonardo/ (archived in DACHS: www.zo.uni-heidelberg.de/boa/digital_resources/dachs/).
17 See Rebecca Hawkes, "Was the Mona Lisa a Chinese Slave?" *The Telegraph*, December 3, 2014 and Raquhel Carvalho, "Did Da Vinci have a Chinese Mother," *South China Morning Post*, November 30, 2014.
18 See Roxann Prazniak, "Menzies and the New Chinoiserie: Is Sinocentrism the Answer to Eurocentrism in Studies of Modernity?" *Medieval History Journal* 13, no. 1 (April 2010), who discusses Gavin Menzies' novel *1434: The Year a Magnificent Chinese Fleet Sailed to Italy and Ignited the Renaissance* (London: HarperCollins, 2008). In this fairytale in the tradition of "alternative" or "conspiracist" history, it is the Chinese Empire, rather than the Italian peninsula, that becomes the Renaissance's birthplace. See also Gavin Menzies, *1421: The Year China Discovered America* (New York: Harper Perennial, 2002).
19 Sri Aurobinda Ghose's (1872–1950) *The Renaissance in India* (1918) and David Kopf's work on the *Bengal Renaissance: British Orientalism and the Bengal Renaissance: The Dynamics of Indian Modernization, 1773–1835* (Berkeley: University of California Press, 1969) are all discussed in detail in Zhou, *Modern Chinese Vernacular*. See also Zhou, "Other Asias, Other Renaissances."

century and – as we have seen in our discussion of repeated uses of Renaissance by Chinese politicians and governments – are still being heard from commentators on world affairs and from politicians today.

The powerful position that European culture assumed in the nineteenth and the first half of the twentieth centuries (a result of the industrial revolution and its imperialist moves which was the result of the rise of the West for which the Italian Renaissance was an important catalyst) granted the term a particular aura that ideas from other places did not have. Thus, to claim the transition from medievalism to modernity, in this sense, meant entering into, or becoming part of, that world of success.[20] Such claims are now quite as, if not more, frequent in Asia than in the West. And in both Asia and Europe, the Renaissance and the Enlightenment are used as important rallying cries and as effective tools in political debate.[21]

In observing and in "showing and telling" all of this, our attention need not be confined to finding and describing the hierarchical (power) relations behind these adaptations: as I have tried to illustrate, it is not really the "subjection to a historical teleology" as Thomas Maissen would call it,[22] that plays a dominant role. Indeed, as Sebastian Conrad contends, the very "globality" of such terms is "a product of, and a response to, global conjunctures; ... the work of many authors in different parts of the world."[23] In this dialogue, I have, therefore, focused on the motives behind, the rationalizations, and eventually the naturalization of China's borrowings of the European Renaissance, and how this clearly demonstrates the "active postures Chinese intellectuals assumed in realizing their own modernization."[24] The protagonists of the New Culture Movement and, more generally, Chinese intellectuals in the late Qing and early Republic (i.e. the early twentieth century) "exercised a great deal of autonomy and control in manufacturing modernity" by carefully choosing European concepts and notions and by "theorizing their [particular] selection and naturalization."[25] Why, then, should our understanding of China's modernization be overshadowed by "continuing attempts to understand this history in terms of its victimization as a semi-colonized nation?"[26] As Frank Dikötter put it:

---

20 Eber, "Thoughts on Renaissance," 193.
21 Gamsa, "Uses and Misuses of a Chinese Renaissance," 651.
22 See Maissen p. 43.
23 Conrad, "Enlightenment in Global History," 1009.
24 Anderson, "Promises," 5.
25 Anderson, "Promises," 15 notes in square brackets have been added by Barbara Mittler.
26 Anderson, "Promises," 5.

Knowledge is never the result of passive reception, but the product of an active subject's industry. Cultural borrowings, then, can never be explained as a passive "exposure to foreign influence"; they can be viewed only as the active creations of a discerning cognitive organism. There is a decision before the borrowing takes place and a decision about what should be borrowed. Foreign ideas were assessed against, and integrated within, a pre-existing framework. From this perspective, any attempt at systematic differentiation between "a native thought" and "Western influence" would seem to be in vain.[27]

The many creative uses of Renaissance, the chronotype, in various geopolitical contexts and their circulation around the world shows the fluidity and mobility of the idea while its particular type of variation in a particular place and circumstance may or may not reveal a power structure that directs the traffic. More importantly, this variation illustrates the transcultural imagination exercised by the people who participate in a complicated network of literary and cultural exchanges. In taking all of these variations and imaginations that now float around the term "Renaissance" seriously, taking them to be part of a pool of "Renaissances-in-common" that would and could engage in a dialogue on Renaissance as equals, we make a start in enriching those vocabularies "devised to think the world"[28] which we have discussed throughout. Indeed, we may consider differentiating their particularities perhaps more carefully than has been done before: when, why, and how do the actors speak of "Renaissance," what do they mean when they refer to it selectively as a "rebirth" (e. g. *zaisheng* 再生), a "rejuvenation" (e. g. *fuxing* 復興), a "new tide" (e. g. *xinchao* 新潮), or yet something rather different (such as a "return to the old," e. g. *fugu* 復古)? What is it that they are talking about in their specific historical and social circumstances and what are the relational patterns in which these categories stand to each other? All of this would entail taking seriously the actor's stance, perspective, and (magic and powerful) linguistic performance in a dialogue of equals where questions of who was first and who came after no longer play a role, and where the many unique and colorful manifestations of a "Renaissance-in-common" which need not be squeezed into one "rather simple scheme of advancement," as Thomas Maissen would put it,[29] but which, to the contrary, may thus serve to expand it, are brought to the fore. Taking the actors seriously, and accepting their use of Renaissance with a capital R is, I think, therefore, a crucial step in using pe-

---

[27] Frank Dikötter, *The Discourse of Race in Modern China* (Stanford: Stanford University Press, 1992), 65.
[28] Conrad, "Enlightenment in Global History," 1011.
[29] Maissen p. 125.

riodization schemes as specific "regimes of historicity"[30] but on one shared matrix, thus achieving what I would call History-in-common.

Yet we have seen, too, that uses of *the* Renaissance are not just restricted to historical actors. Historians of China, have also resorted to the term: for the sinologist working in a European context, it might sometimes appear pragmatic, even indispensable, to employ vocabularies such as "Renaissance" to intimate and describe Chinese phenomena to a non-Chinese audience to make them better understood. The scholar's function as a mediator may suggest such deportment and practice. Accordingly, if a sinologist likens the Chinese New Culture Movement to the Renaissance (or the Enlightenment), he is primarily doing so by engaging in an intercultural conversation, taking on a mediating, translating function and thus negotiating the knowledge that can be expected of a European counterpart in trying to bring a particular Chinese meaning across. Yet it is precisely this behavior that is, I think, problematic for reasons which we have only just begun to illustrate in this dialogue because every such term always already carries far too much specific baggage, both on the Chinese and on the European side.

Accordingly, it seems to me apt to think twice before arbitrarily using particular and loaded European terms and applying them as analytical tools to Chinese circumstances.[31] This is true for any such terminology, not just "Renaissance." To switch to a term such as "rebirth" as an analytical category of preferred use, a "smallest common denominator," for different "renascences," as Goody would call them,[32] does not truly alleviate the problem, since these terms, too, may be charged, if in different ways.

This is why, while I understand that Thomas Maissen is using "renaissance" in lowercase for the Chinese Renaissances only pragmatically, arguing that one should completely avoid this terminology and better switch to using "rebirth" or "renewal" instead,[33] I would still hold that this usage is confusing and more so than the use of a capital R for those movements fashioning themselves as inspired by the European model. My plight is not in discussing these periods according to a particular European chronologic – in fact, I agree with Thomas Maissen, that this would make just as little sense as simply applying the Zhou Dynasty and its "logic" to Europe. But I am also not really interested in creating

---

30 Hartog, *Régimes d'historicité*
31 To use the epithet Holocaust for the Cultural Revolution, as already mentioned by Thomas Maissen (p. 125), is an example and one which I have always and quite vehemently objected to, see Mittler, *A Continuous Revolution*.
32 Goody, *Renaissances*
33 See Maissen on p. 126.

new and (only seemingly) generalizable periodization schemes, taking "anthropological constants," such as regular periods of rebirth as in nature – blossoming, fall, new blossoming – or movements of renewal, as Maissen suggests,[34] as examples for how to study the Chinese Renaissance.

What I am aiming for is something much more modest, and it boils down to this – respecting the voice of the historical actor. I suggest a rethinking of the old and established periodization schemes and the diverse practices around them by taking global actors' categories seriously and following their leads in interpreting their periods – in this instance, Renaissance in relation to *the* Renaissance. I am convinced that this approach can teach us more about Renaissance than if we begin to create our own analytical categories.

Renaissance is an established term in China, as the many writings on Renaissance in English and Chinese show. Just because a certain concept has first been established and used in one place does not mean that it cannot be established and used by historical actors in another. It is a question of vocabulary and of how willing we are to open up its usage: if I translate *fugu* 復古 (returning to the old) as "Renaissance" and the term *xie* 邪 as "heretic/heterodox," the Europeanist may at first be misled, may think of *the* Renaissance in the first case or of an exclusively religious context in the second when each of these terms have in fact many more levels of signification in Chinese.[35] I do not believe, however, as Thomas Maissen does, that we can avoid confusion by disallowing the use of such terminology if simply because it has already been used in the sources all over. Instead, to avoid confusion means precisely to open ourselves up to the diverse logics of others, to begin to understand their languages, to accept that they have and use categories just as we do, and that sometimes these usages and the terms and vocabularies that go with them converge with our own, and sometimes they do not. To avoid confusion, we need to listen to each other, to know more about the multiple meanings of one particular term, not to forbid each other the use of a particular language or terminology.

By adapting a tripartite division of time from light to dark to light again – prosperity, decline, rebirth – but now in new guise, as Antiquity-Middle Ages-Modernity – the actors in China's Renaissance, for example, adapted a chronologic and accompanying terminology which they saw as a key element of the European success story. It is the actors who created this logic and its genealogy, and it is they who made it work by institutionalizing it. While I would speak up for observing how the chronologics of "Renaissance" have been employed and filled

---

34 See Maissen on p. 130.
35 See Mittler on p. 93.

with particular – indeed, unique – meaning by historical actors all over the world, an act which helps us pluralize our visions of particular historical moments and processes as well as epochs or chronotypes in the making, I would also warn scholars about using "renaissance/renascence/rebirth" or any such term as a critical and analytical term to describe these moments and processes. While the particularist use of terms like "Renaissance" by historical actors and in historical documents may lead us to a truer sense of their transcultural imagination and communication, these same terms must not become our own analytical terms, precisely because they would no longer enable us to see these elements of transcultural imagination.[36] In order to be understood outside of China, and in order to enable a fruitful inter- and transdisciplinary dialogue, we need *not* come up with ever new "renaissances," "rebirths" and the like in our analytical tool box, indeed to do so is to fall into the trap of "we had it first, too," a retaliation perspective that does not relieve us from questions of power asymmetries but instead, and paradoxically, perpetuates them. What we need to do instead, is to begin enriching vocabularies like Renaissance, by taking into account the many variations and possibilities for "Renaissances" as they have been lived by historical actors, thus taking them as seriously as the European Renaissance and using them as much to rethink European – as well as Chinese and other – terminologies, categories, and ideas of what Renaissance may or may not mean. Ultimately, this may even allow us to take a new and fresh view of *the* (European) Renaissance: why was there no Renaissance for women or the people, more generally, in Europe, even when the critical dialogue of the humanists had opened up so many ways of thinking about the verity and truth of established assumptions, even though it had illustrated an open "democratic" spirit in allowing heathen into a discussion among equals, for example?

If to study r/Renaissances as generic concepts and chronotypes encompasses these readings far remote in space and in time from its first "privileged" usage, this make questions of authenticity and realness, and the distinctions between "ours" and "theirs" obsolete. They are replaced with questions about circulation and appropriation, about performativity and affect as well as effect. Thus, privileging processuality and agency, and studying r/Renaissance from a global perspective in order to think instead of r/Renaissance-in-common, has fundamental consequences for understanding the term, it relieves us from the

---

36 In this formulation, I debate with Zhou Gang. Zhou comes to the opposite conclusion and is convinced that for precisely the reasons given here, that the use of terminology such as Renaissance should also be adapted by scholars and that it should become a critical term in scholarship, an idea I object to strongly.

Denkzwang, exerted in every (scientific) community and dictated by a particular usage of certain vocabularies, and it enables new discoveries.³⁷ While the use of periodization schemes such as r/Renaissance across cultural boundaries is always inherently problematic, these problems can be solved if such schemes are made in accordance with the concrete cultural phenomena which they are supposed to explain, and if they are thus understood on the same matrix and ontological level as r/Renaissances-in-common. And thus, China's (and other) r/Renaissances may enable us to reveal new aspects in *the* Renaissance that we are not yet even aware of.

So far, so good. The second argument made by Thomas Maissen in his conclusion is concerned with the particular quality of the European Renaissance and its pivotal importance in the history not just of Europe but of humanity – the rise of the West. He writes: "The period of the Renaissance means more than a fascination with millennia-old authors and artists: it encompasses crucial changes in different fields not just for one nation or one region, but eventually for the history of humanity." I would agree, but call to our attention the fact that this sounds quite similar to the kinds of arguments made by the protagonists of the New Culture Movement, as well. They would not have accepted the notion of the Chinese Renaissance as "just a (minor) chapter in the history of learning,"³⁸ as Maissen does. Instead, the protagonists of the New Culture Movement, in a self-aggrandizing discourse, would have argued that

(2) *the Chinese Renaissance meant much more than the resurrection of long-forgotten authors. Indeed (and in hindsight, this is not untrue), it was the beginning of a significant development that would last a long time (already a good 100 years with more to come?), comprising the introduction of a large number of fundamental changes in many important fields of politics and society with an impact not just on Chinese national history but the history of humanity as well.* All of this cannot be explained by the rise of the system of states (as was the case for Renaissance Europe, so Maissen contends),³⁹ but most importantly by the rise of the Chinese Communist Party. As the New Culture, or, in communist parlance, better, the May Fourth Movement came to be inscribed in the official national history textbooks with the foundation of the People's Republic of China in 1949, it was styled into one of the crucial moments in Chinese history, a decisive turning point, a radical break with the past or, in Chinese communist rhetoric, with the "dark feudal

---

37 Fleck, *Entstehung und Entwicklung einer wissenschaftlichen Tatsache*, see especially 85–86.
38 Maissen on p. 33.
39 See above on p. 127.

ages." The effect of the movement, in and through the communist victory, consisted in a re-evaluation of all previous history, it came to entail a radical break with one part of this past, so radical that even Confucianism had to go (at least temporarily). It became canonized as a movement burying some and then resurrecting other forgotten authors (in this case, not of "pagan classical" but of "heretic vernacular" literature), authors and works that had never before in Chinese history been considered important because they were considered too lowly.

The New Culture Movement in China, then, came to be read as having enabled support for the vernacular as the official written language. For this it took *the* Renaissance as its inspiration (and authority), thus paradoxically highlighting (and utilizing) one aspect of the European experience in particular that had indeed not been at the forefront of (elitist) humanist thinking in the first place. The New Culture Movement also came to stand for a revalidation of foreign literary traditions and their influx into China, and it enabled a new appraisal of China's past, playing up the role of the "common people," the peasants, and the proletariat. It was styled into a "rebirth," to the extent that a new cultural code, informed by new ideas – engendered from the confrontation with a distinct other, in this case, the foreign other – was devised to apply to all things Chinese (and otherwise). Not unlike the European Renaissance, which was so dominated by the voices of the humanists, the Chinese Renaissance, too, was carried out by the elites. But through the work of the Chinese Communist Party it came to be translated into something that had consequences for everyone, even the peasant in a far-away village in Xinjiang, and thus this Chinese Renaissance may have become even more (and certainly no less) all-encompassing than the Renaissance project in Europe could ever have been, not just for China, but for humanity as a whole. The Chinese Renaissance is conceived today, not as a moment but as a process that was to last quite some time, beginning at the end of the nineteenth century and, as we have seen, influential to this day – with Xi Jinping's "Chinese dream" as its last reincarnation.

To fully understand the analogies made with the European Renaissance or other such periodization schemes by historical actors in China within the last century, we must free ourselves from thinking of these periodization schemes as fixed and narrow European "programs" that are superimposed on other cultures. It is true that these ideas had their origins in Europe during very particular historical periods, but it is also true that they were rethought and reimagined again and again in various non-European contexts, and appropriated "second-" or even "third-hand" from one non-European context to another. Goody, in *The*

Theft of History (2006),⁴⁰ claims that most cultural and social developments in Europe had their matches in other parts of the non-Western world by charging Europeans with monopolizing the normative categories in which universal (and not only European) history was to be imagined and narrated: the necessary passage from the Renaissance through the Enlightenment to the Industrial Revolution. As he rejects arguments for European superiority on the basis of temporal precedence, he relies on the logic of "who was first" to claim that China preceded Europe in developing cities and urban culture, *haute cuisine* and much more (one might also add, the significantly inconsequential development of printing with moveable types, as mentioned by Thomas Maissen, above).⁴¹

I would argue that we must stop approaching *the* Renaissance as an ontologically autonomous subject that existed in the remote (and exclusively European!) past: it is time to think of Renaissance as an accumulation of various readings and appropriations practiced by different interpreters in different contexts to be considered on one common plane. It is in this sense that I believe it is possible to abandon the old, European-centered notion of Renaissance and to propose reading uses of Renaissance, as an "open semiosis, subject to change, subject to redefinition and revision" as Zhou Gang suggests.⁴² After all, it is hard to imagine that a great idea would be fixed and defined (dead?) at its birth; it is only natural that this idea would grow and be enriched, blossoming in other places and at other times from when and where it was once engendered. A comparative and transcultural reading of the European Renaissance, the Chinese Renaissance, and other Renaissances in their wake, but on a common matrix, may help reveal new patterns of thinking that have been largely ignored so far and by doing so, unraveling different manners of naming and claiming, we may, paradoxically, even capture the (dialogic!) spirit of the European Renaissance itself.⁴³

Therefore, I suggest that China did not have *the* Renaissance, and this does matter. If we view history in a global context and from the perspective of the historical actor, we realize that China had something else: it had *a* "Chinese" Renaissance which was unique and went according to its own rules, but which was of equally pivotal importance far beyond offering a simple reappraisal of the

---

40 Goody, *The Theft of History.*
41 See Thomas Maissen p. 127 and Barbara Mittler and Thomas A. Schmitz, "'Gutenberg kam nur bis Gonsenheim' – Gründe, warum Gutenbergs Erfindung weder in China noch bei den alten Griechen eine entscheidende Rolle gespielt hat. Ein (nicht ganz ernstgemeinter) west-östlicher Dialog," in *Die innovative Bibliothek. Elmar Mittler zum 65. Geburtstag,* eds. Erland K. Nielsen, Klaus G. Saur and Klaus Ceynowa (Munich: Saur, 2005).
42 Zhou, "Other Asias, Other Renaissances," 96.
43 Zhou, "Other Asias, Other Renaissances," 92.

past. Moving toward greater differentiation, and filling and enriching our vocabularies with multiple meanings, we thus also realize that Europe did not have *the* Renaissance, either, in the sense that it did not remain a singular event. It had a specific and particular "European" Renaissance. If read in a global context, then, we have now seen how all *H*istory becomes *regional* history and accordingly that there are many histor*ies* of Renaissance to tell in the global context. Going one step further, I have suggested that if we are able and willing to accept that actors all over the world may have been engaged as equals in the writing of r/Renaissances and thus in the creation of new periodization schemes, and if we make this the basis of our writing of a new and global *H*istory-in-common, which no longer takes the European case as "the Big (and only original) one" and thus does not treat all other historical experiences as derivative (in its negative copy-cat sense), but instead, is interested in engaging and explaining these other, as well as European experiences, as regionally specific and thus "unique" histories, then we can move from these specific histor*ies* back to *H*istory again. This would then be History on a truly global scale; a History-in-common, which would consider periodization schemes, epochal frames and chronotypes characterized not by their universality and inevitability, but by variation, specification, and differentiation both in terms of space and in terms of time.

In our debate, we have now come to an end. We have marked out diametrically opposed positions: Thomas Maissen would answer the question of whether or not terms such as "Renaissance" or "Enlightenment" could and should be used to describe phenomena in places other than particular parts of occidental Europe where these periodizations and the concepts surrounding them were once engendered, with "no, because they belong to a unique and particular cultural setting and to a specific narrative." My answer would be "yes, because they belong to a unique and particular cultural setting and to a specific narrative." Why this contradiction, and what does this twofold answer mean for our schemes of ordering the past here and elsewhere, or, put differently, for the writing of global history?

Here the third contention in Thomas Maissen's conclusion must be discussed. According to him, "The humanists' approach to rediscovered alterity in the unique form of an open dialogue was a necessary precondition for the rise of the West." This was so, he argues, because humanist dialogue, with its acceptance of several possible solutions and not just one Truth, which allowed its readers to evaluate conflicting heritages that were now being systematically collected and commented on, was accompanied by a number of other important historical phenomena situated in the Renaissance, such as the developing system of states, the democratization of knowledge thanks to the printing press, and the discoveries and the founding of colonies.⁴⁴ I would agree and go one step further. My contention would be that if

(3) *the humanists' approach to rediscovered alterity in the unique form of an open dialogue was a necessary precondition for the rise of the West, then it may also open ways for rethinking and re-centering the writing of global history.* Thomas Maissen would contend this point: he is not convinced by thinking History-in-common, which is my attempt to undo the idea of one binding master narrative by substituting it with a more polyphonic, triangulated narrative, approached and written from multiple perspectives in order to answer to the many different constituencies involved in the co-production of periodization schemes. In his view, one overarching narrative is still needed in the writing of history and in his view, if we truly "open ourselves to the logic of others,"⁴⁵ as I demand, we will no longer be able to really write that overarching narrative. My answer would be that overarching narratives are precisely the problem: they create universalizing, stiff chronologics which do not allow for the kind of variation, specification, and differentiation that is inherent in and thus imperative to the writing of global history.

In a recent article entitled "What is global history now?" Jeremy Adelman explains that global history faces "two seemingly opposite challenges for an inter-dependent, over-heating planet."⁴⁶ In his words, "if we are going to muster meaningful narratives about the togetherness of strangers near and far, we are going to have to be more global and get more serious about engaging other languages and other ways of telling history. Historians and their reader-citizens are also going to have to re-signify the place of local attachments and meanings."⁴⁷ And indeed, a recurrent problem in the writing of global history is language, the conceptual apparatus with which we have come to work habitually, and its local meanings.⁴⁸ Attempts to study r/Renaissance (or f/Feudalism, or c/Capitalism, for that matter) on a world scale have amply shown how extremely difficult it is to avoid circularity in this kind of enterprise. For if we begin by defining the phenomenon to be studied using European terminology, even if it appears "neutral" at first, we will, more often than not, end up "discovering" that the

---

44 See Maissen on p. 129.
45 See p. 156.
46 Jeremy Adelman, "What is Global History now?" aeon.co/essays/is-global-history-still-possible-or-has-it-had-its-moment.
47 Jeremy Adelman, "What is Global History now?" aeon.co/essays/is-global-history-still-possible-or-has-it-had-its-moment.
48 See, very intelligently, Jenco, "Recentering Political Theory."

phenomenon is primarily European after all.⁴⁹ Any term, be it as obviously specific as "Renaissance" or as seemingly unspecific as "portrait" or "novel," as "revolution" or "heretic," for that matter, if it has once been associated with a particular European experience, it will consequently be read in that light and with that experience in mind – not just by European interpretive communities, but even by those from other parts of the world many of whom have – for almost two centuries now – lived with significant epistemic rupture that has made available (as well as intimated) an only seemingly distinct set of European terminologies to them. If we are not carefully reading their particular uses of this terminology, therefore – with open ears and open eyes, so to speak – as a shared terminology that contains a rich variety of possible meanings, only then do we run the danger of forcing their institutions, their artifacts, their texts, or their movements to fit a delimited set of European models – and thus, we are restricting their import to humanity as a whole.⁵⁰

While comparison, by way of specific terminologies, is always risky because, as Peter Burke holds, we might forget the flexibility of vocabularies and languages in using them "our way," (and the example of both "heretic" and "Renaissance" in the context of this dialogue may serve as an illustration), not to engage in it may indeed be even more dangerous.⁵¹ One cannot simply ignore meaning-making in other parts of the globe in the writing of global history.⁵² Is there really no other way between using the European apparatus of comparison on the one hand and refusing to compare at all on the other?⁵³

This book is, in fact, an attempt to uncover other possibilities: I have suggested a rethink of terms such as "Renaissance" through dialogue, with the ultimate aim of offering a path toward something one could call a transdisciplinary hermeneutics, one which allows us – eventually – to re-center, in the sense Leigh Jenco proposes, some of the constitutive vocabularies in our discourse about history in the world.⁵⁴ Using dialogue-as-method, I would argue, allows us to take a closer look at vocabularies other than the European and to engage

---

49 This and the following passages are heavily indebted to Burke, "Jack Goody and the Comparative History of Renaissances."
50 Burke, "Jack Goody and the Comparative History of Renaissances," 17.
51 Burke, "Jack Goody and the Comparative History of Renaissances," 17.
52 Burke, "Jack Goody and the Comparative History of Renaissances," 17, makes this point about Norbert Elias and his reading of the civilizing process.
53 Burke, "Jack Goody and the Comparative History of Renaissances," 17.
54 See Jenco, "Recentering Political Theory," 28.

in something one might call, following Burke, the "principle of rotation."⁵⁵ Thinking about "Renaissance" in Chinese terms, recalling ideas such as *fuxing* 復興 (revival/rejuvenation), *fuhuo* 復活 (resurrection), *fugu* 復古 (returning to the old), or *guangfu* 光復 "recovery" (or, literally, "return of the light"), *xinchao* 新潮 (new tide), *xinchan* 新產 (new production/new birth), *zaisheng* 再生 (re-birth), *zaizao* 再造 (re-creation), or even *qimeng* 啟蒙 (enlightenment), all of which we have seen used as translations for *the* Renaissance and renaissances alike but each with their own particular semantic tinge and resonating body, means taking each unique and particular interpretation of r/Renaissance seriously. Each interpretation is allowed to enter into a dialogue among equals in order to produce a History-in-common for the r/Renaissance on its own terms.⁵⁶ Thus, taking different regional terminologies or terminological variations as norms⁵⁷ not only necessitates that we listen to others as specialists each in their fields, but also to broaden and enrich our own uses of particular "regional" terminology.⁵⁸ The critical dialogue I am suggesting, would be a transformative encounter, one that produces knowledge about the specificity not only of others but also of ourselves. This new knowledge discourages, and indeed, it may even make impossible, an untouched return to an established status quo, with *the* Renaissance firmly in place.⁵⁹

What precisely is the importance of the vernacular, of emancipation and the work of the humanists, for example, in *the* Renaissance? If we take Hu Shi's view seriously that both the Chinese and the European Renaissance had (1) set out to replace classical literature with a new literature in the living language of the people – the vernacular; that (2) both were movements of deliberate protest against

---

55 For Liang's uses of the Renaissance, see Anderson, "Promises," chapter 2. See also Kaske, *The Politics of Language*, chapter 5.
56 For further discussion, see Anderson, "Promises," 51.
57 Burke, "Jack Goody and the Comparative History of Renaissances," 17.
58 Burke, "Jack Goody and the Comparative History of Renaissances," 18, suggests, for example, a discussion of whether the pleasure quarters of early modern Venice or Rome, Paris or London might be analyzed as Western examples of the "floating world" (*ukiyo*) that is found in Japanese cities such as Edo, Kyoto or Osaka. I very much agree that this would be important, but both the work of Burke and Goody show that it must be specialists who engage in this task together. To do this in a dialogue between two or more specialists is far better than to attempt comparisons that are written by one who tries to understand and analyze information from another specialist. Even someone as careful as Burke commits so many mistakes in citing Chinese sources, terms and figures that the result is distorting and embarrassing. See Burke, "Jack Goody and the Comparative History of Renaissances," where it should be *kaozhengxue*, Tao Yuanming, *junzi*, etc.
59 This argument is inspired by, but also takes issue with Jenco, "Recentering Political Theory," 29–32.

established cultural ideas and institutions and of conscious emancipation of the individual from the bondage of tradition; and, most importantly, that (3) both were "humanist" movements,[60] then what does that mean for our interpretation of *the* Renaissance in Europe? Evidently *the* Renaissance, which European actors and scholars would define quite differently, holds these possibilities for interpretation, at least for someone like Hu Shi and his contemporaries. Instead of denigrating this Chinese reading of the European Renaissance as inaccurate, derivative, a misunderstanding, this dialogue has suggested that his understanding can offer possibilities for rethinking *the* Renaissance, thus taking seriously the Chinese interpretation as a legitimate alternative interpretation in a critical intellectual analysis. This kind of critical intellectual analysis, reading and discussing in a dialogue, sources from many different origins on a common matrix, is what I would consider a first step in writing a History-in-common.[61]

Through this dialogue, I thus propose to scholars of the European world to begin to engage with the experience of others as more than just "case studies whose particularities present evidence for interrogating the lapses of existing theories."[62] Doing so introduces the possibility of developing, on this basis, extended vocabularies that are in fact relevant and meaningful to "us" as well as "them." Whether indeed, as Burke argues, one must view the "critical approach to the past practiced by humanists as the equivalent of the Chinese *kaozhengxue* 考證學 (evidential learning)"[63] is obviously debatable. *Kaozhengxue* is, after all – as is the humanist approach in Europe – a very specific and very text-driven phenomenon.[64] But it may be considered useful to ask what it is in the very particular and specific humanist approach to texts (and the Renaissance as a whole) that must be called a characteristically, or predominantly, European phenomenon after all, and if so, why? What is actually unique in the European Renaissance (as well as the Chinese), and why? Already the fact that we have begun to ask this kind of question has the advantage of defamiliarizing the idea of the "humanist" and his "Renaissance," thus preventing us from always taking their

---

60 Hu, *Chinese Renaissance*, 44.
61 See Jenco, "Recentering Political Theory," 33–34.
62 Jenco "Recentering Political Theory," 34.
63 Burke, "Jack Goody and the Comparative History of Renaissances," 18. I have added the characters and the correct *Pinyin* spelling, as mentioned above, Burke mistakingly has *kaozhenghue*. I have also added the underlining of "equivalent."
64 Cf., for China, Benjamin A. Elman, *From Philosophy to Philology. Intellectual and Social Aspects of Change in Late Imperial China* (Cambridge: Harvard University Press, 1984).

specified meanings for granted as "universal."[65] Thus, to read r/Renaissance as History-in-common, we begin defamiliarizing ourselves with what we think we know, opening up possibilities to reconceive it, and thus we might even allow differently formulated manners of thinking about r/Renaissance to become *constituents* of potentially generalizable reflections on its historical value.[66]

Obviously, this kind of approach does not deny the pervasion of European thought and the rise of the West over the last two and a half centuries. But this dialogue affirms that European categories or traditions are as "local" and as "timely" as any others, without for that reason dismissing the possibility of their wider applicability. Re-centering, through dialogue, offers another kind of response to any kind of -centrism, offering up more inclusive "in-common" renderings of knowledge production to counter the inequities and occlusions of what has clearly unmasked itself as a very local – European – "universalism." Engaging in dialogue, we realize the possibility for generalizable claims merging from local contexts outside of Europe, opening up a plurality of ways of knowing and describing the world.[67] While "we need not agree with every possible alternative," as Leigh Jenco put it, "we cannot rule out the possibility that one or more of them will convince some of us to start producing and valuing knowledge in a completely new way."[68]

In elaborating different positions in dialogue, there is no need either to highlight the "Truth" or to debunk some "myth of European cultural superiority," as Goody does,[69] nor is it necessary to be concerned about being "less stubbornly Eurocentric," as Gruzinski does.[70] There is no need to lament a "theft of history" either.[71] The endeavor throughout this book is analytical not moralistic: we are not out to find a final answer to all our questions, but instead to stimulate further discussion. This dialogue is not about right or wrong, it is even less about retaliation in the sense of "we had it first" while it acknowledges European (and other) "firsts," but without the gleefulness possibly attached to it. It is also *not* at all about saying that the rise of the West must be considered more a "re-

---

65 See a similar formulation in Burke, "Jack Goody and the Comparative History of Renaissances," 20.
66 Jenco, "Recentering Political Theory," 42.
67 See Jenco, "Recentering Political Theory," 52–53.
68 Jenco, "Recentering Political Theory," 54.
69 See Goody, *Theft of History*, 127; Brotton, *Renaissance Bazaar*, 20.
70 Gruzinski, *The Eagle and the Dragon*, 4.
71 Goody, *Theft of History*.

sponse to the Rest, but dependent on it,"[72] and it is *not* about global history necessarily being connected history either.[73] Instead, it may be taken as an attempt to offer a new format of thinking global history: as History-in-dialogue. As a decentered antagonistic intervention, History-in-dialogue can open up new avenues for thinking about global history and periodization. Using the genre of dialogue between experts in their respective fields – something that we have tested in this book – might help us come to terms with the many deep histories of global transformations which we have only just begun to know about.

One of the historian's most important tasks is to listen. To write a global history as History-in-common means to listen to other parts of the globe, those who are not Europe, for example, and to begin to understand what they actually mean when they talk in terms that appear quite familiar – but are so, only on the surface.[74] Dialogue is never a one-way but always a two-way exchange (or more): it is constituted by a conversation between equal partners and therefore not an attempt to integrate but rather to expose the other, in an open narrative on each of our own terms, in each of our own tongues.[75] Dialogue may be the only way to get away eventually from the shouting match of "we were first" or "we had it only" (while this dialogue presented here, deliberately contains many instances for showing where, uniquely, one or another indeed had something first or only), and with it the only seeming *inevitability* of the hold of any particular kind of local thought (be it European or not) in universal application.[76] Accordingly, I am inclined to follow Burke in postulating that "the western Renaissance deserves to be viewed as a member of a family."[77]

---

[72] Thus, I take issue with Adelman's "What is global history now?" which argues: "Even the industrial revolution and Europe's great leap forward in the 19th century, the one thing that seemed to separate Europe from others, came under the global historian's macroscope. In *The Great Divergence: China, Europe, and the Making of the Modern World Economy* (2000), Kenneth Pomeranz demolished the view of Europeans as the authors of their own miraculous rise. He revealed how much European enterprise and accumulation shared with China. How Europe's break from the common, Eurasian-Malthusian straightjacket began not with the region's internal uniqueness, but with access to and conquest of what Adam Smith called the wastelands of the Americas. In the same vein, global historians demonstrated how much insurance, banking and shipping startups owed to the African slave trade. The European miracle was, in short, a global harvest." While it is true that this miracle was global, this still does not mean that all such miracles are going to be global and that global history, therefore, must always already be conceived as connected or entangled history.
[73] Subrahmanyam, "Connected Histories."
[74] See Adelman "What is Global History now?"
[75] This challenges the restricted possibilities Adelman sees in "What is Global History now?"
[76] See Jenco, "Recentering Political Theory," 49.
[77] Burke, "Jack Goody and the Comparative History of Renaissances," 27.

In a 2001 review of a volume on renaissances (*Die Gegenwart des Altertums*) outside of Europe,[78] Jan Assmann praised the idea of rethinking r/Renaissance both in space and time.[79] Yet he also criticized that the volume under review had not lived up to its potential. According to him, the articles, presenting different renaissances outside of Europe, did not engage each other and thus failed to fulfill their potential of rethinking and re-centering r/Renaissance as a concept. This could be achieved, I would contend, if global history were written in dialogue – not in an additive manner, with specialists each presenting their own cause and field, while not really listening to each other carefully enough – but instead, in syncretic fashion, with specialists from different fields coming together in an engaged and critical, even antagonistic, dialogue. The China scholar immediately recalls that unlikely but iconic dialogue between the *Three Philosophers* of China, Laozi, Confucius, and Buddha.[80] In an iconic depiction, these three philosophers, or, more correctly, philosophical schools, are engaged in that typical "peaceful dialogue with open outcome – and across space and time." They are shown bowing over the same vat of vinegar and tasting it, but each is offering a radically different interpretation of its taste as manifested in their distinct facial expressions, which are conventionally taken to epitomize

---

[78] Dieter Kuhn and Helga Stahl, eds., *Die Gegenwart des Altertums. Formen und Funktionen des Altertumsbezugs in den Hochkulturen der Alten Welt* (Heidelberg: Edition forum, 2001).

[79] Jan Assmann, "Die Antiken der Anderen. Renaissance im Plural: Ein Sammelband untersucht die Wiederbelebung früher Kulturleistungen quer durch Zeiten und Gesellschaften," *Frankfurter Rundschau*, October 27, 2001. He writes: "In vielen Kulturen dieser Erde lassen sich Epochen ausmachen, die sich in Bezug auf ein 'Altertum' definieren, das sie wiederentdecken und zum Vorbild erheben. Dieses uns aus unserer Tradition als 'Renaissance' vertraute Phänomen stellt also keinen europäischen Einzelfall dar, sondern existiert im Plural und lässt sich in kulturvergleichender Perspektive beleuchten.... Auf den ersten Blick scheint dies eine typisch eurozentrische Fragestellung. Überraschenderweise bildet hier aber China Modell und Ausgangspunkt. Die Fragestellung wird anhand chinesischer Phänomene entwickelt, und die chinesischen Renaissancen, vor allen die der Song-Dynastie (960 – 1279) werden in jener Differenziertheit dargestellt, wie man sie in vergleichbaren Unternehmen in Bezug auf westliche Phänomene gewohnt ist, während die uns vertraute Renaissance gerade einmal in zwei Beiträgen gestreift wird. Schon diese Verschiebung der Perspektive macht den Band interessant: ... Um so aufschlussreicher der Vergleich, um so brisanter die These, dass sich Parallelen rund um den Erdball aufzeigen lassen und das auch noch in einer an Karl Jaspers' These von der 'Achsenzeit' erinnernden Synchronizität."

[80] See the discussion of Giorgione's image by Maissen above on p. 78 for the European counterpart to this "trialogue" which, in China, becomes equally emblematic: accordingly, it is used for many other exchangeable figures, for instance Huiyuan (Buddhist, 334 – 416), Tao Yuanming (Confucian, 365 – 427), and Lu Xiujing (Daoist, 406 – 477) among others. See baike.baidu.com/item/虎溪三笑.

their particular philosophical orientation. In the painting (see fig. 10) by Zhu Jianqiu 诸健秋 (ca. 1891–1964) – a contemporary of the New Culture Movement – the Confucian (according to the inscription, here in the form of the famous poet Su Shi 蘇軾 or Su Dongpo 蘇東坡, 1037–1101), depicted with the large hat in the middle, finds the vinegar sour; the Buddhist (here in the form of Chan/Zen-Monk Foyin 佛印 or Xie Duanqing 谢端卿, 1032–1098), on the left, holding his hand up in a mudra of reassurance (the Abhaya Mudrā) finds it bitter in taste; whereas the Daoist (Huang Tingjian 黃庭堅, 1045–1105), a cloth covering his bun – a traditional Daoist hairdo, as a visible marker (a fashion-statement) of his rejection of official Confucian insignia of power – is shown smiling, as to him the vinegar is sweet. The iconic image is often used to illustrate the Chinese syncretistic tradition of "Three Teachings." Each of the three teachers offers his own particular perspective on the matter at hand (vinegar) while none of these is weighed or judged as more or less truthful than the other. The image shows the three philosophers engaged with each other, reacting to each other in this potentially agonistic but in the end always peaceful syncretic dialogue.[81]

Dialogue as a form allows the participants to scrutinize the other, to enable the other to rethink their premises and standpoints, and even while sticking to some or even all of them, participants in a dialogue may be able to transform themselves (as did the humanists) in an effort to learn from events that are far removed in space and time, but nonetheless relevant to understanding the here and now. If through dialogue, we are willing to open ourselves to the logic of others and to the always already complex and internally contested intellectual communities from which other voices and texts emerge, we allow their lines of argument and concern to lead us to unexpected forms of knowledge and the possibility of reconfirming as well as critiquing our own disciplinary positions.[82] History-as-dialogue, then, is an option to make syncretism – in the sense of the three Chinese philosophers (as stand-ins for their philosophical schools), each of them addressing the same topic and material phenomenon (vinegar) but each in a totally different way and from three different perspectives – a guiding principle in the writing of a global History-in-common. In taking History-as-dialogue to be the principle of historical writing, history can remain history for each and every one in their uniqueness and in their own and

---

81 See Patrick Gray, *Varieties of Religious Invention: Founders and Their Functions in History*, (Oxford: Oxford University Press, 2015), 4 and Y. J. Choi, *East and West. Understanding the Rise of China* (Bloomington: Xlibris Corp, 2010), 195. Thanks to Paola Zamperini, Lothar Ledderose and Julia F. Andrews for their interpretations of images and inscriptions that informed this passage.
82 Jenco, "Recentering Political Theory," 55.

Fig. 10 Zhu Jianqiu 诸健秋 (ca. 1891–1964), *Three Vinegar Tasters* 三嚐酸 *Sanchangsuan*.

very specific interpretation. Personal differences and specific viewpoints remain. Indeed, they are not only acknowledged but employed as starting points for a critical process of rethinking, revising, and redeveloping established opinion on a particular periodization scheme. Global history thus need no longer be written simply as additive, the accumulation of single regional histories. It is also not exclusively written as connected history. It is not a history which is acknowledged to have been suppressed by certain regimes of historicity or systems of periodization, either, but instead, it is a history which grows in significance by being studied and understood on its own terms, but in the comparative context of others. As History-in-dialogue it becomes interactive and no longer additive: an idea, an event, an epochal frame may be presented from a variety of different angles as expressed by vastly different and often dissenting interlocutors. Thus, History-in-dialogue may enable us to escape the dilemma of misunderstanding claims for uniqueness (as made throughout this book by both Thomas Maissen and myself) as claims for precedence or superiority. It will allow for new ways of conceiving a global History-in-common.

Epilogue

Thomas Maissen & Barbara Mittler
Why China did not have a Renaissance – and why that matters: Conflicting approaches to periodization

This book asks why China did not have a Renaissance – and why that matters, or, in a more general sense: whether European periodization schemes can be used adequately in the writing of global history. Thomas Maissen has presented the Italian and, more broadly, the European Renaissance with its particularities, namely its intense, critical and ultimately open dialogue with the heathens, as a consequential element in a rather traditional narrative about the rise of the West. Barbara Mittler has questioned the uniqueness of the European Renaissance, by illustrating how other cultures, such as the Chinese, have adopted existing vocabularies such as "Renaissance" to live and describe their own historical experiences.

Thomas Maissen concluded that the concept of *the* Renaissance has been defined in such a particular way, both by the humanist contemporaries and in historiography since the nineteenth century, that it is not useful to speak of Renaissance or renaissance in China or elsewhere (nor in Europe for other centuries). For him, *the* Renaissance is a particular epoch in European history in the fourteenth to sixteenth centuries that is characterized by, among others factors, its specific appreciation of Antiquity and the classical language that found its form in a critical dialogue across time. Barbara Mittler agreed that China did not have *this* Renaissance, but maintained that China did have *a* Renaissance in the early twentieth century, as Chinese intellectuals were trying to make sense of their present by taking inspiration from what they read into *the* Renaissance as a chronotypical model. They thus engendered the notion of a r/Renaissance that took place in the early twentieth century, was preceded by darkness, and led into Modernity; a r/Renaissance that was characterized by its special appreciation of the vernacular and its contempt for the classical language.

Throughout her chapters, Barbara Mittler has focused on the similarities which her Chinese protagonists saw between their own undertaking and its European inspiration – while creatively and constantly transforming it at the same time. Indeed, she argued that the particular significance that specific epochal movements acquire in different times and localities can be understood as the result of situated co-productions that transgress continental boundaries. Thomas Maissen, on the other hand, has insisted on the manifold differences and distinctions between the two cultural movements. His focus on distinctness is not to claim superiority, however, but may be taken as a reminder that epochal historical phenomena are always equally particular.

Barbara Mittler suggested further that this recognition of equality in distinction may allow us to think Renaissance-in-common, while Thomas Maissen questions this idea and its benefit to historiographical writing. Barbara Mittler would go so far as to say that if there was equality in distinction and if we should be able to juxtapose these antagonistic ideas on a common matrix – as in the critical dialogue practiced by the humanists, a dialogue always conducted among equals – this may eliminate superiorist and originalist claims and preclude the possibility of the now proverbial "theft of history."

In this dialogue, we have disagreed not only on whether or not China *had* a Renaissance, but also on fundamental matters in the writing of global history. The sinologist among us holds that it should be possible or even sensible to write a History-in-common, taking historical experiences from different parts of the world to reflect upon each other and thus, by enriching our ways of questioning, through observing variation in contrasting, comparative detail, to sharpen our definitions. According to Mittler, our understanding of *the* Renaissance and its emphases *not* on the vernacular, nor the emancipation of women, nor democratization and the rationale behind such thinking can be highlighted (and questioned) by seeing China's Renaissance develop precisely these elements from their understanding of *the* Renaissance, for example.

The historian, on the other hand, insists that a comparative approach is indispensable to historiography in order to better understand commonalities and differences. Yet according to Maissen, History-in-common will indeed have the opposite effect: it makes terminologies fuzzier and less distinct, inevitably leading to historical imprecision and ultimately to the making of generic, ideal, universal "types" – renaissances (or "renascences") – that both authors of this book would criticize if used as a scholar's analytical vocabularies or epistemological categories. Why? If "renaissance" is used this way, as an analytical category defined by the smallest common denominator (such as "rediscovery of the past"), it becomes very difficult to observe specific patterns of continuity or distinction, and instead it amounts to simply throwing everything in one and the same category.

Hence, we both agree with the spirited arguments presented by Yu Yingshi in his essay on the New Culture Movement as neither *the* Renaissance nor *the* Enlightenment (both in analytical terms and as copies of a chronotype). He proposes instead

> ...to discard analogy in the study of Chinese history altogether: If we can neither recognize general laws in history nor take the unique pattern of European historical experience as the

universal model for all non-Western societies, why must we bother even to raise the question whether there was a Renaissance or an Enlightenment in Chinese history in the first place? We would do well to see the May Fourth movement as it really was. It was, ... first and foremost a cultural movement in response to the stimulus of Western ideas. May Fourth intellectuals did consciously borrow ideas from the Renaissance and the Enlightenment. This is precisely why one can interpret May Fourth in terms of either with some justification. But May Fourth was neither *The* Chinese Renaissance nor *The* Chinese Enlightenment for the simple reason that a great variety of western ideas and values other than Renaissance and Enlightenment were also introduced into China during the same period. If we carry analogical thinking to its logical extreme, then we would have to crowd many centuries of European history into the brief space of one or two decades of twentieth-century China which, needless to say, amounts to monstrous absurdity.[1]

In presenting this book in the form of an open-ended dialogue, we deliberately close with a number of irreconcilable conclusions. Our hope, however, is that our fundamental differences in approaching one single term, Renaissance/renaissance as highlighted in this dialogic format, reveals how important this kind of intense interdisciplinary exchange may be, as it brings different fields of expertise and different sensibilities to the same table; and this matters. Such a dialogue does not have to lead to consensus automatically, but it sensitizes us to the cultural imprint of the hermeneutic tools we often use without reflection. Thus, we would hope that this kind of antagonistic dialogue, presenting, rather than hiding fundamental disagreement, may in fact open new avenues of thinking about Renaissance/renaissance in particular and periodization in global history in general.

---

1 Yu, "Neither Renaissance nor Enlightenment," 311.

Appendix

This appendix contains fuller excerpts from some of the more important sources only partially quoted above. These sources illustrate the particular ways in which their authors dealt with the past, presented their own time as a "Renaissance," and fashioned their particular position within this epochal moment.

Sources from the European Renaissance

Petrarca, Letters on Familiar Matters, 15, 3 (1353)[1]

To Zanobi, Florentine grammarian

I know that you are surprised and saying to yourself: "Where in the world is he battling now?" unless perchance that alter ego of mine in name and in fact, who is keeping watch over my nest in my native land as I wander far away, sent you from Florence to Naples my letter addressed to him, which dealt more or less with this subject. If he has done so, the present letter is useless. But since I fear he may be very busy, and know your desire to hear from me, I decided it was preferable to spend an hour writing an unnecessary letter than to withhold news about myself from a friend because of my greed for time. Where I am, what I am considering, what I am doing you have heard; and rumor had it that I was fleeing the storms of the Curia to return to Italy where the fates seemed to offer a quiet retreat. I was making my way along the road to Genoa with the sole purpose of seeing after five years my only brother, dearer to me for his virtue than for our common blood, who has chosen a solitary and wooded place named Montrieux near that road to become a servant of Christ and to mortify the flesh. At the western boundary of Italy near the river Var I learned that the road was blocked by a war caused by certain armed Alpine peoples who had poured down onto the shore. Moved by these reports and by friends' entreaties, I was about to change my plans and take another route. I was already mentally turning leftward in order to go to Mont Genèvre when an unexpected cloudburst poured down everywhere – and this was all the stranger because before and ever since that storm we have had a great drought in the heavens and on the land such as we have never seen and can hardly find recorded. I stopped anxiously. Rarely had I ever realized more clearly what Virgil meant by his fear for a dear burden. I had with me a precious bundle of books, and in with the old books was a small number of my own trifles with which I too cover sheets of Egyptian parchment, not because doing so is the best of occupations, but because for me doing anything else is difficult, and doing nothing at all is harmful, almost impossible, and against my nature. In that situation I feared not for my body, hardened enough for anything and long accustomed to bear not only rain but ice, heat and hail, and experienced in all labors or danger; I feared not for myself *and*

---

[1] Francesco Petrarca, *Letters on Familiar Matters*, ed. Aldo S. Bernardo (New York: Italica Press, 2005), vol. 2, 254–257.

for my burden as Aeneas did, but only for my burden as Metabus did; for I confess that my fear was for that little bundle so dear to me. What could I do? "Turning all things over in my mind," as he says, it seemed evident that God's will was somehow forbidding me to depart at that time; it would seem almost irreverent if I, on my own authority, resisted divine prohibition. Recalling the saying of Cleanthes, "the fates lead on the willing, but drag the unwilling," I willingly yielded in order not to yield unwillingly, and sent several of my servants to Italy, not so much to attend, with their presence, to certain urgent matters for me, as to afford me, with their departure, a more perfect solitude and a more tranquil idleness. They had scarcely departed and had proceeded just so far that there was no way to recall or overtake them, when the skies suddenly cleared. It has now been this way for several months, as it had been previously, and it seems likely it will continue thus, unless the heavenly ruler changes His mind or, since the will of the Lord remains in eternity, decides to reveal His will in a new way. Therefore, the more I think about it, the more it becomes evident that my strong desire attracting me to Italy has been checked by God with earthly and celestial obstacles in order to counteract human dangers; for what we desire is merely pleasing, whereas for God it is also known. What else could I think, given the war in regions where in the memory of our fathers there had never been one, and given the only cloudburst this year on the very day at the very hour of my departure? And so, checked in this fashion, I returned to the source of the Sorgue a few days after my departure. Before the swift moon had twice completed its immense course, one of the servants whom I had sent ahead, as you heard, returned. "What in the world," he said, "are you trying to do? While fleeing Charybdis, you turn your prow toward Scylla: you shudder at the problems in the Curia, as you should, but you do not know what a mass of troubles await you if you set foot in Italy. What a bevy of friends the rumor of your return has created for you; in how many ways you will have to divide your mind, which you hope to collect; in how many affairs it will have to become involved that are really not concerns of yours but of your friends; and how much time you will have to lose, of which you have so little and need so much; how many annoyances you will have to bear in order to satisfy the desire of others!" After this rather general statement, he carefully elaborated each point, presenting explanations that were brighter than the sun, and added much else which must remain unsaid. Why do I detain you any longer? He seemed to me to be speaking not as a servant, but as a philosopher and a divine being. And so, pondering and reconsidering much within myself, perceiving that where I had believed to find a port was a turbulent sea, and forced by the storm of affairs to redirect the ship of my mind, I tied the halyards, dropped anchor, tied fast the helm, and moored amidst these cliffs the ship of my life, wearied by storms, until a port appears, with no intention of returning to the Curia or of seeking Italy unless I hear otherwise.

If you were to ask what I am doing here, I would answer, "I am alive – to be sure." Do you expect me to complete the verse with: "I spend my life amidst all kinds of adversities?" God forbid! Indeed I am well and happy, and I reject everything that distresses most men. Here is how I live: I rise in the middle of the night, so outdoors at sunrise, but both in the fields and at home I study, think, read, and write; I keep sleep from my eyes as long as possible, softness from my body, pleasures from my mind, sluggishness from my actions. Every day I wander over the rocky mountains, through the dewy valleys and caverns; I often walk along both banks of the Sorgue without meeting anyone who disturbs me, without a companion or guide except my cares, which day by day grow less insistent and troublesome. Mindful of the past, I deliberate on things to come and consider them from every angle. Let Him decide how wisely I do this about whom it is written: "In Your light we shall see the light," without whom blind humanity peers in vain through the shadows. My every hope lies in His guidance, certainly with all my might I strive to make my spirit ready and willing, forgetting as did the Apostle the past as best I can and turning my attention to the future. One important consolation has been granted me in each place of exile, just as I seem to have succeeded in adapting myself to this place, I could do the same in any other as required, with the exception of Avignon which overhangs the windy and turbulent waters of the Rhone. I could no longer bear your not knowing all this, my dear friend, if it was indeed unknown to you until now, for fear of having your letters perchance wandering in search of me here and there over uncertain paths. As I said, I am at the source of the Sorgue; and since fortune has so decreed, I seek no other place, nor shall I do so, until she shifts her changeable edicts as is her wont. Meanwhile here I have established my Rome, my Athens, and my spiritual fatherland, here I gather all the friends I now have or did have, not only those who have proved themselves through intimate contact and who have lived with me, but also those who died many centuries ago, known to me only through their writings, wherein I marvel at their accomplishments and their spirits or at their customs and lives or at their eloquence and genius. I gather them from every land and every age in this narrow valley, conversing with them more willingly than with those who think they are alive because they see traces of their stale breath in the frosty air. I thus wander free and unconcerned, alone with such companions; I am where I wish to be. As much as possible, I remain alone with myself; often too I am with you and with that illustrious man whom, strange to say, I see at all hours although I have never met him. Whenever you are able to speak with him, I beg you to keep my name alive for him. Farewell.

At the source of the Sorgue, 22 February [1353].

Petrarca, Letters on Familiar Matters, 24, 2 (1345)[2]

To Pulice da Vicenza, poet, concerning the contents of and the occasion for the following letters addressed to Cicero, Seneca, and others.

While an overnight guest in a suburb of Vicenza, I found a new subject to write about. After my departure about noon from Padua, I happened to reach your city gates as the sun was setting; while I stood deliberating whether to stay there for the night or to push onward since I was in a hurry and there was still a good deal of daylight remaining, suddenly – for who can remain hidden from loving friends? – all my doubts were resolved by your arrival in the company of several eminent men, with whom the city abounds. You so ensnared my wavering spirit with your cheerful and interesting conversation that, even as I planned to proceed, I lingered, and no sooner had the day waned than night was upon us. On that day as on past occasions, I discovered that nothing so robs us of time without our perceiving it than conversations with friends; friends are the great thieves of time, although no time ought to be viewed as less stolen, less lost than that which, next to God, we spend with friends. Without recounting all that happened, you perhaps remember that someone made mention of Cicero, as so often happens among learned men, which at once put an end to our random conversation. To him alone we all turned, discussing nothing afterward except Cicero; we rallied around him, taking turns celebrating him in palinode or in panegyric, if you prefer. But since in human affairs nothing is perfect, and no man exists undeserving of criticism or even a modest critic, it happened that while I expressed almost unreserved admiration for Cicero, a man I loved and honored above all others, and amazement too at his golden eloquence and heavenly genius, I had no praise for his weak character and his inconstancy, which I had discovered from various bits of evidence. When I noticed the astonishment of all present at my novel opinion, and especially that old man whose name escapes me but whose face I remember well since he is a fellow townsman of yours and a venerable scholar, it seemed an opportune time for me to fetch from its box the manuscript containing my letters.

When it was brought in, it provoked even more discussion, for along with many letters to my contemporaries, a few are addressed to illustrious ancients

---

2 Francesco Petrarca, *Letters on Familiar Matters*, ed. Aldo S. Bernardo (New York: Italica Press, 2005), vol. 3, 314–316.

for the sake of variety and as a diversion from my labors; and thus, an unsuspecting reader would be amazed at finding such outstanding and honorable names mingled with those of contemporaries. Two are addressed to Cicero: one expresses reservations about his character, the other praises his genius. When you had read them to the attentive onlookers, a friendly argument ensued, in which some agreed with me that Cicero deserved the criticism. Only the old gentleman became more obstinate in his opposition; so taken was he with Cicero's fame and so filled with love for him that he preferred to applaud even his errors and to accept his vices together with his virtues rather than condemn anything in a man so worthy of praise. Thus, his only response to me or to others was to contrast the splendor of Cicero's name with everything being said, thereby substituting authority for reason. With hand outstretched, he repeatedly exclaimed, "Gently, please, gently with my Cicero!" When asked whether he thought that Cicero could have erred, he shut his eyes, and as if smitten by the words he would turn aside groaning. "Alas, are they denouncing my Cicero?" as though we were dealing not with a man but with a god. I then asked whether in his opinion Tullius was a god or a man; immediately he responded, "A god," but then realizing what he had said, he added, "really a god of eloquence." I said, "Quite so, for if he is a god, he could not have erred; still, I had not heard him called a god, but if Cicero called Plato his god, why should you not call Cicero yours except that our faith does not allow us to fashion gods arbitrarily?" He said, "I was joking: I know that Tullius was a man, but with divine genius." "This," I said, "is certainly better, for Quintilian called him a divine man in eloquence; but if he were a man, he surely could err, and in fact, did." As I said this, he shuddered and turned away as though the words were directed not at another's reputation, but at his own. Indeed, what could I say, being myself such an admirer of Cicero? I congratulated the old gentleman for his great devotion and ardor despite its Pythagorean flavor, I rejoiced in his reverence for such genius and in his awe that made any suspicion of human weakness in Cicero almost a sacrilege, and I marveled at finding a man who loved him more than I did since I had always loved him above all others. The old man held the same deep-seated opinion of Cicero that I recall having as a boy, and even at his age was incapable of entertaining the thought that if Cicero were a man, it followed that in some things, perhaps not in many, he must have erred. This I now believe in part and know in part, although up to the present no one else's eloquence has so delighted me; nor was Tullius himself, about whom we are speaking, unaware of this, having often and seriously deplored his own faults. Unless we admit his awareness of them, in our eagerness to praise him we deny him self-knowledge and modesty, which are significant reasons for his renown as a philosopher. That day following our lengthy discussion, given the late hour, we rose and departed without settling the question; but you made me promise, since time was then too short, to send you a copy of both letters so that, after considering the matter in depth, you could become either a mediator between the factions or possibly a defender of Cicero's steadfastness. I commend your spirit and forward the requested letters, fearing, strange as it may seem, to be the winner, and indeed wishing to be the loser so that you will realize that by winning you will be assuming a greater task than you think. For in a similar conflict, Anneus Seneca asks you to be his champion since the following letter in fact criticizes him. I have dealt lightly with these great geniuses, perhaps boldly, but lovingly, sorrowfully, and, I believe, truthfully, in fact somewhat more truthfully than I wanted to. Many things delighted me in their writings, a few troubled me; it was the latter few that prompted me to write with a vigor that I would perhaps not have had today, for although these letters are relegated to the last book because they are so unlike the others, I had hammered them out long before. The fact ist that I still mourn the fate of such men, but I grieve no less over their faults; and please note that it is not my purpose to condemn Seneca's private life or Cicero's attitude toward the Republic. Lest you confuse the two cases, I am now dealing with Cicero, whom I know to have been a most vigilant, worthy, and effective consul, always the most patriotic of citizen. And yet? I cannot praise his inconstancy in friendship and his serious and destructive quarrels upon slightest provocation, which availed neither himself nor anything else; his inability to understand his own position and the condition of the Republic, strange indeed for a man with his keen mind; and finally his childish mania for wrangling, all of which are so unseemly in a philosopher. And remember that neither you nor anyone else can pass fair judgment on these matters until you thoroughly and slowly read all of Cicero's correspondence, which suggested this controversy. Farewell.

13 may [1345], en route.

Petrarca, Letters on Familiar Matters, 24, 3 (1345)[3]

To Marcus Tullius Cicero

Francesco sends his greetings to his Cicero. After a lengthy and extensive search for your letters, I found them where I least expected, and I then read them with great eagerness. I listened to you speak on many subjects, complain about many things, waver in your opinions, O Marcus Tullius, and I who had

---

[3] Francesco Petrarca, *Letters on Familiar Matters*, ed. Aldo S. Bernardo (New York: Italica Press, 2005), vol. 3, 317–318.

known the kind of preceptor that you were for others now recognize the kind of guide that you were for yourself. Now it is your turn, wherever you may be, to hearken not to advice but to a lament inspired by true love from one of your descendants who dearly cherishes your name, a lament addressed to you not without tears. O wretched and distressed spirit, or to use your own words, O rash and ill-fated elder, why did you choose to become involved in so many quarrels and utterly useless feuds? Why did you forsake that peaceful ease so befitting a man of your years, your profession, and your fate? What false luster of glory led you, an old man, into wars with the young, and into a series of misfortunes that then brought you to a death unworthy of a philosopher? Alas, forgetful of your brother's advice and of your many wholesome precepts, like a wayfarer at night carrying a lantern before him, you revealed to your followers the path where you yourself stumbled most wretchedly. I make no mention of Dionysius, of your brother or of your nephew, and, if you like, even of Dolabella, all men whom you praise at one moment to the high heavens and at the next rail at with sudden wrath. Perhaps these may be excused. I bypass even Julius Caesar, whose oft-tested clemency proved a haven of refuge for those very men who had assailed him; I likewise refrain from mentioning Pompey the Great, with whom you seemed able to accomplish whatever you liked by right of friendship. But what madness provoked you against Mark Anthony? Love for the Republic, I suppose you would say, but you yourself confessed that it had already collapsed. But if it were pure loyalty, if it were love of liberty that impelled you, why such intimacy with Augustus? What would your answer be to your Brutus who says, "If you are so fond of Octavius, you seem not to have fled a tyrant, but rather to have sought a kindlier one." There still remained your last, lamentable error, O unhappy Cicero: that you should speak ill of the very man whom you had previously praised, not because he was doing you any harm, but merely because he failed to check your enemies. I grieve at your destiny, my dear friend, I am filled with shame and distress at your shortcomings; and so even as did Brutus, "I place no trust in those arts in which you were so proficient." For in truth, what good is there in teaching others, what benefit is there in speaking constantly with the most magnificent words about the virtues, if at the same time you do not give heed to your own words? Oh, how much better it would have been, especially for a philosopher, to have grown old peacefully in the country, meditating, as you write somewhere, on that everlasting life and not on this transitory existence; how much better for you never to have held such offices, never to have yearned for triumphs, never to have had any Catilines to inflate your ego. But these words indeed are all in vain. Farewell forever, my Cicero.

From the land of the living, on the right bank of the Adige, in the city of Verona in transpadane Italy, on 16 June in the year 1345 from the birth of that Lord whom your never knew.

Leonardo Bruni, Life of Petrarch (1436)[4]

Francesco Petrarca, a man of great genius and no less virtue, was born at Arezzo in the Borgo dell'Orto, shortly before sunrise on the twenty-first of July, 1304. The name of his father was Petracolo; his grandfather was named Parenzo; they were originally from Ancisa. Petracolo, the father, lived in Florence and was very active in the Republic: he was sent out as an ambassador of the city on many very serious occasions, often he was employed with other duties of great importance, and in the court he was for a time a scribe of the Riformagioni.[5] He was a worthy man, active and quite prudent.

In that disaster suffered by the Florentine citizenry, when there came the division between White and Black [Guelfs], this man was believed to sympathize with the White party and consequently was driven from Florence along with the others. Thus he was reduced to living in Arezzo where he stayed, vigorously aiding his party and his faction according to his hope of returning home. Then when his hopes lessened, he left Arezzo and went to the Roman court, which was newly transferred in those times to Avignon. In the court he was well employed with considerable honor and income. There he brought up two sons, one named Gherardo and the other Checco, who was then called Petrarca as we shall observe in this biography.

Petrarca, then, was raised at Avignon and as he began to grow up he showed a gravity of manner and high intellect. He was very attractive in appearance, and his handsomeness lasted throughout his life. After learning letters and finishing his first childhood studies, he gave himself over to the study of civil law, according to the orders of his father. In these studies he persevered several years, but he considered this material too low for his aptitude, for his nature was drawn to higher things and did not much esteem the law and litigation. Secretly he directed all his study to Cicero, to Virgil and Seneca, to Lactantius and to other philosophers, poets and historians. He was already set to write prose, ready for sonnets and edifying canzoni; gentle and gracious in all his speech, he despised the law

---

4 *The Italian Renaissance. The essential sources*, ed. Kenneth Gouwens (Malden: Blackwell Publishing, 2004), 43–48.
5 Part of the Florentine government.

and its tedious and gross explanatory glossing. He did not pursue the law, and even if the law had pursued him, he would not have accepted it, had his reverence for his father not held him to it.

After the death of his father he became his own master and dedicated himself openly and entirely to those studies of which he had earlier been a disciple in secret for fear of his father. Quickly his fame began to spread; he came to be called not Francesco Petracchi, but Francesco Petrarca, his name made greater out of respect for his virtues. He had such grace of intellect that he was the first to bring back into the light of understanding the sublime studies, so long fallen and ignored. Having grown since then, they have reached their present heights, of which I want to tell briefly. So that I may be better understood, I would like to turn to earlier times.

The Latin tongue and its perfections and greatness flourished most at the time of Cicero, for previously it was neither polished nor precise nor refined; but its perfection increased slowly until at the time of Cicero it reached its summit. After the age of Cicero it began to fall, and sank as in his time it had risen; not many years passed before it had suffered a very great decadence and diminution. It can be said that letters and the study of Latin went hand in hand with the state of the Roman Republic, since it increased until the age of Cicero, and then after the Roman people lost their liberty in the rule of the emperors, who did not even stop at killing and ruining highly regarded men, the good disposition of studies and letters perished together with the good state of the city of Rome. Octavian, who was the least fierce of the emperors, killed thousands of Roman citizens; Tiberius and Caligula and Claudius and Nero left not one who had the appearance of a man. Then followed Galba and Otho and Vitellius, who in a few months undid one another. After these there were no emperors of Roman blood, for the land was so devastated by the preceding emperors that no man of worth remained. Vespasian, who was emperor after Vitellius, was from Rieti and so too were Titus and Domitian his sons; the emperor Nerva was from Narni, his adopted son Trajan from Spain; Hadrian too was Spanish, Severus from Africa, Alexander from Asia, Probus from Hungary, Diocletian from Slavonia and Constantine from England. Why do I bother with this? Only to show that as the city of Rome was devastated by perverse tyrannical emperors, so Latin studies and letters suffered a similar destruction and diminution, so that at the last hardly anyone could be found who knew Latin with the least sense of style. And there came over into Italy the Goths and the Lombards, barbarous and foreign nations who in fact almost extinguished all understanding of letters, as appears in the documents drawn up and circulated in those times; for one could find no writing more prosaic or more gross and coarse.

When the Lombards, who had occupied Italy for 240 years, were chased out and the Italian people thus recovered their liberty, the Tuscan cities and others began to recuperate. They devoted work to studies and began to polish their coarse style somewhat. Thus little by little they regained their vigor, although they were weak and lacked real judgment for any fine style, since they paid attention mainly to vernacular rhyme. In this way until the time of Dante few knew the literate style and those few knew it rather poorly, as we said in the *Life of Dante*.

Francesco Petrarca was the first with a talent sufficient to recognize and call back to light the antique elegance of the lost and extinguished style. Admitted it was not perfect in him, yet it was he by himself who saw and opened the way to its perfection, for he rediscovered the works of Cicero, savored and understood them; he adapted himself as much as he could and as much as he knew how to that most elegant and perfect eloquence. Surely he did enough just in showing the way to those who followed it after him. Having given himself to these studies and thus showing his virtue, Petrarca was much honored and favored while still young, and was called by the Pope to be secretary of his court; but Petrarca never agreed, nor did he value money. Nevertheless, so that he could lead an honorable life with leisure, he accepted benefices and became a regular cleric; he did this not so much by his own choice as constrained to it by necessity, for little or nothing remained from his father, and in marrying off his sister almost all the paternal inheritance was spent, Gherardo his brother became a Carthusian monk and persevered in that order to the end of his life.

Petrarca's honors were so great that no man of his age was more highly thought of, not only beyond the mountains but also here in Italy; having gone to Rome, he was solemnly crowned poet. He wrote in one of his own epistles that he came to Rome for the Jubilee in 1350. Returning from Rome, he took his way to Arezzo in order to see the place where he was born; the citizens had heard of his arrival and came out to meet him, as if a king had come to visit. The fame and honor attributed to him by every city and province and by all the people throughout Italy were so great that it seemed an incredible miracle. Not only the citizens and the farmers, but also the noble and great princes and lords, sought and honored him and made extraordinary provisions for his welcome. For with Prince Galeazzo Visconti he resided some time, having been asked most graciously to deign to stay with him; similarly, he was honored by the lord of Padua; and his reputation and the respect offered him by those gentlemen was so great that there were often great disputes whether to send him along in his journey, or to send him to some place and favor him with more honors. Thus Petrarca lived honored and esteemed to the end of his life.

In his studies, Petrarca had one particular gift: he was very much suited to both prose and verse, and he wrote a good deal in each. His prose is graceful and elegant, his verse polished and finished and elevated in style. This gift for both the one and the other has been found in few if any but in him, for it seems that natural talent tends toward one or the other, and man usually gives himself over to that one which has the natural advantage. So it happens that Virgil, most excellent in verse, wrote or is worth nothing in prose; Cicero, grand master of prose, is worth nothing in verse. We see the same in other poets and orators, that one of the two styles has been their source of excelling praise, but I remember having read none of them in both. Petrarca alone has been excellent in the one and the other style, through his singular gift, and he composed many works in prose and in verse, which there is no reason to enumerate, for they are known.

Petrarca died in Arquà, a village in the province of Padua, where he had chosen to live in his old age, retiring to a quiet and leisurely life separated from all complications. While he lived he kept up a very close friendship with Giovanni Boccaccio, who at that time was famous for the same studies as Petrarca; so it came about that with the death of Petrarca, the Florentine Muses became the property of Boccaccio, as if by hereditary succession; and in him then resided the fame of the previously discarded studies. It was also a succession in time, since when Dante died Petrarca was seventeen years old, and when Petrarca died Boccaccio was nine Years younger than he. Thus go the Muses by succession.

Poggio Bracciolini, Letter to Guarinus Veronensis (1416)[6]

Although I know well that no matter how busy you are each day, your kindness to all and your affection for me in particular always make the arrival of my letters a pleasure to you, I ask you especially to pay most particular attention to this one; not that there is anything in me which would have any claim even on a person who was completely at leisure, but because of the interest of the subject of which I am about to tell you. I know it will bring the utmost pleasure to you, who have long been an expert, and to other learned men. For what, for Heaven's sake, is there that could be more delightful, more pleasant, and more agreeable to you and the rest of the learned world than the knowledge of those things whose acquaintance makes us more learned and, what seems even more important, sty-

---

6 *Two Renaissance Book Hunters: the letters of Poggius Bracciolini to Nicolaus de Niccolis*, ed. Phyllis Walter Goodhart Gordan (New York: Columbia University Press, 1974), 193–196.

listically more polished. When Mother Nature gave the human race mind and reason, two wonderful guides to a righteous and happy life, she could think of nothing finer to give. Then she gave us one thing that perhaps may be the greatest gift of all, the use and understanding of speech, without which mind and reason would not have been of any use to us. For it is speech alone which we use to express the power of our mind and which separates us from the other beings. And so we must be deeply grateful to the pioneers in the other liberal arts and especially to those who by their concern and efforts have given us rules for speaking and a pattern of perfection. They have made it possible for us to excel other men in the ability in which all men excel beasts.

You know that while there were many writers in the Latin tongue who were renowned for elaborating and forming the language, there was one outstanding and extraordinary man, M. Fabius Quintilian, who so cleverly, thoroughly, and attentively worked out everything which had to do with training even the very best orator that he seems in my judgment to be perfect in both the highest theory and the most distinguished practice of oratory. From this man alone we could learn the perfect method of public speaking, even if we did not have Cicero, the father of Roman oratory. But among us Italians, he so far has been so fragmentary, so cut down, by the action of time I think, that the shape and style of the man has become unrecognizable. So far you have seen the man only thus:

> "Whose face and limbs were one continued wound,
> Dishonest, with lopp'd arms, the youth appears,
> Spoil'd of his nose, and shorten'd of his ears."

Surely we ought to feel sorrow and anger that we have done so much damage to the practice of oratory by our careless destruction of a man so eloquent. But the more we regret and blame ourselves for the damage that was formerly done to him, the more we should congratulate ourselves that by our energetic search he has now been restored to us in his original appearance and grandeur, whole and in perfect condition. For if Marcus Tullius rejoiced so fervently when Marcus Marcellus was returned from exile, and that at a time when Rome had a great many able and outstanding men like Marcellus both at home and abroad, what should men do now in learned circles, and especially men who devote themselves to oratory, when the one and only light of the Roman name, except for whom there was no one but Cicero and he likewise cut to pieces and scattered, has through our efforts been called back not only from exile but from almost complete destruction? By Heaven, if we had not brought help, he would surely have perished the very next day. There is no question that this glorious man, so elegant, so pure, so full of morals and of wit, could not much longer have endured the filth of that prison, the squalor of the place, and the savage cruelty of his keepers. He was sad and dressed in mourning, as people are when doomed to death; his beard was dirty and his hair caked with mud, so that by his expression and appearance it was clear that he had been summoned to an undeserved punishment. He seemed to stretch out his hands and beg for the loyalty of the Roman people, to demand that he be saved from an unjust sentence, and to feel it a disgrace that he who had once preserved the safety of the whole population by his influence and his eloquence could now not find one single advocate who would pity his misfortunes and take some trouble over his welfare and prevent his being dragged off to an undeserved punishment. But how often things turn out spontaneously which you dare not hope, as Terence says.

For by good luck, as much ours as his, while we were doing nothing in Constance, an urge came upon us to see the place where he was being kept prisoner. This is the monastery of St. Gall, about twenty miles from Constance. And so several of us went there, to amuse ourselves and also to collect books of which we heard that they had a great many. There amid a tremendous quantity of books which it would take too long to describe, we found Quintilian still safe and sound, though filthy with mold and dust. For these books were not in the Library, as befitted their worth, but in a sort of foul and gloomy dungeon at the bottom of one of the towers, where not even men convicted of a capital offense would have been stuck away. As I know for certain, if there ever had been any other men who explored these prison houses of the barbarians where they confine such men as Quintilian and if they had recognized them after the custom of our ancestors, they would have found a treasure like ours in many cases where we are now left lamenting. Beside Quintilian we found the first three books and half of the fourth of C. Valerius Flaccus' *Argonauticon*, and commentaries or analyses on eight of Cicero's orations by Q. Asconius Pedianus, a very clever man whom Quintilian himself mentions. These I copied with my own hand and very quickly, so that I might send them to Leonardus Aretinus and to Nicolaus of Florence; and when they had heard from me of my discovery of this treasure they urged me at great length in their letters to send them Quintilian as soon as possible. You have, my dearest Guarinus, all that a man who is devoted to you can send you just now. I wish I could send you the book itself but I had to satisfy Leonardus; but you know where it is, so that if you want it and I expect that you will want it as soon as possible, you can get it easily. Farewell and love me as I do you.

At Constance, 15 December, A.D. 1416.

Matteo Palmieri, Civil Life, Book Two (ca. 1438)[7]

To summarize, we discussed briefly in the first book how to raise a child to become an outstanding citizen, and we guided this child through a liberal education to the ripeness of adulthood. The second book continues our discussion. In it, we shall offer advice on what steps a person must take in civil life to prepare for worthy deeds and virtuous actions. We shall also show how to live with prudence, moderation and fortitude – three of the main principles of civic integrity. ...

Let no one be fooled into thinking that, since he has heard Socrates, Diogenes or Democritus praised for their extraordinary severity, he can become a celebrity by aping them. In order to live as they did, one would need to combine their many excellences and to demonstrate their proven and constant integrity over many years. Otherwise, the incredible gravity which won glory and immortal fame for such great thinkers – men born as an example and lesson to others – will appear ridiculous and base in lesser men.

There is little need to caution you against actions which greatly disrupt and depart from accepted behaviour, for they are easily noticed. A person of sound mind avoids behaviour such as continual laughter or singing and dancing in public. People of little wit who close their ears to such advice deserve compassion. But we must guard most diligently against minor faults, first because they are more difficult to notice, and second because good people are blamed more for minor faults than the wicked for major sins. The old proverb says. 'The whiter and brighter the surface, the more we see the stain.' We often see dissolute persons engaging openly in their vices – hedonists, gamblers, adulterers and others full of bad habits. But having seen them, we soon forget and neglect them. Once we have judged them depraved in our minds, we pay them no heed, but merely regard them as plying their trade, no more and no less. Yet when a person of good reputation is seen at the gaming tables, the entire populace murmurs at what seems a serious lapse. We pay more attention to the good man and reproach him more for al small mistake than a bad person who always does wrong.

It is useful to observe carefully the actions of others, imitating what we deem good and avoiding what we recognize as blameworthy. Such observations can greatly benefit our behaviour, for although I am unable to explain it, experience (our teacher in all matters) makes clear that we are better at judging the mistakes

---

[7] Matteo Palmieri, "Civil Life," in *Cambridge Translations of Renaissance Philosophical Texts*, vol. 2: *Political Philosophy*, ed. Jill Kraye, trans. David Marsh (Cambridge: Cambridge University Press, 1997), 150, 165–167.

of others than our own. However excellent the person we choose to imitate, we shall always find some objectionable trait and shall often feel superior in some respect to our model. We must not adhere so closely to one model, even one of excellent learning and morals, that we cannot strive to adopt what is best in someone else who surpasses our model.

We should imitate the example of the great painter Zeuxis, who was hired for a large sum at Croton, the most prosperous Italian city of his day. For their famous and noble temple, he wanted to paint a likeness of Helen of Troy, the most celebrated beauty on earth. Observing that the women of Croton were more beautiful than all the others in Italy, Zeuxis asked to view the form and delicate features of the fairest virgins of the town while he was painting. The townspeople agreed to let him see naked all the virgins of Croton. Zeuxis chose five of them, whose fame still lives on, for they were the best of the beauties chosen by an expert in beauty. Since he could not find in one body the completely perfect elegance of nature, he took from each the feature which was most excellent. And from all of them, he created in image so completely perfect in every detail that the greatest painters of the entire world came to see the painting as a marvel and declared it more an object sent from heaven than one created on earth.

In like manner, by imitating the moderation, order and laudable habits of praiseworthy living, we shall adopt from each virtuous person that quality in which he excels. Imitating many people, each the best in respect to one quality, we shall strive to become as perfect as we can in every virtue. If we are in doubt, we shall avoid mistakes by consulting older people, whose long years make them experts in the art of living. Whenever several people reproach our behaviour, we must correct and improve it, as is expected of wise persons. We should not imitate anything, no matter how good itself, so obstinately that we cannot abandon it for something better. In this, let us imitate good painters, who submit their works to the people for judgement and correct whatever the majority criticizes, sometimes giving general opinion preference over their art and acting in accordance with the majority. Above all, we should listen to our elders by imitating, revering and honouring them, by obeying magistrates in public office and by conversing amicably with civic officials in concord and peaceful harmony. It is not our task to counsel in matters prescribed by civic ordinances and statutes, for they constitute the laws by which we must live.

Niccolò Machiavelli to Francesco Vettori (1513)[8]

To the Magnificent Francesco Vettori, His Patron and Benefactor, Florentine Ambassador to the Supreme Pontiff in Rome.

Magnificent Ambassador. "Divine favors were never late." I say this because it seemed to me that I had lost – no, rather, strayed from – your favor; it has been a long time since you wrote me, and I was unclear about what the reason might be. And I paid little attention to all those reasons that came to mind except for one: I was afraid that you might have ceased writing to me because someone had written you that I was not a good steward of your letters, I knew that, except for Filippo and Paolo, no one else had seen them through my doing. I am reassured by your recent letter of the 23rd of last month, from which I am extremely pleased to see how methodically and calmly you fulfill your public duties. I exhort you to continue in this manner, because whoever forgoes his own interests for those of others sacrifices his own and gets no gratitude from them. And since Fortune is eager to shape everything, she wants people to let her do so, to be still, not to trouble her, and to await the moment when she will let men do something. That will be the moment for you to persevere more unfailingly, to be more alert about matters, and for me to leave my farm and announce, "Here I am." Since I want to repay you in the same coin, therefore, I can tell you nothing else in this letter except what my life is like. If you decide you would like to swap it for yours, I shall be happy to make the exchange.

I am living on my farm, and since my latest disasters, I have not spent a total of twenty days in Florence. Until now, I have been catching thrushes with my own hands. I would get up before daybreak, prepare the birdlime, and go out with such a bundle of birdcages on my back that I looked like Geta when he came back from the harbor with Amphitryon's books. I would catch at least two, at most six, thrushes. And thus I passed the entire month of November. Eventually this diversion, albeit contemptible and foreign to me, petered out – to my regret. I shall tell you about my life. I get up in the morning with the sun and go into one of my woods that I am having cut down; there I spend a couple of hours inspecting the work of the previous day and kill some time with the woodsmen who always have some dispute on their hands either among themselves or with their neighbors. I could tell you a thousand good stories about these woods and my experiences with them, and about Frosino da Panzano and other men who wanted some of this firewood. In particular, Frosino

---

[8] James B. Atkinson and David Sices, eds., *Machiavelli and his Friends. Their Personal Correspondence* (DeKalb: Northern Illinois University Press, 1996), 262–265.

sent for some loads of wood without saying a word to me; when it came time to settle, he wanted to withhold ten lire that he said he had won off me four years ago when he had beaten me at cricca at Antonio Guicciardini's house. I started to raise hell; I was going to call the wagoner who had come for the wood a thief, but Giovanni Machiavelli eventually stepped in and got us to agree. Once the north wind started blowing, Battista Guicciardini, Filippo Ginori, Tomaso del Bene, and some other citizens all ordered a load from me. I promised some to each one; I sent Tommaso a load, which turned into half a load in Florence because he, his wife, his children, and the servants were all there to stack it – they looked like Gaburra on Thursdays when he and his crew flay an ox. Consequently, once I realized who was profiting, I told the others that I had no more wood; all of them were angry about it, especially Battista, who includes this among the other calamities of Prato.

Upon leaving the woods, I go to a spring; from there, to one of the places where I hang my birdnets. I have a book under my arm: Dante, Petrarch, or one of the minor poets like Tibullus, Ovid, or some such. I read about their amorous passions and their loves, remember my own, and these reflections make me happy for a while. Then I make my way along the road toward the inn, I chat with passersby, I ask news of their regions, I learn about various matters, I observe mankind: the variety of its tastes, the diversity of its fancies. By then it is time to eat; with my household I eat what food this poor farm and my minuscule patrimony yield. When I have finished eating, I return to the inn, where there usually are the innkeeper, a butcher, a miller, and a couple of kilnworkers. I slum around with them for the rest of the day playing *cricca* and backgammon: these games lead to thousands of squabbles and endless abuses and vituperations. More often than not we are wrangling over a penny; be that as it may, people can hear us yelling even in San Casciano. Thus, having been cooped up among these lice, I get the mold out of my brain and let out the malice of my fate, content to be ridden over roughshod in this fashion if only to discover whether or not my fate is ashamed of treating me so.

When evening comes, I return home and enter my study; on the threshold I take off my workday clothes, covered with mud and dirt, and put on the garments of court and palace. Fitted out appropriately, I step inside the venerable courts of the ancients, where, solicitously received by them, I nourish myself on that food that alone is mine and for which I was born; where I am unashamed to converse with them and to question them about the motives for their actions, and they, out of their human kindness, answer me. And for four hours at a time I feel no boredom, I forget all my troubles, I do not dread poverty, and I am not terrified by death. I absorb myself into them completely. And because Dante says that no one understands anything unless he retains what he has understood, I have jotted down what I have profited from in their conversation and composed a short study, *De principatibus*, in which I delve as deeply as I can into the ideas concerning this topic, discussing the definition of a princedom, the categories of princedoms, how they are acquired, how they are retained, and why they are lost. And if ever any whimsy of mine has given you pleasure, this one should not displease you. It ought to be welcomed by a prince, and especially by a new prince; therefore I am dedicating it to His Magnificence Giuliano. Filippo da Casavecchia has seen it. He will be able to give you some account of both the work itself and the discussions I have had with him about it, although I am continually fattening and currying it.

Magnificent Ambassador, you would like me to abandon this life and come and enjoy yours with you. I shall do so in any case, but I am kept here by certain commitments that I shall attend to within six weeks. What makes me hesitate is that those Soderinis are in Rome; were I to come there, I would be obliged to visit and to talk with them. I am afraid upon my return that I might not count on dismounting at home but rather that I should dismount at the Bargello. For although this regime has extremely strong foundiations and great security, it is still new and, consequently, suspicious. There are plenty of rogues like Paolo Bertini who, in order to be impressive, would order a meal for others and leave the tab for me to pick up. I beg you to make this fear evaporate, and then, come what may, I shall come and see you in any case at the time mentioned.

I have discussed this little study of mine with Filippo and whether or not it would be a good idea to present it [to Giuliano], and if it were a good idea, whether I should take it myself or should send it to you. Against presenting it would be my suspicion that he might not even read it and that that person Ardinghelli might take the credit for this most recent of my endeavors. In favor of presenting it would be the necessity that hounds me, because I am wasting away and cannot continue on like this much longer without becoming contemptible because of my poverty. Besides, there is my desire that these Medici princes should begin to engage my services, even if they should start out by having me roll along a stone. For then, if I could not win them over, I should have only myself to blame. And through this study of mine, were it to be read, it would be evident that during the fifteen years I have been studying the art of the state I have neither slept nor fooled around, and anybody ought to be happy to utilize someone who has had so much experience at the expense of others. There should be no doubt about my word; for, since I have always kept it, I should not start learning how to break it now. Whoever has been honest and faithful for forty-three years, as I have, is unable to change his nature; my poverty is a witness to my loyalty and honesty.

So I should like you, too, to write me what your opinion is about all this. I commend myself to you. Be happy.

10 December 1513, Niccolò Machiavelli, in Florence

Niccolò Machiavelli, Discourses on Livy, Preface of the First Book (ca. 1517)[9]

Although the envious nature of men has always made it no less dangerous to find new modes and orders than to seek unknown waters and lands, because men are more ready to blame than to praise the actions of others, nonetheless, driven by that natural desire that has always been in me to work, without any respect, for those things I believe will bring common benefit to everyone, I have decided to take a path as yet untrodden by anyone, and if it brings me trouble and difficulty, it could also bring me reward through those who consider humanely the end of these labors of mine. If poor talent, little experience of present things, and weak knowledge of ancient things make this attempt of mine defective and not of much utility, it will at least show the path to someone who with more virtue, more discourse and judgment, will be able to fulfill this intention of mine, which, if it will not bring me praise, ought not to incur blame. Considering thus how much honor is awarded to antiquity, and how many times—letting pass finite other examples—a fragment of an ancient statue has been bought at a high price because someone wants to have it near oneself, to honor his house with it, and to be able to have it imitated by those who delight in that art, and how the latter then strive with all industry to represent it in all their works; and seeing, on the other hand, that the most virtuous works the histories show us, which have been done by ancient kingdoms and republics, by kings, captains, citizens, legislators, and others who have labored for their fatherland, are rather admired than imitated—indeed they are so much shunned by everyone: in every least thing that no sign of that ancient virtue remains with us—I can do no other than marvel and grieve. And so much the more when I see that in the differences that arise between citizens in civil affairs or in the sicknesses that men incur, they always have recourse to those judgments or those remedies that were judged or ordered by the ancients. For the civil laws are nothing other than verdicts given by ancient jurists, which, reduced to order, teach our present jurists to judge. Nor is medicine other than the experiments performed by ancient physicians, on which present physicians found their judgments. Nonetheless, in order-

---

9 Niccolò Machiavelli, *Discourses on Livy*, trans. Harvey C. Mansfield and Nathan Tarcov (Chicago: Chicago University Press, 1995), 5–6.

ing republics, maintaining states, governing kingdoms, ordering the military and administering war, judging subjects, and increasing empire, neither prince nor republic may be found that has recourse to the examples of the ancients. This arises, I believe, not so much from the weakness into which the present religion has led the world, or from the evil that an ambitious idleness has done to many Christian provinces and cities, as from not having a true knowledge of histories, through not getting from reading them that sense nor tasting that flavor that they have in themselves. From this it arises that the infinite number who read them take pleasure in hearing of the variety of accidents contained in them without thinking of imitating them, judging that imitation is not only difficult but impossible—as if heaven, sun, elements, men had varied in motion, order, and power from what they were in antiquity. Wishing, therefore, to turn men from this error, I have judged it necessary to write on all those books of Titus Livy that have not been intercepted by the malignity of the time whatever I shall judge necessary for their greater understanding, according to knowledge of ancient and modern things, so that those who read these statements of mine can more easily draw from them that utility for which one should seek knowledge of histories. Although this enterprise may be difficult, nonetheless, aided by those who have encouraged me to accept this burden, I believe I can carry it far enough so that a short road will remain for another to bring it to the destined place.

Erasmus to Johann van Vlatten (1523)[10]

Erasmus of Rotterdam to the Honourable Johann von Vlatten, Provost of Cranenburg and Scholaster of Cologne, Greeting.

When Johann Froben, honoured sir, was preparing to print Cicero's *Tusculan Questions*, and had asked me to put something of my own work into it as best I could, so that the book when it appeared might have some useful novelty to recommend it, I set about the task all the more readily since for some years I had had either no contact with the more humane among the Muses or very little. I therefore entrusted the business of comparing copies of the text to members of my household, and took upon myself the duties of a critic; and having read through the whole work with some attention, I marked off in lines the verse which he collects from Greek and Latin poets, with some precedent, it is true, from Plato and Aristotle, but till one almost tires of them. Where the copies dif-

---

[10] *The Correspondence of Erasmus*, vol. 10: *Letters 1356 to 1534, 1523 to 1524*, R.A.B. Mynors and James M. Estes, eds. (Toronto: University of Toronto Press, 1992), 96–101 (no. 1390).

fered, I either adopted what I thought best or, if it seemed a difficult decision, maintained both readings, one in the text and the other in the margin. Some places I have restored without the help of manuscripts, but not very many, and only where there would be no problem for a good scholar with some experience; and I have also added a few notes. While so engaged, I was obliged to suffer the loss of two or three days in the other studies by which I do what I can to advance the gospel cause.

And so far am I from regretting this expenditure of time that it is my ambition, if it is permitted me, to make my way back to those old friends of mine and spend some months in their intimate society. So great is the profit I felt I derived from rereading these books, not only in rubbing the rust off my prose style (though that too is far from negligible, in my view at least), but much more in learning to moderate and control my passions. How often, as I read, I felt a gush of contempt for those blockheads who are always repeating that there is nothing notable in Cicero except the splendour of his language! What a choice of reading he gives us there from the books left behind them by the best Greek writers on the subject of the good and happy life! What power and plenty in the way of sound and truly moral precepts! What a range of knowledge and what a memory for ancient and modern history at the same time! And again, what profound reflections on the true felicity of man, which clearly show that he practised what he preached! And in expounding subjects far removed from the sentiments and language of the ordinary man, where many men used to despair of the possibility of treating them in Latin, the clarity, the openness of mind, the easy movement, the ready flow of words, and last but not least the lightness of touch!

Philosophy at first was absorbed in the contemplation of the natural world and had little contact with life; it was Socrates, we read, who first brought her down to earth and even into the homes of men. Plato and Aristotle tried to introduce her to the courts of kings, to the legislature, and even to the law-courts. But Cicero seems to me to have brought her almost onto the stage, for with his help she has learned to speak in such a fashion that even a miscellaneous audience can applaud. And in this field that great man wrote so many books in a time of great crisis when his country was in the utmost confusion and some of them he wrote when public affairs were in the most desperate state. Surely we ought to be ashamed of our casual conversations and our dinner-table talk, when we see how pagans devoted to such high moral considerations even such leisure as they were allowed by the downfall of their country, not seeking an anodyne for the mind in brainless pleasures but trying to find a remedy in the most exalted precepts of philosophy.

What others experience, I do not know; but for myself, as I read Cicero, especially when he treats of the good life, he affects me in such a way as to leave me no doubts that something divine dwelt in the bosom whence all this proceeded. And this my judgment seems to me the more likely to be right, when I consider how immeasurable, how far beyond conjecture is the goodness of the eternal God, which some men, judging it I suppose by their own natures, try to constrict within such narrow limits. The present dwelling-place of Cicero's soul is not perhaps a subject for human judgment to pronounce on. I at least shall not be found actively in opposition, as they count the votes, by those who hope that he lives peacefully among the heavenly beings. No one can doubt that he believed in the existence of some supreme power, the greatest and the best thing that can be. And as for his opinions on the immortality of the soul, on the different lots and different rewards in a future life and the great confidence inspired by a clear conscience – if these are not clear enough from all the books he wrote, that one letter at least quite proves the point, which he wrote to Octavius, apparently when his death had already been decided on.

If the Jews before the appearance of the gospel found a kind of rough and confused credulity about divine subjects sufficient for salvation, why should not an even more rudimentary knowledge suffice for the salvation of a pagan ignorant even of the Mosaic law, especially one whose life was of a high standard, and not merely high but holy? Very few Jews before the light of the gospel dawned upon them had any exact knowledge of the Son and the Holy Spirit; many did not believe in the resurrection of the body; yet that was not in the eyes of the older generation a reason for despairing of their salvation. What if a pagan's creed went no further than this, that God, whom he is convinced is almighty, perfectly wise, and perfectly good, will reward the good and punish the bad on some system which seems to him the most appropriate? If someone were to make an objection of the blemishes in his life, I for my part do not suppose that either Job ore Melchizedek was entirely devoid of all faults all his life long. But it is inexcusable that he should have sacrificed to idols. So he did, maybe; only it was not from conviction but in accordance with public custom, and since that was established by law, there was no stopping it. That the stories about the gods were inventions he could learn from, among other places, the *Sacred History* of Ennius. But, they say, he should have convinced the public of its folly by the sacrifice of his life if need be. Such stamina was not to be found among the apostles themselves, before they received the Spirit from heaven, so that it would be grossly unfair to demand it of Cicero.

But on this topic let each man be free to use his own judgment. I come back to those blockheads who think that beyond the empty music of the words there is nothing important in the works of Cicero. How can he possibly expound so many recondite subjects so clearly, so fully, and with so much feeling, unless he really understands what he is writing? Who ever took up one of his books without having more peace of mind when he rose from the reading of it? Who went to him in a time of mourning and was not more cheerful when he came away? What you read seems to be happening, and your mind feels the breath of a kind of enthusiasm in the style, exactly as though you had heard it coming from the heart and the eloquent lips of the living man. This is why I often think that among all the discoveries that enterprise has made for the profit of mortal life, nothing is more profitable than the use of writing, and no art more valuable than the craft of printers. What blessing can be greater than to converse at will with the most eloquent and the most saintly of men, and to have as clear a view of their gifts and character and thoughts and ambitions and actions as if you had lived in their company for many years?

Never have I more wholly approved of Quintilian's remark that a man may know he has made progress when he begins to take great pleasure in Cicero. When I was a boy Cicero attracted me less than Seneca, and I was already twenty before I could bear to read him at any length, although I liked almost all other writers. Whether I have progressed with advancing years, I do not know; at any rate, I never enjoyed Cicero more, in the days when I had a passion for these studies, than I do now in my old age, not only for his almost divine felicity of style but for the combination of learning and high moral tone. I find in him a direct inspiration, and he gives me back to myself a better man. And so I should have no hesitation in urging the young to spend long hours in reading him and even in learning him by heart, rather than on the captious and quarrelsome books which abound everywhere nowadays. As for myself, although now getting on in years, I shall find it neither embarrassing nor tedious, as soon as I can extricate myself from the work I have in hand, to resume close relations with my old friend Cicero, and to renew for a few months that original intimacy which has now been too long interrupted.

And I decided to dedicate this work, such as it is, to you, dear Vlatten, man of many and great gifts, partly to make clear by this piece of evidence that I have not yet forgotten that delightful association through which, when I was in Freiburg, I first learned to know really well your exceptional kindness and rare subtlety of character, and partly to provide you with a correct text of these books of Cicero, which you might order to be studied by the intelligent young; for you used to say that concern for the school was your special province. In any case, that there should be a chorus of frogs in your part of the world ready to croak against the humanities should surprise no one, for there is no shortage anywhere of such creatures to interrupt with their song from the old comedy *brekekekex koax koax*; but you must boldly pay them no attention, and follow what is most in the interests of the young. To this end it will be a great help to have in charge of the school a man of good character no less than good education, whose salary can be increased if he deserves it. Once he has laid the first foundations of both Greek and Latin, he should read all the best authors with the boys; and this means Cicero, and the others in proportion as they approach him. Among the poets he must choose those who are respectable; and in any case those who are worth reading for the amount they can tell us but are objectionable for their obscenity, of whom Martial is one, must in my view be presented in excerpts which can safely be read with the boys.

But of these things I may perhaps say more on another occasion; though no one will give you better advice than Leonardus Priccardus, a man of various learning and high character, whose great experience makes his advice of great value. I should be very sorry to see Konrad Heresbach taken from us – for my life upon it, I never yet saw a more rounded character than that young man, whether you consider his knowledge of Latin and Greek or his fertile intelligence or the courtesy of manners which is a match for his integrity – did I not know what miserly characters he has left behind him, and what sort of a prince he has for a master. Farewell.

From Basel, [October] 1523

Sources from the Chinese Renaissance

1 Edith Sichel, The Renaissance (1914)[11]

This text illustrates very cleary why the description of the Renaissance in Burckhardtian tradition, proffered by Edith Sichel, was so attractive to the protagonists of the New Culture Movement *in China: Its emphasis on emancipation and expression, on the reawakening of a new culture, built on heretic writings and the vernacular and spread by great men and forerunners (such as Dante, here described as,* "an individual cut after no pattern") *to the people at large, and finally, the migration of the Renaissance, out from Italy to other parts of Europe (and by extension, the world), spoke very much to the concerns and the self-fashioning of Chinese intellectuals in the early twentieth century, who were convinced that they could taste their own Renaissance. For did not Rabelais tell of "how, when the seekers after the Temple of Bacbuc at last reached the shrine and entered, the wine that the priestess gave them, though it came from the same fountain, tasted different in the mouth of every man.*[12] *So it was with the subtle wine of the Renaissance."*

[7] MICHAELANGELO'S great painting of the newly created Adam on the ceiling of the Sistine Chapel might be taken as a symbol of the Renaissance, of the time when man was, as it were, re-created more glorious than before, with a body naked and unashamed, and a strong arm, unimpaired by fasting, outstretched towards life and light.

Definitions are generally misleading, and it is easier to represent the Renaissance by a symbol than to define it. It was a movement, a revival of man's powers, a reawakening of the consciousness of himself and of the universe – a movement which spread over Western Europe, and may be said to have lasted over two centuries. It was between 1400 and 1600 that it held full sway. [8] Like other movements it had forerunners, but, unlike other movements, it was circumscribed by no particular aim, and the fertilizing wave which passed over Italy, Germany, France, England and, in a much fainter degree, over Spain, to leave a fresh world behind it, seems more like a phenomenon of nature than

---

11 Edith Sichel, *The Renaissance* (New York, London: Henry Holt and Company, 1914). Page numbers given within the text in square brackets are references to the page numbers in this edition.
12 This scene must have resonated in particular with Chinese readers who would immediately have the *Three Vinegar Tasters* in mind (discussed above in Mittler's conclusion on p. 155) who would also come up with each a different interpretation of taste for their wine.

a current of history – rather an atmosphere surrounding men than a distinct course before them. The new birth was the result of a universal impulse, and that impulse was preceded by something like a revelation, a revelation of intellect and of the possibilities in man. And like the Christian revelation in the spiritual world, so the Renaissance in the natural, meant a temper of mind, a fresh vision, a source of thoughts and works, rather than shaped results. When it crystallized into an aesthetic ritual, it fell into decadence and corruption.

But before that happened, its real task had been accomplished – a complex task, in which certain elements stand out. Two main things there were which the Renaissance of Western Europe signified: it signified Emancipation and Expression. The Renaissance is a loose term which has served to cover [9] many issues – the Revival of Learning, the regeneration of art, the revolt against the Schoolmen, the expansion of men's thought with the expansion of the world beyond the seas. And it has been ascribed to many external causes greater and less. The death of feudalism had given free play to the individual and had weakened authority. The famous taking of Constantinople by the Turks in 1453, which put an end to the Greek Empire, had sent Greek scholars wandering over he world and shipped west into Italy a glorious cargo of looted manuscripts and sculptures. The discovery of printing, with the consequent circulation of books and of thought, produced a change that was immeasurable; while the discovery of America and the obvious effect that it produced upon trade profoundly modified the laws of wealth and the possibilities of transit. But all these outward events were only visible signs of a great motive power that grew from within; of the reassertion of Nature, and of her rights, against asceticism; of the disinterested desire for knowledge for its own sake – not the Schoolman's desire for logical results, or that of the alchemist who regarded science as a [10] means to find the philosopher's stone, but for something far wider. Rabelais' giant baby, Prince Gargantua, born in the open air, in the midst of a festival, waking to life parched with thirst and calling loudly for drink, must have been a conscious symbol of the child of the Renaissance, who came forth into the world unswaddled, and a thirst, to drink deep and grow strong enough for the overturning of false barriers, and the reinstatement of those senses which religion had taught him to condemn. Beauty was manifested to man afresh – beauty and joy which he had learnt to regard as the deadly foes of Christianity. And, inspired by new-found marbles and manuscripts, in a kind of intoxication, he once more embraced Paganism and Nature, and acknowledged man's body to be the exponent, not the adversary, of his soul.

Here there comes in the second great element of the Renaissance – Expression. Expression implies a consciousness of that which is expressed. In the Middle Ages expression in words or stone or painting was naif, a matter of narrative and of symbols prescribed mostly by tradition. If personal [11] force pierced through, it was accidental – when men of exceptional gifts happened to be employed. But as people became more conscious of themselves and the world, and began to want to define their relations towards it, and when they finally reawakened to a sense of beauty, emotion was kindled and expression sought and found. There arose, first in Italy, then in other lands, a perfect passion for language. The fuel was ready, the re-discovery of the classics set it alight. The unearthing of manuscripts in remote and forgotten monasteries, the publication of the works of Virgil and Seneca, Plato and Aristotle, with a score of other ancient authors, acted upon men's imaginations. Scholarship in those days was no set science; it involved risk, it unfolded unknown vistas. Like all else, like science itself, it was bathed in an atmosphere of poetry. Men approached new-found manuscripts with excitement and reverence.

When Poggio Bracciolini (1380 – 1459) discovered an ungarbled text of Quintilian's *Institutions*, there was an almost religious exaltation; while the great Lorenzo Valla (1406 – 1457) urged the claims of Latin with [12] the zeal of a propagandist. Scholars and students unknown to one another corresponded all the world over, formed friendships, compared texts, communicated fresh niceties of erudition. The Scaligers in Verona, the Estiennes in France, the pre-eminent Erasmus of the Netherlands, the rest of that wonderful band of men who tried to apply learning to life and went by the name of Humanists, revealed and increased a hundredfold the powers and possibilities of language. And in doing so they performed a work more important for the nations than scholarship. They increased vocabulary, and with it the national mind. Few words mean few ideas, and vocabulary is a fairly safe index of a country's intellectual outlook. Literature is, foremost, a sweetening and civilizing influence. But, unconsciously, it has a further power, not deeper, but more far-reaching – the faculty to propagate words and widen the horizon. This is what happened in the early Renaissance; presently scholarship ceased to be emotional, it became prosaic, and then it grew formal. Words fresh from the mint were over-used and, turning against themselves, finally hardened [13] into shibboleths or eupheuisms. Humanists gave place to pedants. But the words introduced by scholars quickly filtered into common speech; the vulgar tongue was enriched; and the spirit of research went outside the classics, revising old folk-songs, forming schools of popular poets. The *Stornelli* and *Rispetti* (songs of the country-side, many of which are still existent), the *Ballate* (dance-songs), the sacred songs, or *Laude*, and such-like traditional verse, served as a ready means for the ripening of the Italian mother-tongue and the rehabilitation of homely themes. And in France Fables, and Romances of chivalry did much in the same fashion to keep the French language alive. The exclusive employment of Latin in the world of letters had been the link between the Middle Ages and the Renaissance. The growth of national speech and its gradual encroachment upon Latin as a literary medium was the link with modern times. [...] Literature became what it was meant to be, the property of the people.

[14] Language, however, is but one part of expression, and art was, perhaps, the most potent and enduring means of self-revelation chosen by the Renaissance. In painting, in sculpture, in chiselled gems and goldsmiths' work, that wonderful period flowered and seeded, as fertile as if it were a second Nature with its own laws and seasons, until expression degenerated into over-expression and art grew decadent and died of surfeit. This emancipation, this power of expression, were manifest in every direction. Men's minds were in love – there was not a dry place throughout the realm of knowledge. If the investigation of language was poetic, the study of grammar was a high adventure and the science of the Law became romantic. [...] [15] [...] on the physical side, the discovery of the Western world – the voyages of Columbus (1492) and Sebastian Cabot (1497, 1499, 1526), of Vasco da Gama to India by the Cape of Good Hope (1497–1498), and of Vespucci over the Atlantic (1499), with the later expeditions of Drake and Hawkins – enlarged men's horizons, widened their national sympathies, enriched their purses. Physical science, which can hardly exist till thought has advanced far enough to provide it with a starting-point, was the last branch of knowledge to develop. It was not the least. The upheaval produced by Copernicus when (1507) he proclaimed that the earth was not the centre of the universe, but only one of many planets revolving round the sun, was perhaps the greatest blow that intellect dealt to orthodoxy – an assault followed up by Galileo (1564–1642) and his famous *Pur si muove*. [...] [16] [...] All these men, setting out in small vessels on the high seas of knowledge, were as much explorers as any Drake or Hawkins who sailed, big with hope, for El Dorado. But the Renaissance could never have been the true Renaissance, the spread of knowledge among the many, had not this intellectual enthusiasm arisen at the same time as a means of diffusing it. It almost seems indeed, as if the enthusiasm itself produced the invention of printing, as a strong current forces a passage. In a day when the dissemination of literature depended on copyists of manuscripts, even though there were hundreds of them, ideas were bound to remain in the possession of the few. The printing press of Gutenberg – the inventor of the art – in partnership with Fust or Faustus, set up in Mayence (1450); that of William Caxton in London (1474); the great Aldine Press in Venice (1494), which first published books under folio size – in itself an inestimable service – and the House of Plantin in Antwerp [17] (1549), began a new era for the world. Whoever has been over the House of Plantin, with its simple Renaissance front, its spacious rooms – a perfect hostelry for learning – its garnered memories of furred and

blackrobed scholars and printing-presses ever at work, and gold-tooled brown leather folios, has gained some notion of the patient knowledge, the fine taste and criticism which went to make the printers of those days; and whoever has seen or read descriptions of the Aldine editions of the Greek classics will realize that Aldus Manutius was a genius. They will understand how great was his contribution to knowledge at a time when he had often no more than a single manuscript, badly defaced, from which to reconstruct his version; when, in any case, a choice of readings of these garbled documents meant an act of daring when the very fact of publication meant a lifelong devotion. The printing of books in those days was in itself expression, perfect in each part, from the text and paper to the binding – a noble art which ranked with the highest. And it was the same when, as speedily happened, books grew cheaper and more numerous when the [18] Aldine press sold them at what amounted to a shilling or half-crown in our currency. Printing remained the source of irrigation which fertilized the world of intelligence.

It is always an interesting question whether men produce movements or movements men. The answers may be equally true. Every great movement is heralded by forerunners, each following each, each often influenced by each, till the single figures mass into groups first, later into throngs, and what was exceptional is universal. Men make movements, and then it would seem that the movement, once created, makes the men. For with the general need there spring up the people to fulfil it, one, magnet-like, drawing others.

The Renaissance had many forerunners, growing, indeed, so frequent between 1300 and 1400 that some historians prefer to date its rise earlier by a century than we have done. But even long before that there were prophetic messages. There were, to begin with, all the heretics: the Breton Abelard (1079–1142), the foe of the Schoolmen; and their other enemy, the Arabian, Averroes (1120–1198), who tried to restore the true text of Aristotle, so [19] mutilated by theologians; and his great patron, Frederick II, the arch-heretic, the friend of heretics and of artists, who initiated a brief and premature Renaissance at his court in Sicily. After his day the names come more quickly, first in literature and the arts, and afterwards in thought. The *Divina Commedia* of Dante (1265–1321) revealed behind its medieval theology the mind of an individual cut after no pattern; and in that colossal work and in the *Vita Nuova* he built up the national language – always the first step towards emancipation. [...] [20] [...] literature did not lie fallow after Dante. He was succeeded by Petrarch (1304–1374) and Boccaccio (1313–1375), two complete men of the Renaissance before their time: Petrarch, almost the first collector, and the loving student of Latin manuscripts, the Christian who adored the pagan thinkers, who said he stood between Augustine and Virgil (the fragmentary

Virgil of those days, for no complete Virgil saw light till 1469); Boccaccio, the frank child of beauty and the senses, whose starry meadows and greenrobed, myrtle-wreathed ladies foreshadow the painters to come; whose vivid, marvellous prose continued the work of Dante and helped to mould the mother-tongue.

"What life dost thou live?" says Petrarch in his Imaginary Letter to Virgil, "... how near the truth were thy earthly dreams and imaginings? Hast thou been welcomed by the wandering Aeneas, and hast thou passed [21] by the ivory portal? ... Or, rather, dost thou dwell in that quiet region of heaven which receives the blessed, where the stars shine benignly upon the peaceful shades of the famous? Wert thou received thither after the conquest of the Stygian abodes – on the arrival of that Highest King who, victorious in the great struggle, crossed the unholy threshold with pierced feet, and, irresistible, beat down the unyielding bars of hell with His pierced hands, and hurled its gates from their ... hinges."

In this passage the Renaissance was born – with its passionate feeling for the past, its determination to reconcile the old gods with Christianity. And while Petrarch was writing thus, Chaucer (1328–1400) was singing in England, running tilt against asceticism and hypocrisy, striking blows for the "trouthe" that "shal delivere"; and Langland was giving us *Piers Plowman,* with its cry for sincerity and equality.

After the dawn came the day. Its first glory passed quickly, its noon and evening brought about unexpected results. The Renaissance began with an almost fanatical [22] revival of classical learning; it ended in anti-classicism and the triumph of the Romantic Movement. It opened with Poggio and Lorenzo Valla, it closed with Shakespeare. For while it was worshipping antique forms, it bore within itself a new life which was pushing towards birth; it involved paradoxes of which it was unconscious. The embracing of Paganism meant the reassertion of Nature; the reawakening of art and learning, a revived sense of beauty and enjoyment. And enjoyment, which is vitality can bear no bonds; it is spontaneous, it must make its own laws and live. It must live in the present, not in the past. By 1600, the world was on the side of Shakespeare.

Every nation played its part in the Renaissance, but Italy came first of all. Italy was the well-spring from which the other countries drew life. That life was the enduring fruit of conquest which the French invaders, Charles VIII, Louis XII, Francis I, carried back to France between 1494 and 1515. Germany and England caught the same inspiration from the same source. And in each land, shaped by its own qualities, the Renaissance took a particular form. Rabelais tells how, when the seekers after the Temple of Bacbuc at last reached the shrine and entered, the wine that the priestess gave them, though it came from the same fountain, tasted different in the mouth of every man. So it was with the subtle wine of the Renaissance.

In Italy the movement was practically over by 1500. [...] The Renaissance had a sense of beauty, a conviction of man's power, of his dignity; it had no conscience, no rudder to steer by. And yet it has bequeathed to us a noble heritage. Before it ended, what was enduring in it had already passed into common existence. [...] In Autumn, when all seems most mortal, the dying leaves make the mould from which the flowers will grow the next Spring; and in the decay of the Renaissance was hidden the secret of the future – the rich seed of modern thought.

2 Hu Shi Some Modest Proposals for the Reform of Literature (1917)[13]

Hu Shi's Eight-No-Manifesto 八不主義 *(Ba-Bu Zhuyi) for the renewal of the Chinese literary language is modelled on Ezra Pound's "A few don'ts" (1913). The essay advocates the use of the vernacular and openly links times of foreign influence in Chinese history with its rise – ultimately in order to draw parallels between past and present, of course. The essay also clearly contains elements taken directly from Hu's reading of Sichel, especially in the final passages on the importance of Dante.*

[123] Those engaged in the present discourse on literary reform are myriad. How am I, unlearned and unlettered, qualified to speak on the subject? Yet I have over the past few years, with the benefit of my friends' argumentation, pondered and studied this matter a fair degree and the results achieved are perhaps not unworthy of discussion. So I summarize the opinions I hold and list them in eight points; I have divided them in this fashion for the investigation of those interested in literary reform.

It is my belief that those wishing to discuss literary reform today should begin with eight matters, which are as follows:
1. Writing should have substance
2. Do not imitate the ancients
3. Emphasize the technique of writing

---

[13] Hu Shi, *Wenxue gailiang chuyi* 文學改良芻議 (Some Modest Suggestions for Literary Reform) in *Xin Qingnian* 新青年 (New Youth) 2, no. 5 (January 1, 1917). The translation follows the translation by Kirk Denton: Hu Shi "Some Modest Suggestions for Literary Refom," *Modern Chinese Literary Thought. Writings on Literature, 1893–1945*, Kirk Denton (ed.) 123–139 (Stanford: Stanford University Press 1996). Page numbers given here in square brackets are linked to this translation.

4. [124] Do not moan without an illness
5. Eliminate hackneyed and formal language
6. Do not use allusions
7. Do not use parallelism
8. Do not avoid vulgar diction

[...]

[125] II. Do Not Imitate the Ancients

Literature has changed from dynasty to dynasty, each dynasty having its own literature. The Zhou and Qin dynasties had their literatures, the Wei and Jin had theirs, as did the Tang, Song, Yuan, and Ming. This is not just a personal opinion held by me alone, but a truth of the progression of civilization. As for prose, there are the styles of the Book of History, the philosophers of the pre-Qin period, the Han historians Sima Qian and Ban Gu, the essayists Han Yu, Liu Zongyuan, Ouyang Xiu, and Su Shi, the dialogues of Zhu Xi, and the fictional narratives of Shi Nai'an and Cao Xueqin.

This is the progression of literature. To turn our attention to verse, poems such as *The Pushpin Song* and *Song of Five Sons* constitute the earliest period. Then follow the poems in the Book of Songs, Qu Yuan's *Sao*, and Xunzi's rhyme-prose. From Su Wu and Li Ling of the Western Han to the Wei-]in period, and the *paibi* parallel style of the Southern dynasties, to the flourishing of regulated verse in the Tang and Du Fu and Bai Juyi's realism (as in Du Fu's *Recruiting Officer of Shihao* and *Jiang Village* or Bai Juyi's *New Ballads*). The regulated verse form flourished in the Tang, but was later replaced by the lyric meter and the dramatic song (*qu*). From the Tang and Five Dynasties period to the *xiaoling* form in the beginning of the Song marks one period of the lyric meter. The lyrics of Su Shi, Liu Yong, Xin Qiji, and Jiang Kui form another period. The *zaju* and *chuanqi* dramas of the Yuan are another. All these periods have changed [126] with the times, and each has its own characteristics. Our generation, looking back with a historical, progressive perspective, is most certainly unable to say that the literature of the ancients is superior to that of the present.

The prose of the *Zuo Commentary* and *Records of the Grand Historian* is miraculous indeed, but do they cede much to that of Shi Nai'an's *Water Margin*. And the rhyme-prose of the *Three Capitals* and *Two Capitals* is but dregs in comparison to the Tang regulated verse and the Song lyric meter.

We see from the above that literature develops and does not stand still. Tang people should not write poems of the Shang and Zhou, and Song people should not write rhyme-prose like Sima Xiangru or Yang Xiong. Were they to do so, their results would certainly not be fine. One cannot be skillful if one goes against Heaven, turns one's back on one's age, and defies the footsteps of progress.

Since we now understand the principle of literary development, I can proceed to a discussion of what I mean by *Not imitating the ancients*. In contemporary China, in creating a literature for today, one must not imitate the Tang, Song, Zhou, or the Qin. I once saw the *Inaugural Remarks of the National Assembly* and it read: "Most glorious National Assembly, the end of penumbrous times is nigh."[14] This is evidence that today there is a desire to model literature after the Three Dynasties of antiquity. When we look at today's "great writers," the lesser writers model themselves after Yao Nai and Zeng Guofan of the Tongcheng School, the greater writers take the Tang – Song essayists Han Yu and Ouyang Xiu as their masters, while the greatest follow the prose of the Qin – Han or Wei – Jin periods and feel that there is no literature to speak of after the Six Dynasties. But the difference between these is like the difference between one hundred steps and fifty steps; they all belittle literature. Even if it resembles the ancients in spirit, it still amounts to nothing more than adding several "realistic counterfeits" to a museum. Is this literature? Yesterday I saw a poem by Chen Boyan[15] that reads as follows:

> In the Garden of Waves I copied lines from Du Fu,
> Half a year passed, many brushes worn thin.
> All I have to show for myself are tears,
> [127] Though friends passed by commenting on my "skillful creations."
> The myriad souls are all silent,
> The more I look up to Du Fu the higher he becomes.
> I turn these feelings over in my bosom
> And leisurely read Qu Yuan's tragic *Sao*.

This amply represents the imitative psychology of today's "poets of the first rank." The root of their sickness lies in spending "half a year passed with many brushes worn thin" in being slavish scriveners to the ancients, resulting in sighs about "the more I look up to him the higher he becomes."

---

14 The language is from the *Book of Songs*. The phrase as it appears in the original poem is used to convey the idea that one waits until one's time is right to take action, in this case military action. The sense in the "Inaugural Remarks of the National Assembly" is that the time is now ripe for this democratic institution.

15 Chen Boyan 陳伯嚴 (1852–1937) is a late Qing reformer who participated in the Hundred Days Reform of 1898. After being banished from government service, he devoted himself to old-style poetry (in the *Jiangxi* style) and prose writings.

If we free ourselves from this kind of slavery and no longer write poems of the ancients and only write our own poems, we will not end with this sort of defeatism.

Whenever I mention contemporary literature, only vernacular fiction (Wu Woyao, Li Baojia, and Liu E) can be compared without shame to the world's literary "first rank." This is for no other reason than that they do not imitate the ancients (although they owe much to *The Scholars*, *The Water Margin*, and *The Story of the Stone*, they are not imitative works). And it is only because they faithfully write about the contemporary situation that they can become true literature. All other poets or ancient-style essayists who study this or that style have no literary value. Those today with a determination to pursue literature should understand precisely the nature of that in which they are engaged.

[...]
[137]
[...]

VIII. Do Not Avoid Vulgar Diction

Since my literary canon is composed only of Shi Nai'an, Cao Xueqin, and Wu Woyao, I have the theory of "do not avoid vulgar diction." And yet for a long time the spoken and literary languages in our country have been turning their backs on each other. Ever since the importation of Buddhist scriptures, translators have been aware of the fact that the classical language is deficient in conveying meaning, so they have used in their translations an ordinary and simple language, whose style verged on the vernacular. Later, Buddhist lectures and catechisms mostly made use of the vernacular, which gave rise to the dialogue (*yulu* 語錄) form. When the Song neo-Confucians used the vernacular in the scholarly lectures of their dialogues, this form became the standard in scholarship. (Ming scholars later followed this style.) By this time, the vernacular had already long since entered rhymed prose, as can be seen in the vernacular poetry and lyrics of the Tang and Song. By the end of the Yuan dynasty, northern China had already been under the occupation of a foreign race for more than three hundred years (Liao, Jin, and Yuan dynasties). In these three hundred years, China developed an incipient popular literature, out of which emerged the novels *The Water Margin*, *The Journey to the West*, and *The Romance of the Three Kingdoms* and innumerable dramas (Guan Hanqing et al. each produced more than ten different dramas; no period in the history of Chinese literature exceeded this in terms of wealth of productivity). Looking back from our contemporary perspective, the Yuan should without doubt be seen as the most vigorous period of Chinese literature, producing the greatest number of immortal works. At that time, Chinese literature came closest to a union of spoken and written languages, and the vernacular itself had nearly become a literary language. If this tendency [138] had not been arrested, then a "living literature" might have appeared in China and the great endeavor of Dante and Luther might have developed in old Cathay. (In the Middle Ages in Europe, each country had its own vulgar spoken language and Latin was the literary language. All written works used Latin, just as the classical language was used in China. Later, in Italy appeared Dante and other literary giants who first used their own vulgar language to write. Other countries followed suit, and national languages began to replace Latin. When Luther created Protestantism, he began by translating the *Old Testament* and the *New Testament* into German, which ushered in German literature. England, France, and other countries followed this pattern. Today the most widely circulated English Bible is a translation dating from 1611, only 300 years ago. Hence, all contemporary literature in the various European nations developed from the vulgar languages of that time. The rise of literary giants began with a "living literature" replacing a dead literature in Latin. When there is a living literature, there will be a national language based on the unity of the spoken and written languages.) Unexpectedly, this tendency was suddenly arrested during the Ming. The government had already been using the "eight – legged essay" to select its civil servants, and scholars like Li Mengyang [1472–1529] and the followers of the "former seven masters" raised "archaism" (*fugu* 復古) as the most lofty of literary goals. So the once-in-a-millennium opportunity to effect the unity of the spoken and written languages died a premature death, midway in the process. Yet, from today's perspective of historical evolution, we can say with complete certainty that vernacular literature is really the canonical and will be a useful tool for developing future literature. (My "certainty" is only my opinion, one shared by few of my contemporaries.) For this reason, I propose the appropriate use of vulgar diction in the writing of prose and poetry. It is preferable to use the living words of the twentieth century than the dead words of three millennia past (like "Most glorious National Assembly, the end of penumbrous times is nigh"); it is preferable to use the language of *The Water Margin* and *The Journey to the West*, which is known in every household, than the language of the Qin, Han, and Six Dynasties, which is limited and not universally understood.

Conclusion

The eight points related above are the result of my recent investigation and contemplation of this important question. Since I am studying in a far-off foreign land[16] I have little leisure for reading, so I must ask my learned [139] elders back home for their scrutiny and circumspection, for there may well be places in need of severe rectification. These eight points are all fundamental to literature and merit investigation. So I have drafted this essay and hope that it elicits some response from those who care about this issue, both here and in China. I have called them "modest proposals" to underscore the sense of their incompleteness and to respectfully seek the redaction of my compatriots.

3 Hu Shi, The Renaissance in China (Address given at the Royal Institute of International Affairs, Chatham House, London, on November 9th, 1926)[17]

Hu Shi in this address gives a genealogy of his "Chinese Renaissance" by explaining how mechanical and political changes in the late nineteenth and early twentieth centuries had necessitated the cultural changes to follow, which the New Culture Movement *would now address. He sees this movement as the dawn of a new beginning, a new birth for China and a movement that is responsible for something he calls a "transvaluation of values," one in which Western civilization, at least temporarily, takes first position while Chinese civilization is criticized. In this address, Hu also describes the entanglement of the Chinese Renaissance or New Culture Movement with politics, the Nationalist and Communist Parties and the May Fourth Student Movement.*

[265] IT is a great honour to me to be invited to speak at Chatham House, which, I am told, was the residence of three Prime Ministers of England, and to address the Royal Institute of International Affairs, an Institution devoted to the study of problems affecting the intercourse and interdependence of nations.

[...]

The subject chosen for me to-night is the "Chinese Renaissance." Such a title may sound a little conceited, especially from the lips of one who has taken a personal part in this new movement. The Renaissance is, of course, the term usually associated with that great movement in Western history which heralded modern Europe. The same name has been accorded to the far-reaching changes in

---

16 Hu was studying at Cornell University when he wrote this essay.
17 The text follows Hu Shi, "The Renaissance in China," *Journal of the Royal Institute of International Affairs* 5 (1926), 265–283; page numbers are in square brackets.

thought and action which have swept over China during the last ten years, and for the sake of [266] convenience I will use that name and try to tell you something of the movement for which it stands.

The Chinese Renaissance movement represents a new stage in the process of modernising our country and our people, and in that process three stages have already been manifested. The first may be described as the mechanical stage – the introduction of mechanical implements, of battleships, guns and steamships. The second was the stage of political reform. Then came the third stage, the movement of which I am to speak to-night.

In the last hundred years, the period of our close contact with the West, China has shown an unfortunate resistance to the new form of civilisation which has been knocking at our door. We resisted for a hundred years, and started our effort to modernize alrnost at the point of the bayonet. Perhaps it is hardly to be wondered that our first efforts lay in the direction of mechanical devices. Our mechanical experience started in 1850 with the weapons of war introduced during the Taiping Rebellion, which swept over the country like a cyclone and devastated almost half the provinces of China. The old army was powerless largely because it had been demoralised and weakened by opium smoking. There arose in the province of Hunan certain Chinese leaders of high courage and character who tried to organise a volunteer army and a volunteer navy. In the course of a few years they recovered from the rebels a number of cities and provinces; but even this new army, this volunteer army, proved quite inadequate in equipment and organisation for its great task.

Then one of these leaders, Li-Hung-Chang, realised that assistance could be secured from the West in the form of munitions, of organisation and of leadership. In the Lower Yangtse territory a new army was organised, equipped with modern arms and trained under modern Western military officers, among whom was General Gordon. This new force, which soon acquired the name of the "Ever-Victorious Army," recovered practically all the provinces in the Lower Yangtse Valley, and finally besieged and recaptured Nanking, the seat of the rebellion.

This event brought home to the Chinese in a practical way the superiority of certain phases of Western civilisation. The introduction of modern armaments paved the way for a general reorganisation of the Chinese navy and of part of the Chinese army. Arsenals were erected and a big dockyard was established.

But in all these innovations, these attempts to introduce Western ways, there was no attempt and indeed no desire on the [267] part of the Chinese to understand the basic ideas underlying the civilisation which had produced these wonderful new weapons of war and the new methods of commerce which became conspicuous at about the same time. There was not even a desire to understand the language of the foreigners. When at last a School of Languages was established by order of the Government, even the sons of the men who had originated the idea refused to enter the new school, and scholars had to be recruited from poor families who were attracted by a small monthly gratuity. There was no desire on the part of the Chinese Government or people to train leaders for a new and more modern form of civilisation in China. Their activities were confined to the training of young boys in the mastery of a foreign language, in order that they might become interpreters to the great Mandarins.

Throughout this first stage indeed, this stage of mechanical experiment, there was no attempt to understand or to introduce those finer elements which constitute the genius of Western civilisation. There was, it is true, some attempt to translate scientific text-books with the help of foreign missionaries, but the whole tone of the age was represented by the demand for only two things from the West – wealth and power. In the newspapers and publications of the last generation these two factors stand out as the sole requirements of the first reformers.

But we soon began to realise that it would be impossible to achieve even those desired objects of wealth and power without political reorganisation. The wars of 1860, of 1884 and of 1885, and the war with Japan in 1894, demonstrated that the introduction of modern weapons of war and of commerce, unaccompanied by the transformation of outworn political machinery, was not sufficient to save China. The new navy, which had cost China vast fortunes, was swept away during the Sine-Japanese War in the final decade of the last century. And at last the more far-seeing of our leaders began to realise and to preach the need for a thorough reorganisation of our political machinery. China thus entered the second stage in the process of her modernization – the stage of political reform.

The drama of Chinese political reform divides itself into four acts. Act I, to make a long story short, was the reform of 1898, based on a programme of the Manchu Emperor Kwang-Hsu, who was convinced that China needed certain basic reforms if she was to retain her independence. When he came into power he called to his service a number of the more radical leaders of the time and, in the course of a few months, proclaimed a series of drastic [268] reforms. But this movement was short-lived. The forces of reaction soon gathered together and rallied round the person of the Empress-Dowager. The reforms were swept away, the Emperor was imprisoned by the Dowager and six of the reformers were executed.

China then entered on the second Act of this political drama, which consisted of reaction and culminated in the appalling tragedy of the Boxer Rising of 1900. That episode so disgraced the nation that for many years China was not considered a respectable member of the Family of Nations. But the humiliation which China suffered in those days was sufficient to convince the people that political reform could no longer be neglected, and even the reactionary Court of the Manchus was persuaded to proclaim a few important reforms during the years from 1901 to 1910. When the Russo-Japanese War was being fought on Chinese soil in 1904–5, the Chinese had a striking illustration of the efficacy of modernisation. A small nation of the East defeated Russia, one of the greatest Powers of Europe, and modern organisation was recognised as the cause of her success. Thousands of students accordingly flocked to Japan, hoping to discover the means for a second and similar miracle. The Government was compelled to send an Imperial Commission to Europe and America to study constitutional reform, and in 1908 a scheme of Constitutional Government was proclaimed, allotting a period of nine years to the gradual fulfilment of a programme of Constitutional Monarchy. The Council of State, which was to be the father of the future Parliament, opened in 1910. But these reforms, which constituted Act III of the political drama, were approached half-heartedly; there was no genuine change on the part of the Court, the nobility or the officials, the Government was still in the hands of intriguing princes, eunuchs and old women.

There was no genuine leadership in the direction of a more healthy and more vigorous national life.

During those years a new activity had manifested itself, a revolutionary movement which was directed against the Manchus. The Manchus, who had been reigning in China for 270 years, had now proved themselves incompetent, incapable of meeting the needs of the nation either in its internal or external affairs. The Taiping Rebellion provided the first definite evidence of the demoralisation of the reigning race. It was followed by the period of reaction, by the coup d'état of 1898 and by the tragedy of 1900.

A conviction was growing among the people that, so long as the Manchu Court and nobility remained in power, there was little [269] hope of effective transformation. The spirit of unrest grew deeper and broader in those years between 1900 and 1911, until in 1911 it showed itself in open rebellion. The dynasty offered no effective resistance. The old loyalties had been shaken by those years of revolutionary agitation. The dynasty abdicated in 1912, and thus the first popular revolt, the anti-Manchu Rebellion, won a complete and almost bloodless success.

But there remained the more important task of establishing a Republican Government. The forces that set it in motion have been in evidence for fifty years, but we must confess that the first efforts at popular government have so far proved a failure. The Republic has failed, not because modern China has failed – there has never been a modern China – but because in all these processes the changes have been superficial and have hardly touched the fundamental issues of political transformation. There has been practically no modern leadership, practically no genuine admission of our real weaknesses, no recognition of the spiritual possibilities of the new civilisation. Such reforms as were carried out were regarded as a necessary evil and were never directed by men trained for such great tasks. If we look at the list of men who have played an important part in the history of the last fifty years, there is not one who had received even the rudiments of a modern education, not one who was qualified to govern a modern State, for to govern a modern State in a constitutional way requires a modern education.

In the first years of the Republic the old forces were taken by surprise and the old officials hurried to Shanghai or Tsingtau [Qingdao] to seek refuge and retirement, thinking probably that their day had passed. But in the course of a few years they were recalled one by one to participate once more in the Government of the country.

The reactionary forces rallied round one man, Yuan Shikai, the incarnation of reaction, and it was impossible for the infantile new forces to maintain an effective resistance against the shrewdness and experience of men who were pastmasters at the Chinese official game. In a very short time the new forces had been swept out of sight and Yuan Shikai had proclaimed himself Emperor of China.

In 1914, 1915 and 1916 there was an all-pervading sense of despair. A number of young men committed suicide because they could think of no way out, could see no ray of light ahead. It was not like those last years of the Manchu Dynasty, when people knew that somewhere and some time a rebellion would come. Now it had come, had been swept out of the path and had [270] left only depression and despair. One of my young friends jumped into the West Lake at Hang-Chow, leaving letters of farewell to his friends expressing his joy at escape from a situation without hope. In those years people began at last to realise the futility of superficial political change, and to seek for some new factor which could be made the corner-stone of a new age.

May I read to you an extract from a letter of Huang Yuanyung, one of the leading publicists of the day, written just before leaving the country in 1915 at the height of Yuan Shikai's power. "Politics are in such confusion that I am at a loss to know what to talk about. Ideal schemes will have to be buried for future generations to unearth. . . . As to fundamental salvation, I believe its beginning must be sought in the promotion of a new literature. We must endeavour to bring Chinese thought into contact with the contemporary thought of the world and thus accelerate its radical awakening. And we must see to it that the basic ideals of the modern World produce some direct effect upon the life of the average man. The method seems to lie in using simple language and literature for the wide dissemination of ideas among the people. Have we not seen that historians regard the European Renaissance as the foundation of the overthrow of mediaevalism in Europe? "

That letter was addressed by Huang to his friend, the editor of a paper called *The Tidings*,[18] who wrote an editorial comment pointing out that it was impossible to have a new literature without first having some political order. He said that social reforms presuppose a certain general level of political stability and order, and that the new literature could not be an exception. Events have proved that he was wrong and that Huang was right.

Huang Yuanyung was assassinated in 1915, and he died without ever becoming aware that at about the time of his death a new movement was coming into being which would verify and vindicate his prophetic message.

It was at that time that the new movement began which forms the title and the topic of my address to-night. In the years 1915 and 1916 groups of Chinese students in American Universities were carrying on a controversy on problems of literature. The controversy began on a question of poetic diction and it gradually extended to the larger problem of Chinese literature. The results of the controversy were published in the early days of 1917, and formed the first declarations of a movement which has created a revolution in Chinese literature. This literary revolution marks the first stage in the Chinese Renaissance, for here will be [271] found a spirit essentially different from the earlier stages of modernisation. In the early days we wanted to be modern, but we were afraid of losing the other things which we were told were good. We had been constantly flattered, even by the missionaries, that we were heirs to a great heritage, and we were adjured to cherish it and cling to it – at whatever cost. Even to-day we are hypnotised continually by praises of our old civilisation. We want to be modernised, and we are expected to become modern. But at the same time we are requested not to lose what we have.

We are expected to perform a miraculous task – to change and to remain the same. There is little wonder then that the Chinese have continued to live in comfortable dreams of compromise, accepting certain externals from the Western Barbarians whilst preserving the restrictions and negations of the past.

But a new age has dawned. We have realised at last that certain things must be given up if China is to live. If we really want education, general and universal education, we must first have a new language, a language which can be used and understood by tongue and ear and pen, and which will be a living language for the people. For years and years we tried to have education, but we feared to

---

18 This is the journal *Xinchao*.

use the spoken language. We tried to compromise in various ways, but we clung as scholars to the scholarly language. It was impossible to preach a language, to ask people to accept a language, which was not good enough for us. China went through a stage of contradictions and remained unconscious of the fact.

At last the new movement began in earnest, the Literary Revolution. It advocates the adoption of the spoken language, the vulgar tongue of the people, as the lay medium for all official and literary composition. Its aim is to elevate the despised vulgar tongue of the people to the dignified position of the literary language of the nation. It is a revolution in a sense because it has involved a reassessment of the vulgar literature of the past and of the classical tradition. It seeks to introduce the spoken language of the people as the medium of expression in all text-books, in all the newspapers, in all respectable branches of literature. It has achieved its success through two methods, through historical justification and through constant experiment. The historic argument has aimed to demonstrate that the classical literature, the classical tradition, of China, did not represent the whole historical development of Chinese literature; it represented only the stereotyped phase of the development of Chinese literary genius; side by side with this classical tradition there has always [272] existed a continuous current of popular literature in the form of folk-songs, poems, epic recitals, the drama and the novel. It based its claims on those great masterpieces of literature which have become so popular among the people. One of the greatest critics of the seventeenth century was inspired to declare that one of the popular novels was superior to any work of classical diction in literary beauty. The masterpieces of the popular literature have proved conclusively that the vulgar language is capable of being used as the literary language of the people. The historical argument has been supplemented by conscious experimentation. It has been shown that in the long historical development of popular literature there was lacking one great factor-conscious endeavour. The great writers, the people, the street singers, the rustic lovers, the tavern entertainers have accepted and used this living language to express their feelings and their aims, but there has been in the past no conscious effort to adopt the language, no conscious effort to defend it.

In the history of the rise of Modern Literature in Europe there were great writers who wrote in the vulgar dialects; and at the same time they were men who defended those languages in a conscious and articulate manner. Dante, for example, wrote a defence of Italian; and the early French poets wrote a defence of the use of French. But this conscious effort was lacking in the history of Chinese literature. The leaders of the Literary Revolution tried to supply this need by resolving never to write anything except in this new language. In the course of a few years a number of young writers have succeeded in producing presentable specimens of literary experiment. And so, by means of the indisputable facts of history and by the fruits of conscious experiment, the Literary Revolution has won its way to success in the course of less than ten years. It has succeeded in revolutionising all the school texts, and it has succeeded in making the school life of millions of children easier than that of their fathers.

It has given to the youth of the nation a new instrument for the expression of their emotions and ideas. It has formally established what was once the despised vulgar tongue of the people as the legitimate and even the fashionable medium of literary composition.

This Literary Revolution formed the first phase of the Chinese Renaissance. It marked a new phase, a new life. It was not a complete breaking away from the past, it was an historical development; it was a conscious effort to make articulate all the valuable elements we already possessed. At the same time the [273] methods were modern, the inspirations were modern. It thus presented to the people a new and living idea.

As language is the most important vehicle of thought and of expression, any radical and fundamental change in a national language could not but involve a great change in other phases of social and intellectual life. During the last ten years, this Literary Revolution has spread and has affected various phases of Chinese life. I shall not describe those different phases in great detail. I shall confine myself to two particular phases: first, the intellectual changes, and secondly, the social and political developments. However multifarious these tendencies may seem, there are certain general characteristics which unite them more or less into one great National Movement. The whole movement may be characterised, in the words of Nietzsche, as a movement of the transvaluation of all values. It is a movement in a way to make everything upside down; to try, to judge, to criticise, to doubt, to revalue old things according to new standards. Nothing is too high or too low to be subjected to this process of transvaluation. Marriage, concubinage, widowhood, Confucianism, Christianity – nothing is too sacred to be allowed to pass without criticism. It is for us an age of doubt, of criticism, of protest.

The first phase, the most important effect of this age, is shown in the world of intellectual life. For the first time in history we begin to recognise a new attitude, a desire to understand the basic meaning of modern civilisation, to understand the philosophy behind the civilisation of the West. As the best example of this new consciousness I may cite the work of a Chinese scholar, Liang Shouming.[19] Mr. Liang's father committed suicide during the early years of the Republic because he could not bear to see the incoming of a new order and the passing away of the Manchu régime, to which he had been always loyal. The young Mr. Liang, who had apparently inherited an impulsive and courageous character from his father, was disturbed by the imminent conflict between the civilisations of the East and West. He spent years of thought on this problem, and in 1920 published a book called *The Civilizations of the East and the West and their Philosophies* – quite an ambitious title. In his introductory chapter he points out that Oriental civilisation has come into sharp and fundamental conflict with the civilisation of the West, and that we cannot escape the imperative necessity of seeking a fundamental solution. "Other people may not feel the pressing demand for the solution of this great problem," says he, "but it is not so with me. If no [274] satisfactory answer can be found to this question, I shall not know how to live my own life." Then he goes on to postulate what he considers the only three possible alternative outcomes of this cultural conflict. He says, " First, if the two cultures are incapable of co-existence and inter-assimilation, and if Oriental civilisation must be replaced by modern culture, then we must consciously hasten our basic reforms and not wait to perish together with our civilisation. "Secondly, if the invasion and aggression of Western civilization is not to be feared, and if our own civilisation may yet ultimately triumph, then we must earnestly and actively work for its revival, and we must not waste time in daydreams and idleness and bring ruin upon ourselves and our culture. And, thirdly, if the two cultures are capable of mutual assimilation and compromise, then we should directly seek a clear and definite solution and fight out a new road of life; we cannot meet the urgencies of the situation by half-hearted adoption of certain non-essentials from the West."

That is his impulsive statement of the case. He is voicing the yearning of a new age. His book was widely read and much has been written since on the same subject. The most surprising thing in the writings on this question is the almost entire absence of any apologetic tone in defence of the civilisation of the East. Even Mr. Liang, whose words I have just quoted – probably the most apologetic of these writers – condemned the philosophy of life of the Hindus and frankly admitted that the Western civilisation must become the world civilisation of our day. Of course Mr. Liang had his pious hopes. He admitted that the Western must be the world civilisation to-day, but he prophesied that this Western civilisation would be replaced by Chinese civilisation, which in turn would

---

19 Liang Shuming 梁漱溟 (1893–1988), philosopher, teacher and leader of China's *Rural Construction Movement*.

be ultimately replaced by the civilisation of India. But he said that for the present we must get rid of all the weaknesses of the East and frankly adopt, thoroughly adopt, modern civilisation – to use his own words, the modern "democratic and scientific civilisation of the West."

We will not bother about those pious wishes, but may I suggest that in these discussions we find a completely new attitude, an attitude on the one hand of frank admission of our own weaknesses, all the weak points in Oriental civilisation; and on the other hand the attitude of a frank, a genuine understanding of the spirit, not only the material prosperity, but also the spiritual possibilities of the Western civilisation.

These modern Chinese thinkers, among whom I may mention [275] Mr. Wu Chingheng,[20] an old scholar of sixty who has been some years in this country and in France – men who know their own civilisation as well as modern civilisation – have come to some general conclusions, which may be stated as follows. They recognise that the civilisations of India and of China have not only failed to give proper emphasis to the physical well-being of mankind, but have failed also to satisfy the spiritual demands of the human race. For example, the desire to know, the demand for knowledge – certainly a legitimate and spiritual demand of mankind – has always been discouraged by the great sages of the East. This desire, this yearning for knowledge, has been suppressed either by scepticism or by resort to a so-called deeper wisdom through meditation and contemplation. The sceptics – Chuang-tse [Zhuangzi 莊子], for example – say that life is finite and knowledge is infinite; how dangerous then is it to pursue the infinite with the finite! Then the esoteric mystics tell us to meditate and seek a deeper wisdom through the processes of introspection. We have been accustomed to regard these forms of deeper wisdom as forms of spirituality. But, the modern Chinese are asking, what spirituality really exists in these forms of deeper wisdom, what spirituality is there in a civilisation which has maintained a caste system for thousands of years, or which has bound the feet of its women for a thousand years, and has sought justification in claims of duty and beauty?

These are some of the judgments which the modern thinkers of China are frankly passing upon their own civilisation. On the other hand, there is a growing understanding of and a desire to appreciate the spiritual possibilities of Western civilisation.

---

20 Wu Jingheng 吳敬恆 or Wu Zhihui 吳稚暉 (1865–1953), a linguist and philosopher, had anarchist leanings during his youth but later became the staunchly anti-communist senior leader of the Nationalist Party *Guomindang*.

The ideals of equality and liberty are certainly spiritual. Science, the idea of seeking truth by verifiable methods, is certainly spiritual. The emancipation of women, the extension of the franchise, the protection of the labourer, and all that social legislation which is centred upon the idea of extending the greatest happiness to the greatest number – all these are certainly spiritual. And Socialism, whether we like it or not, is certainly the highest spiritual idea of social organisation.

Even material progress is spiritual, if we only regard it as the necessary condition for liberating humanity from the pitiful struggle for a mere subsistence and for uplifting it for higher and more valuable things. All those who have been in the Far East and have seen those millions of human beings toiling under that peculiarly Oriental form of human slavery, the rickshaw, or "man-power carriage," cannot fail to agree with us modern [276] Chinese thinkers, that there is much spirituality in material progress which has at least relieved that much of human slavery by means of mechanical inventions.

These judgments may be wrong, they may sound even more eulogistic than the Westerners themselves are willing to admit. But I must add that we are not blind to the shortcomings of modern civilisation, to certain phases of nationalism, the means of warfare, the use of machinery for manslaughter and war, the inhuman phases of industrialism, and so on. We are not blind to these things, but we have come to an understanding of the spiritual possibilities, and we are prepared to work for the realisation of those potentialities when modernisation does come to us.

I will not discuss at any great length the other phases of the intellectual change. They include the development of a scientific scholarship, of a critical study of past learning, of movements for mass education. I might even cite the great controversy which took place several years ago on the relation of science to the view of life, a controversy which in the course of a year produced a literature amounting to 250,000 words. These things I will pass over and come to the second phase, the social and political unrest. When the Literary Revolution began in 1917, some of us resolved not to take an active part in politics; some of us indeed declared that we would not talk politics for twenty years. I was one of them, but I broke my vow long ago, so it will be all right for me to talk politics to-day. We were convinced of the importance of non-political work, of the work of literary and intellectual change which was to become the cornerstone of a new revolution.

But this movement can only be carried on by process of education, and education is always too slow a process for impulsive and impatient souls. Even in the early days of the revolution some of my colleagues were so anxious to talk politics that, during my temporary absence from Peking, they started a political paper. That was the beginning of a division in this new movement.

Some of the original leaders of the movement became leaders of political parties. The present leader of the Chinese Communist party was the co-editor with me of that paper, *The New Youth*, which was responsible for the first launching of the language movement.

At first there were two phases of politics. One school represented a willingness to work in non-political movements and wait for years before tangible results could be expected in the political order. On the other side was the impatient school who were [277] anxious to go on with political activities at the same time as with the non-political movement. Political disturbances, internal politics and international relations gradually forced the political problem upon us, and in the course of a few years we were convinced that we could not possibly refrain from talking politics or even from taking an active part in politics. That difference remains amongst us to-day. On the one side you have the moderates, the workers who devote their attention to literature, to new philosophy and new views of life. On the other side you have the men who are taking their part in politics.

I should like to say a few words about the part played by the students in recent years. The Student Movement began in 1919 as a protest against the decision of the Versailles Peace Conference in regard to the Chinese province of Shantung. The constant interference of students in politics is regarded as strange in foreign countries, but when you come to think of it, it is quite a usual phenomenon in the history of mankind. It is almost a universal rule that, whenever abnormal conditions of society exist, whenever there is lacking a regular channel for the expression of popular wishes and ideas, whenever the older generation fails to satisfy the desires of the people, the burden of political interference almost invariably falls upon the shoulders of the younger generation of intellectuals – the students. The Chinese students participated actively in politics in the second century A.D., in the tenth century, and in the seventeenth century. Whenever you find an abnormal state of affairs, there you find the Student Movement. In European history I believe that you find the same thing. In mediaeval times such movements were not uncommon.

In the year 1848, the year of revolutions throughout Europe, revolutions were started by students in almost every country. In India, in Korea, in Turkey, in Persia, in Russia, whenever you find a set of abnormal conditions and the existing order of things no longer satisfies the people, or wherever the older generation has failed to live up to the expectation of the younger generation, you find an active Student Movement. And the reverse is equally true. In those countries where conditions are tolerably normal, as in America and in England, we shall find the students more deeply interested in football and cricket than in politics.

The Chinese Student Movement began as a spontaneous movement in 1919. It became so suddenly strong that the Government was soon forced to dismiss three pro-Japanese officials of the highest rank. There was no Russian propaganda, no organisation of any kind behind it; it was a spontaneous [278] patriotic movement. Though it gradually spread and became a national movement, it lacked any efficient form of organisation. But the events of 1919, 1920 and 1921 so clearly demonstrated the usefulness and power of this new element in Chinese life that political parties began to understand and try to use that power. In the years 1920 and 1921 many political parties threw open the columns of their papers to student contributions; student editors and reporters were employed in an attempt to get students interested in political life. Then in 1924 the KwominTang [*Guomindang* 國民黨 Nationalist Party] – probably the only Chinese party that deserves the name of a political party – officially adopted the policy of enlisting students among its members. From that time onward party organisations have existed in the Colleges and Universities throughout the country, and wherever you find an educational centre you will find a party organisation of some kind.

The first stage of student activity found them without any organisation. The second stage was one of political organization. Then came a third stage, when the students were no longer a loose organisation, but a highly organised body under the influence of Soviet Russia and of the Third International. The Chinese as a race have always shown a lack of organisation. Even in literature we find in the whole literary harvest of 2500 years no single book written with a plot, with an organisation, with a desire for architectonic structure. Even the novels and dramas show a lack of plot, of organisation. The early unorganised efforts of the Student Movement soon died away. Any great emotional crisis would be sufficient to call up a Student Movement, but as soon as the issue passed the movement died away.

But the new phase of the movement is different. The new KwominTang, or National Party, has adopted a highly developed organisation, a new army, a new discipline. The army became a part of the party, and the party became the directorate, the teacher, the soul, the brain of the army. The whole organization of the military arm and of the party itself is practically identical, at least interlocked. There is a party representative in every unit of the army. At the same time, the whole party is more or less under a military type of discipline. This, I think, is a very remarkable and very important fact. The Japanese received a great deal of inspiration from the Germans in the early days of their enlightenment. The Chinese have not yet learned any serious lesson from any Western country.

But we are beginning to be schooled in the matter of organisation. We do not know what will be the result, but, so far as we can judge by the events [279] of the last few months, we can see that the movement is taking shape. The army thus organised has certainly won victories over the older armies which were not organised.

Thus the movement of Chinese Renaissance swings back to politics. This is, perhaps, inevitable. The political anarchy had become intolerable and the outside world, as well as Young China, has grown quite impatient. It may be that we were wrong in trying to avoid politics. It may be that the new political movement was after all not so premature as it had once seemed to us. Recent events seem to point to the possibility of an early success of the new political revolution under the leadership of the Nationalist Party. The old forces set loose by the revolution of 1911 have gradually exhausted themselves and are offering no serious resistance to the new forces which have the advantage of organisation and the inspiration of political ideals. As an impartial and non-partisan liberal, I wish them success and welcome it.

I am sorry that I have taken so much time. I was advised not to read a paper, so I have tried to speak without notes. But I have been tempted to speak for longer than I had intended.

HU SHIH. Professor of Philosophy at the University of Peking.

4 Zhu Jinpan, The Chinese Renaissance (1930)[21]

This text, from a school journal published in Canton, shows, first, the enormous breadth of this intellectual movement, and second, it points to the importance of English (or generally foreign) language writings and vocabularies in the discussion of the Chinese Renaissance, even within China.

THE CHINESE RENAISSANCE
We, The Young Chinese, is (sic) awakening to the need of crticising (sic) the traditional values of centuries, and is bringing to China a renaissance such as Europe went through. Within a decad e (sic) there has been telescpüed the conscious eulmination of this movemet (sic). All of Chinese tradition, ancestor worship, the family institution, has been subjected to instance (sic) and earnest criticism much of which has resulted in definite protest. Nothing is too sacred to

---

21 Zhu Jinpan 朱錦盤 "The Chinese Renaissance," *Taizhong* 台中 (Canton) 18 (1930), 56.

be submitted to the scrutiny of intelligent criticism. It is an age of transvaeuation (sic) of uolues (sic).

The Revolution of 1911 was an attempt to create a new government which should be strong enough to cope with aggression from without, and to conque (sic) the forces of reaction within. It failed, because there was never a revolution in the sense that the French Revolution was a revolution, or the Russian Revolution was a revolution, It did not touch the fundamental life of the people. It never touch (sic) the thought, the beliefs, the ideals oft he people. It was merely a chang (sic) of government, a change of dynasty. But during these last ten years we have seen the gradual spread of an intellectual reformation which affects the religious life, the social life, the family customs, and the fundamental attitude in scholarshig (sic) and in thinking.

The Literary Revolution has succeeded in revolutionizing the whole language of China, has succeeded in writing over all the textbooks in the schools, has succeeded in producing a literature capable of being understood by the vast majority of the people.

The Youth Movement of 1919, which arose as a protext against the action of Paris Convention on German possessions in China, found expression in this new language, and in 1920 the government was persuade (sic) to require its use in all newly printed textbooks. The developmnt (sic) of this new language is but one phase of the Chinese Renaissance, which is the *conscious development* of an (sic) unconscious movement that has been gathering force for two thousand (sic) years, 朱錦盤 (Zhu Jinpan).

5 Prefaces to Hu Shi's Haskell Lectures (1933; 1963)[22]

Much has been cited from Hu Shi's lectures in this book. It is very illuminating, however, to see how his text – and with it, his Renaissance – was paratextually framed by foreigners, at the time of its first appearance in 1933/34, and then again, three decades later, when it was reprinted in 1963. Hu is depicted as an ambassador and as someone "between the worlds" of East and West, well-versed in the histories and cultures of both. It is for this reason that his interpretation of "Renaissance" is rather uncritically accepted.

---

22 Hu Shi. *The Chinese Renaissance* 中国的文艺复兴 (*The Haskell Lectures*, 1933), Chicago: The University of Chicago Press; London: Cambridge University Press, 1934, (reprinted New York: Paragon Book Reprint Corp., 1963).

A. EUSTACE HAYDON: FOREWORD TO THE 1934 PUBLICATION

A long deferred hope was fulfilled when Dr. Hu Shih of the National Peking University accepted appointment as Haskell lecturer for the summer of 1933. His lectures on cultural trends in modern China are here presented under a title selected by him expressly to characterize the nature of the cultural transformation described – *The Chinese Renaissance*.

The Haskell Foundation was established by Mrs. Caroline E. Haskell as an aid to mutual understanding among the peoples of the world, separated so long by their varied heritages of culture and religion. She intended the Barrows Foundation to provide a scholarly presentation of Christianity to the Orient and completed the circle by the Haskell Foundation which brings a sympathetic interpretation of the religions of the East to the Christian West.

During the last decade all religions, in all parts of the World, have been awakened from the slow rhythm of past ages by new forces compelling startling and revolutionary change. Since all cultures are penetrated by the same influences and all religions are of necessity wrestling with the same problems, it seemed wise and in line with the intention of the founder to devote the Haskell Lectures during this period of transition to an interpretation of the process of re-embodiment through which old religions and cultures are assuming new and vital forms.

Both as an interpreter of China's cultural renaissance and as an ambassador of interracial and intercultural understanding Professor Hu was an ideal Haskell lecturer.

Culturally he belongs to both East and West. The vast changes in the cultural life of China are so recent as to fall within the span of his youthful age and in many of these movements he has been a pioneer and a trusted leader. His western education and his work in the field of international conciliation have given him the background and the detached vision necessary to an evaluation of the processes of intercultural penetration at work in his native land. The personal note in some of the chapters was retained at the urgent request of members of the committee who won in the contest with Dr. Hu's self-effacing modesty.

A. Eustace Haydon, University of Chicago

HYMAN KUBLIN: PREFACE TO THE 1963 REPRINT

Twenty five years ago, when I was a student at Boston University, I first read *The Chinese Renaissance* by Dr. Hu Shih. I can still recall vividly the intellectual excitement roused by the book. From its little more than one hundred pages I acquired a far richer understanding of the epochal changes then overtaking China than had been possible from the study of dozens of books and literally hundreds of periodical articles. Rereading his lectures today, thirty years subsequent to their delivery at the University of Chicago, I find that my initial enthusiasm for Dr. Hu's scholarship and historical insight has not waned.

It was characteristic of the late Dr. Hu that, at a time when his country was cruelly wracked and torn by civil wars, Communist subversion, and foreign invasion, he sought to place these tragic events in a broad historical setting. In an era when it was so easy for China's leaders to succumb to political despair and intellectual cynicism and to wring their hands over their nation's plight and prospects who but Dr. Hu could have used so optimistic a phrase as the "renaissance in China"? It was not that he was oblivious to the tides of nationalism that were rolling over his age-old country or that he dismissed lightly the titanic struggles for political and military power that all too often mesmerised the observer seeking rhyme and reason in the transient affairs of the day. On the contrary, he took these phenomena as seriously as he believed history itself would take them.

Dr. Hu had a wary regard for the nature and meaning of revolution and, insofar as China was concerned, he invoked the word sparingly and asvisedly. He himself strove to grasp and transmit understanding of history, as it had been and as it was becoming. Revolutions, however defined, were, he knew, not without precedent in China nor was cultural renaissance alien to the history of his country. If Dr. Hu preferred to categorize the mighty transformation in China during modern times as a "renaissance" rather than as a revolution, it was doubtless because he himself placed a value upon the changes to which he himself was a primary witness. Revolution implied metamorphosis, for better or for worse, while "renaissance" signified rebirth and, hopefully, new life.

Chronologically Dr. Hu was still a young man when The Chinese Renaissance was published in 1934. Still, it is clear that the basic ideas and personal experiences which he presented reflected a life that was already mature. Long before he was invited to present the Haskell Lectures in Comparative Religion at the University of Chicago, he had made his mark internationally as a scholar, philosopher, critic, and educator. His many addresses and publications had won him unstinting renown in China and the West. To single out but a few of the factors conditioning his views of the nature and implications of the widespread changes occurring in modern China would surely leave one open to the charge of oversimplification. Nevertheless, it would perhaps not be inappropriate to take note of the following circumstances.

Dr. Hu was in many ways a prototype of the new Chinese intellectual who inspired and was inspired by the Chinese renaissance. Born in 1891 in a small village in Anhwei province in eastern China, it was still not too late for him to have a traditional upbringing and education. Unlike many Chinese intellectuals of later generations it could never be said of him that he was ignorant of or alienated from his own cultural heritage. He was, thus, never at a disadvantage in academic jousts with even the most conservative Confucian scholars; he was ever prepared to match quotations from the Classics and the commentaries with the most erudite of pundits.

But Dr. Hu also boasted, in the narrower sense of the term, a sound and solid Western training and education. He was at ease in the realm of Western history, literature, and thought. These two cultural traditions, the Chinese and the Western, did not constitute separate and distinct sectors of his mind but were rather integrated into a philosophical whole. He was, accordingly, able to view the Chinese Revolution in its many manifestations from the perspectives of both the centuries-old civilization of China and of world history. It becomes immediately apparent to the reader of his works that he never suffers from cultural parochialism or strident nationalism.

If Dr. Hu possessed a finely rounded view of history, he also had a favored point of departure in his intellectual inquiry, especially as it related to matters of the Chinese Revolution. During his years as a graduate student in the United States he became intimately involved in the pai hua [*baihua* 白話 vernacular language] movement, the campaign to replace usage of the classical with the colloquial language. Once he became wedded to the premise that the promotion of literacy among the masses of his countrymen, traditionally illiterate and unlettered, would ultimately work a revolution, a renaissance of inconceivable dimensions, his orientation towards the vast upheaval in China was affected accordingly. He took it as axiomatic that the wars and politics, the science and technology, of the modern world would inevitably alter the nature of Chinese civilization but he also believed with equally firm conviction that acquisition of the instruments of basic literacy by China's millions of people would lastingly shape the character of the revolution in the older way of life. While his fellow revolutionaries battled against warlords, subverters, and aggressors, Dr. Hu sought to arm his countrymen for an all-out war against ignorance.

One last determinant of the thought of Dr. Hu might well be stressed, namely, the circumstances of his own life. Even during his adolescent years he was not oblivious to the erosive effects of Western civilization upon the traditional Chinese way of life. Not simply cultural change but, as importantly, its unprecedentedly quick tempo captured his attention. In his essay, "Social Disintegration and Readjustment" (*The Chinese Renaissance*, page 96), he himself has neatly summed up his marvel at the intrusions of modernity into his own familiar world. "And the rapidity of it all," he exclaimed.

> Within my own life, I read all the beloved novels by lamps of vegetable oil; I saw the Standard Oil invading my own village, I saw gas lamps in the Chinese shops in Shanghai; and I

saw their elimination by electric lights. In the field of locomotion, I traveled in sedan chairs, wheelbarrows, and small river boats rowed by men . . . I saw the first tramway operated in Shanghai in 1909, and wrote a poem protesting against its dangers to the ricksha. My first trip on a steamship was when I was only two years old, but I never rode in a motor car before coming to the United States in 1910, and did not travel in the air until 1928. And my people have traveled with me from the vegetable oil lamp to electricity, from the wheelbarrow to the Ford car, if not to the aeroplane, and this in less than forty years' time.

Dr. Hu was an indefatigable scholar but he also sought to learn the lessons of life. Dr. Hu Shih has justly been acclaimed as one of modern China's foremost scholars, philosophers, and educators. He was revered not only in his native land but also in the United States where for years he carried on his work. The republication of *The Chinese Renaissance*, the book by which he is best known in this country, thirty years after its first appearance is a fitting tribute to this inimitable scholar and man.

Brooklyn College, June 18, 1963
Hyman Kublin
Professor of History

Acknowledgements

Different versions of this dialogue have been presented at the City University in Hong Kong, the Humanities Center in Stanford and Gut Siggen (Töpfer-Stiftung) as well as twice in Heidelberg: first as a keynote for the Conference *Rethinking Early Modern Europe in a Global Perspective* in 2015, and later, in 2017, as an Interdisciplinary Seminar at the Heidelberg Graduate School for the Humanities and Social Sciences. We are deeply grateful to the conveners, the discussants and the participants at these events for their curiosity as well as for their critical contributions. Susan Richter and Sebastian Meurer kindly invited us to develop our paper into the inaugural book of their new series. Throughout this project, we were fortunate in receiving support from Felicitas Eichhorn, Erika Lokotsch, Oliver Plate, Li Shuang, Valentin Harder, Sebastian Vogt and Tobias Ertl. They helped us track down sources, format the text, check translations and create the digital repository. Angela Roberts has cast her careful eye over the text as our copy-editor and has transformed our Germanisms into proper English. We owe all of them a huge debt of gratitude.

The first conversations on which this text is based stretch back more than a decade. They have involved many colleagues from Heidelberg and beyond and have culminated in sustained discussions within the Heidelberg Cluster "Asia and Europe in a global context," now the Heidelberg Centre for Transcultural Studies (HCTS). We would like to extend our heartfelt thanks to this institution and to its members, our colleagues, fellows and graduate students, for the countless stimulating debates that we were fortunate enough to be a part of. We dedicate this volume to them.

Works cited

All digital titles have been archived in a repository which can be reached here: dx.doi.org/10.25354/2017.08.3.

Adelman, Jeremy. What is Global History now? aeon.co/essays/is-global-history-still-possible-or-has-it-had-its-moment.

Alanus ab Insulis (Alain of Lille). *Anticlaudianus* (= *Textes philosophiques du môyen âge*, vol. 1), R. Bossuat (ed.). Paris: J. Vrin, 1955.

Alcuin. *Epistolae Karolini aevi* (vol. II) (= *Epistolarum*, vol. 4), Ernst Dümmler (ed.). Munich: Monumenta Germaniae Historica, 1895.

Ampère, Jean-Jacques. Histoire littéraire de la France avant le XIIe siècle. *Revue des Deux Mondes* 5 (1836), 24–38. http://fr.wikisource.org/wiki/Histoire_litt%C3%A9raire_de_la_France_avant_le_XIIe_si%C3%A8cle.

Ampère, Jean-Jacques. *Histoire littéraire de la France avant le XIIe siècle*. Paris: Hachette, 1840.

Anderson, Kyle D. Promises of Modern Renaissance. Italian Presences in Chinese Modernity. PhD diss., Pennsylvania State University, 2010.

Assmann, Jan. Die Antiken der Anderen. Renaissance im Plural: Ein Sammelband untersucht die Wiederbelegung früher Kulturleistungen quer durch Zeiten und Gesellschaften. *Frankfurter Rundschau*, 27 October, 2001.

Atkinson, James B. and David Sices (eds.). *Machiavelli and his Friends. Their Personal Correspondence*. DeKalb: Northern Illinois University Press, 1996.

Austin, John L. *How to Do Things with Words*. Oxford: Clarendon Press, 1962.

Bacci, Orazio. *La critica letteraria*. Milan: Vallardi, 1910.

Bakhtin, Mikhail. *The Dialogic Imagination: Four Essays*. Austin and London: University of Texas Press, 1981.

Balzac, Honoré de. Le bal de Sceaux. In *La Comédie humaine* (La Pléiade), vol. 1, Marcel Bouteron (ed.), 72–127. Paris: Gallimard, 1951.

Baron, Hans. *The Crisis of the Early Italian Renaissance: Civic Humanism and Republican Liberty in an Age of Classicism and Tyranny*. Princeton: Princeton University Press, 1955.

Batkin, Leonid. *Die italienische Renaissance. Versuch der Charakterisierung eines Kulturtyps*. Basel/Frankfurt am Main: Stroemfeld, 1981.

Batkin, Leonid. *Gli umanisti italiani. Stile di vita e di pensiero*. Rome: Laterza, 1990.

Bec, Christian. De Pétrarque à Machiavel. À propos d'un 'topos' humaniste (le dialogue lecteur/livre). *Rinascimento* 16 (1976), 3–17.

Belon, Pierre. *Observations de plusieurs singularitez et choses memorables*. Paris: Guillaume Cavellat, 1553.

Bembo, Pietro. Gli asolani. In *Prose e rime*, Carlo Dionisotti (ed.), 310–504. Turin: Unione Tip.-Ed. Torinese, 1966.

Bender, John B. and David D. Wellbery (eds.). *Chronotypes: The Construction of Time*. Stanford: Stanford University Press, 1991.

Bentley, Jerry H. Cross-Cultural Interaction and Periodization in World History. *The American Historical Review* 101, no. 3 (1996), 749–770.

Berling, Judith A. *The Syncretic Religion of Lin Chao-en*. New York: Columbia University Press, 1980.
Bielenstein, Hans. Is there a Chinese Dynastic Circle? *Bulletin of the Museum of Far Eastern Antiquities* 50 (1978), 1–23.
Blumenberg, Hans. *Aspekte der Epochenschwelle*. Frankfurt am Main: Suhrkamp, 1976.
Blumenberg, Hans. Licht als Metapher der Wahrheit. In *Ästhetische und metaphorologische Schriften*, Anselm Haverkamp (ed.), 139–171. Frankfurt am Main: Suhrkamp, 2001.
Boccaccio, Giovanni. *The Decameron* 十日談 *Shiritan*. Translated by Huang Shi and Hu Zanyun. Shanghai: Kaiming shudian, 1932.
Bodde, Derk. Cyclical and Linear Time. In *Chinese Thought, Society and Science. The Intellectual and Social Background of Science and Technology in Pre-modern China*, Derk Bodde (ed.), 122–133. Honolulu: University of Hawaii Press, 1991.
Boucheron, Patrick (ed.). *Histoire du monde au XVe siècle*, Paris: Fayard, 2009.
Boucheron, Patrick and Nicolas Delalande. *Pour une histoire-monde*. Paris: PUF, 2013.
Brindley, Erica. *Individualism in Early China: Human Agency and the Self in Thought and Politics*. Honolulu: University of Hawaii Press, 2010.
Brotton, Jerry. *The Renaissance Bazaar: From the Silk Road to Michelangelo*. Oxford: Oxford University Press, 2002.
Brotton, Jerry. *The Renaissance: A Very Short Introduction*. Oxford: Oxford University Press, 2005.
Bruni, Leonardo. *Dialogi ad Petrum Paulum Histrum*. Stefano Ugo Badassari (ed.). Florence: Olschi, 1994.
Bruni, Leonardo. *History of the Florentine people*, vol. 1. Edited and Translated by James Hankins and D.J.W. Bradley. Cambridge, Mass.: Harvard University Press, 2001.
Bruni, Leonardo. *Life of Petrarch*. In *The Italian Renaissance. The essential sources*, Kenneth Gouwens (ed.), 43–48. Malden: Blackwell Publishing, 2004.
Buck, August. *Zu Begriff und Problem der Renaissance* (= *Wege der Forschung*, vol. 204). Darmstadt: Wissenschaftliche Buchgesellschaft, 1969.
Buck, August. *Humanismus: Seine europäische Entwicklung in Dokumenten und Darstellungen*. Freiburg/Munich: Alber, 1987.
Burckhardt, Jacob. *Die Cultur der Renaissance in Italien*. Basel: Schweighauser, 1860.
Burckhardt, Jacob. *The Civilization of the Renaissance in Italy*. Translated by S. G. C. Middlemore. London: C. K. Paul & Co., 1878.
Burioni, Matteo. Vasari's rinascita. History, anthropology or art criticism? In *Renaissance? Perceptions of Continuity and Discontinuity in Europe, ca. 1300–1550*, Harry Schnitker, Pierre Péporte and Alexander C. Lee (eds.), 115–127. Leiden: Brill 2010.
Burke, Peter. *The Renaissance*. London: Longman, 1964.
Burke, Peter. *The Renaissance Sense of the Past*. London: Edward Arnold, 1969.
Burke, Peter. The Renaissance Dialogue. *Renaissance Studies* 3, no. 1 (1989), 1–12.
Burke, Peter. *The European Renaissance: Centres and Peripheries*. Oxford: Blackwell, 1998.
Burke, Peter. Western Historical Thinking in a Global Perspective – 10 Theses. In *Western Historical Thinking. An Intercultural Debate*, Jörn Rüsen (ed.), 15–30. New York: Berghahn Books, 2002.
Burke, Peter. Renaissance Europe and the World. In *Palgrave Advances in Renaissance Historiography*, Jonathan Woolfson (ed.), 52–70. Basingstoke: Palgrave Macmillan, 2005.

Burke, Peter. Jack Goody and the Comparative History of Renaissances. *Theory, Culture & Society* 26, no. 7–8 (December 2009), 16–31.
Buron, Emannuel, Philippe Guérin and Claire Lesage (eds.). *Les États du dialogue à l'âge de l'humanisme*. Rennes: Presses Universitaires de Rennes, 2015.
Calinescu, Matei. *Five Faces of Modernity: Modernism, Avant-garde, Decadence, Kitsch, Postmodernism*. Durham: Duke University Press, 1987.
Cardelle de Hartmann, Carmen. *Lateinische Dialoge 1200–1400. Literaturhistorische Studie und Repertorium* (= Mittellateinische Studien und Texte, vol. 37). Leiden: Brill 2007.
Carvalho, Raquhel. Did Da Vinci have a Chinese Mother? *South China Morning* Post, November 30, 2014.
Chang, Maria Hsia. *The Chinese Blue Shirt Society. Fascism and Developmental Nationalism*. Berkeley: Center for East Asian Studies, 1985.
Chen Duxiu. *Wenxue geming lun* 文學革命論 (On Literary Revolution). *Xin Qingnian* 新青年 (New Youth) 2, no. 6 (February 1, 1917).
Chen Pingyuan. *Zhongguo xiandia xueshu de jianli* 中國現代學術的建立 *(The Establishment of Modern Chinese Scholarship)*. Beijing: Beijing University Press, 1998.
Choi, Y. J. *East and West. Understanding the Rise of China*. Bloomington: Xlibris Corp, 2010.
Chun, Allen. From Nationalism to Nationalizing: Cultural Imagination and State Formation in Postwar Taiwan. *Australian Journal of Chinese Affairs* 31 (January 1994), 49–69.
Condorcet, Nicolas de. *Esquisse d'un tableau historique des progrès de l'esprit humain*, P.-C.-F. Daunou and Mme M.-L.-S. de Condorcet (eds.). Paris: Agasse, 1794.
Conrad, Sebastian. Enlightenment in Global History: A Historiographical Critique. *The American Historical Review* 117, no. 4 (2012), 999–1027.
Cooper, Frederick. Modernity. In *Colonialism in Question: Theory, Knowledge, History*, 113–149. Berkeley: University of California Press, 2005.
Curtius, Ernst Robert. *Europäische Literatur und lateinisches Mittelalter*. Bern: Francke, 1948.
Davis, Edward L. (ed.). *Encyclopedia of Contemporary Chinese Culture*. London and New York: Routledge Taylor & Francis Group, 2005.
Davis, Kathleen and Nadia Altschul (eds.). *Medievalisms in the Postcolonial World: The Idea of "The Middle Ages" Outside Europe*. Baltimore: John Hopkins University Press, 2009.
Denton, Kirk A. (trans.). *Modern Chinese Literary Thought: Writings on Literature, 1893–1945*. Stanford: Stanford University Press, 1996.
Denys Hay (ed.). *The Renaissance Debate*. New York: Holt, Rinehart, Winston, 1965.
Dikötter, Frank. *The Discourse of Race in Modern China*. Stanford: Stanford University Press, 1992.
Dirlik, Airif. The Ideological Foundations of the New Life Movement: a Study in Counter-Revolution. *Journal of Asian Studies* 34, no. 4 (August 1975), 945–980.
Duara, Prasenjit. *Rescuing History from the Nation: Questioning Narratives of Modern China*. Chicago: University of Chicago Press, 1995.
Duara, Prasenjit. *The Global and Regional in China's Nation-Formation*. London: Routledge, 2009.
Eber, Irene. Thoughts on Renaissance in Modern China: Problems of Definition. In *Studia Asiatia. Essays in Asian Studies in Felicitation of the Seventy-Fifth Anniversary of Professor Ch'en Shou-yi*, Laurence G. Thompson (ed.), 189–220. San Francisco: Chinese Materials Center, 1975.

Edelman, Nathan. The Early Uses of Medium Aevum, Moyen-Âge, Middle Ages. *Romanic review* 29 (1938), 3–25.

Eisenstadt, Shmuel N. (ed.). *Multiple Modernities*. New Brunswick: Transaction Publishers, 2002.

Elliott, Mark. The Historical Vision of the Prosperous Age (shengshi). *China Heritage Quarterly* 29 (March 2012), online publication, no pages, www.chinaheritagequarterly.org/articles.php?searchterm=029_elliott.inc&issue=029

Elman, Benjamin A. *From Philosophy to Philology. Intellectual and Social Aspects of Change in Late Imperial China*. Cambridge: Harvard University Press, 1984.

Erasmus of Rotterdam. *The Correspondence*, vol. 10: *Letters 1356 to 1534. 1523 to 1524*, R.A.B. Mynors and James M. Estes (eds.). Toronto: University of Toronto Press, 1992.

Farago, Claire (ed.). *Reframing the Renaissance: Visual Culture in Europe and Latin America 1450 to 1650*. New Haven and London: Yale University Press, 1995.

Febvre, Lucien. Comment Jules Michelet inventa la Renaissance. In *Studi in onore di G. Luzzatto*, vol. 3, 1–11. Milan: Giuffrè, 1950.

Feldman, David and Rebecca L. Spang. Periodization, Then and Now. *History Workshop Journal* 63 (Spring 2007), 189–191.

Ferguson, Wallace K. *The Renaissance in Historical Thought. Five Centuries of Interpretation*. Boston: Houghton Mifflin Co., 1948.

Fetscher, Justus. Zeitalter/Epoche. In *Ästhetische Grundbegriffe, Historisches Wörterbuch in sieben Bänden*, vol. 7, Karlheinz Barck et al. (eds.), 774–810. Stuttgart: J. B. Metzler, 2005.

Flasch, Kurt. Epoche. In *Philosophie hat Geschichte*, vol. 1: *Historische Philosophie. Beschreibung einer Denkart*, 129–53. Frankfurt am Main: Klostermann, 2003.

Fleck, Ludwik. *Entstehung und Entwicklung einer wissenschaftlichen Tatsache. Einführung in die Lehre vom Denkstil und Denkkollektiv*. Frankfurt am Main: Suhrkamp, 1980.

Gamsa, Mark. Uses and Misuses of a Chinese Renaissance. *Modern Intellectual History* 10, no. 3 (November 2013), 635–654

Garin, Eugenio. *Italian Humanism. Philosophy and Civic Life in the Renaissance*. Oxford: Blackwell, 1965.

Garin, Eugenio. Raffaello e la 'pace filosofica'. In *Umanisti artisti scienziati. Studi sul Rinascimento italiano*, 171–181. Rome: Editori Riuniti, 1989.

Gatto, Ludovico. *Viaggio intorno al concetto di Medioevo. Profilo di storia della storiografia medievale*. Rome: Bulzoni, ^{5}2002.

Gentz, Joachim. Long Live the King! The Ideology of Power between Ritual and Modernity in the *Gongyang zhuan*. In *Ideology of Power and Power of Ideology in Early China*, Paul R. Goldin, Martin Kern and Yuri Pines (eds.), 69–117. Leiden: Brill, 2005.

Gibert, Stéphane, Jean Le Bihan and Florian Mazel (eds.). *Découper le temps. Actualité de la périodisation en histoire* = *Atala. Cultures et sciences humaines* 17 (2014).

Gibert, Stéphane, Les enjeux renouvelés d'un problème fondamental: la périodisation en histoire. In *Découper le temps. Actualité de la périodisation en histoire*, Stéphane Gibert, Jean Le Bihan and Florian Mazel (eds.), 7–31. *Atala. Cultures et sciences humaines* 17 (2014).

Goody, Jack. *The Theft of History*. Cambridge: Cambridge University Press, 2006.

Goody, Jack. *Renaissances: The One or the Many*. Cambridge: Cambridge University Press, 2010.

Gordan, Phyllis Walter Goodhart (ed.). *Two Renaissance Book Hunters: the Letters of Poggius Bracciolini to Nicolaus de Niccolis*. New York: Columbia University Press, 1974.

Grafton, Anthony, *Joseph Scaliger. A Study in the History of Classical Scholarship*, vol. 2. Oxford: Clarendon Press, 1993.

Grataloup, Christian, Les périodes sont des régions du Monde. In *Découper le temps. Actualité de la périodisation en histoire*, Stéphane Gibert, Jean Le Bihan and Florian Mazel (eds.), 65–81. *Atala. cultures et sciences humaines* 17 (2014).

Gray, Patrick. *Varieties of Religious Invention: Founders and Their Functions in History*. Oxford: Oxford University Press, 2015.

Grazia, Margreta de. The Modern Divide: From Either Side. *Journal of Medieval and Early Modern Studies* 37/3 (Fall 2007), 453–467.

Grendler, Paul F. Renaissance. In *Encyclopedia of the Renaissance*, vol. 5, 259–268. New York: Charles Scribner's Sons, 1999.

Gruzinski, Serge. *Quelle heure est-il là-bas? Amérique et islam à l'orée des temps modernes*. Paris: Seuil, 2008.

Gruzinski, Serge. *The Eagle and the Dragon: Globalization and European Dreams of Conquest in China and America in the Sixteenth Century*. Translated by Jean Birell. Cambridge: Polity Press, 2014.

Guarino Veronese. *Epistolario*, vol. 1, Remigio Sabbadini (ed.). Venice: A spese della Società, 1915.

Guthmüller, Bodo and Wolfgang G. Müller. *Dialog und Gesprächskultur in der Renaissance*. Wiesbaden: Harrassowitz, 2004.

Hall, Marcia (ed.). *Raphael's 'School of Athens.'* Cambridge: Cambridge University Press, 1997.

Harbsmeier, Christoph. Some Notions of Time and of History in China and in the West. In *Time and Space in Chinese Culture*, Chun-Chieh Huang and Erik Zürcher (eds.), 49–71. Leiden: Brill, 1995.

Hartog, François. *Régimes d'historicité. Présentisme et expériences du temps*. Paris: Seuil, 2002.

Haskins, Charles. *The Renaissance of the Twelfth Century*. Cambridge, Mass.: Harvard University Press, 1927.

Häsner, Bernd and Angelika Lozar. Providenz oder Kontingenz? Antonio Galateos Eremita und die ‚Lukianisierung' des religiösen Diskurses. In *Grenzen und Entgrenzungen des Renaissancedialogs*, Klaus W. Hempfer (ed.), 13–57. Stuttgart: Steiner 2006.

Hawkes, Rebecca. Was the Mona Lisa a Chinese Slave? *The Telegraph*, December 3, 2014.

Hegel, Georg Wilhelm Friedrich. China. In *The Philosophy of History*. Translated by John Sibree, 176–202. New York: American Home Library, 1902.

Hegel, Georg Wilhelm Friedrich. *Grundlinien der Philosophie des Rechts* (1821) (= *Sämtliche Werke*, ed. Hermann Glockner, vol. 7). Stuttgart-Bad Canstatt: Frommann-Holzboog, 1964.

Hegel, Georg Wilhelm Friedrich. *Vorlesungen über die Philosophie der Weltgeschichte* (1837) (= *Sämtliche Werke*, ed. Hermann Glockner, vol. 11). Stuttgart-Bad Canstatt: Frommann-Holzboog, 1971.

Hempfer, Klaus W. Probleme traditioneller Bestimmungen des Renaissancebegriffs und die epistemologische 'Wende.' In *Renaissance. Diskursstrukturen und epistemologische*

Voraussetzungen. Literatur – Philosophie – Bildende Kunst, Klaus W. Hempfer (ed.), 9–46. Stuttgart: Steiner, 1993.

Hempfer, Klaus W. Die Poetik des Dialogs im Cinquecento und die neuere Dialogtheorie. Zum historischen Fundament aktueller Theorie. In *Poetik des Dialogs. Aktuelle Theorie und rinascimentales Selbstverständnis*, Klaus W. Hempfer (ed.), 67–96. Stuttgart: Steiner, 2004.

Hempfer, Klaus W. Zur Interdependenz und Differenz von 'Dialogisierung' und 'Pluralisierung' in der Renaissance. In *Pluralisierungen. Konzepte zur Erfassung der Frühen Neuzeit*, Jan D. Müller, Wulf Oesterreicher and Friedrich Vollhardt (eds.), 71–94. Berlin/New York: De Gruyter, 2010.

Hennings, Anne. The National Museum of China. Building Memory, Shaping History, Presenting Identity. PhD diss., Universität Heidelberg, 2012.

Hideo, Kiyama. The 'Literary Renaissance' and the 'Literary Revolution'. *Acta Asiatica* 72 (March 1997), 27–60.

Hon Tze-ki, *Revolution as Restoration:* Guocui xuebao *and China's Path to Modernity, 1905–1911*. Leiden: Brill, 2013.

Honnacker, Hans. *Der literarische Dialog des Primo Cinquecento. Inszenierungsstrategien und Spielraum* (= *Saecula Spiritalia*, vol. 40). Baden-Baden: Verlag Valentin Koerner, 2002.

Hu Shi. *Wenxue gailiang chuyi* 文學改良芻議 (Some Modest Suggestions for Literary Reform) in *Xin Qingnian* 新青年 (New Youth) 2, no. 5 (January 1, 1917).

Hu Shi, The Renaissance in China. *Journal of the Royal Institute of International Affairs* 5 (1926), 265–283.

Hu Shi. *The Chinese Renaissance* 中国的文艺复兴 *Zhongguo de wenyi fuxing* (*The Haskell Lectures*, 1933). Chicago: The University of Chicago Press; London: Cambridge University Press, 1934. (reprinted New York: Paragon Book Reprint Corp., 1963).

Hu Shi. 39th May Fourth Celebration in 1958. *The Chinese Renaissance Movement* 中國文藝復興運動 *Zhongguo wenyi fuxing yundong*, no pages given, Taipei: Wentan, 1961.

Hu Shi. The Literary Renaissance. In *Symposium on Chinese Culture*, Sophia H. Chen Zen (ed.), 150–164. Shanghai: China Institute of Pacific Relations, 1931 (reprinted New York: Paragon Book Reprint Corp., 1969).

Huizinga, Jan. The Task of Cultural History. In *Men and Ideas: History, the Middle Ages, the Renaissance*. Translated by James S. Holmes and Hans van Marle, 17–76. London: Eyre and Spottiswoode, 1960.

Hume, Robert D. Construction and Legitimation in Literary History. *Review of English Studies, new series* 56, no. 226 (2005), 632–661.

Jeans, Roger B. *Democracy and Socialism in Republican China: The Politics of Zhang Junmai (Carsun Chang), 1906–1941*. Lanham, MD: Rowman & Littlefield, 1997.

Jenco, Leigh K. Recentering Political Theory: The Promise of Mobile Locality. *Cultural Critique* 79 (2011), 27–59.

Jiang Fangzhen, *Ouzhou wenyi fuxing shi* 歐洲文藝復興史 (A History of the European Renaissance) (= Collection of Republican Texts *Minguo congshu*, vol. 61). Shanghai: Shangwu Press 1921. (reprint Shanghai: Shanghai shudian, 1989).

Jordheim, Helge. Against Periodization: Koselleck's Theory of Multiple Temporalities. *History and Theory* 51 (2012), 151–71.

Kamp, Andreas. *Vom Paläolithikum zur Postmoderne. Die Genese unseres Epochen-Systems*, vol. 1: *Von den Anfängen bis zum Ausgang des 17. Jahrhunderts* (= Bochumer Studien zur Philosophie, vol. 50). Amsterdam: Benjamins, 1982.

Kang Youwei, *Yidali Youji* 義大利遊記 (Italian Travelogue). In 歐洲十一國遊記 *Ouzhou Shiyi Guo youji* (A Reportage of Eleven European Nations), Li Bingtao (ed.). Shanghai 1905 (reprint: Beijing: Shehui kexue wenxian, 2007).

Kaske, Elisabeth. *The Politics of Language in Chinese Education, 1895–1919*. Leiden: Brill, 2008.

Kelly-Gadol, Joan. Did Women Have a Renaissance? In *Becoming Visible. Women in European History*, Renate Bridenthal and Claudia Koonz (eds.), 137–164. Boston: Houghton Mifflin, 1977.

Kirby, William C. *Germany and Republican China*. Stanford: Stanford University Press, 1984.

Koestler-Grack, Rachel. *Leonardo da Vinci: Artist, Inventor and Renaissance Man*. New York: Chelsea House Publishers, 2003.

Kopf, David. *British Orientalism and the Bengal Renaissance: The Dynamics of Indian Modernization, 1773–1835*. Berkeley: University of California Press, 1969.

Koselleck, Reinhart. Begriffsgeschichtliche Probleme der Verfassungsgeschichtsschreibung. In *Der Staat* Beiheft 6 (1983), 12–13.

Koselleck, Reinhart. A Response to Comments on the Geschichtliche Grundbegriffe. In *The Meaning of Historical Terms and Concepts: New Studies on Begriffsgeschichte*, Hartmut Lehmann and Melvin Richter (eds.), 59–70. Washington D.C.: German Historical Institute, 1996.

Koselleck, Reinhart. Historia Magistra Vitae. The Dissolution of the Topos into the Perspective of a Modernized Historical Process. In *Futures Past. On the Semantics of Historical Time*. Translated by Keith Tribe, 26–42. New York: Columbia University Press, 2004.

Kristeller, Paul Oskar. The Humanist movement. In *Renaissance Thought. The Classic, Scholastic, and Humanistic Strains*, 3–23. New York: Harper & Row, 1961.

Kublin, Hyman. Preface to Hu Shi, *The Chinese Renaissance*. New York: Paragon Book Reprint Corp., 1963.

Kuhn, Dieter and Helga Stahl (eds.). *Die Gegenwart des Altertums. Formen und Funktionen des Altertumsbezugs in den Hochkulturen der Alten Welt*. Heidelberg: Edition forum, 2001.

Kuhn, Thomas S. *The Structure of Scientific Revolutions*, 2. ed., enlarged. Chicago: University of Chicago Press, 1970.

Lai Chen-chung (ed.). *Adam Smith across Nations: Translations and Receptions of The Wealth of Nations*. Oxford: Oxford University Press, 2000.

Le Goff, Jacques. *Faut-il vraiment découper l'histoire en tranches?* Paris: Seuil, 2014.

Lee, Seung-hwan. *A Topography of Confucian Discourse: Politico-philosophical Reflections on Confucian Discourse since Modernity*. Translated by Jaeyoon Song and Seung-hwan Lee. Paramus, NJ: Homa and Sekey Books, 2008.

Lee, Thomas H. Must History Follow Rational Patterns of Interpretation? Critical Questions from a Chinese Perspective. In *Western Historical Thinking. An Intercultural Debate*, Jörn Rüsen (ed.), 173–177. New York: Berghahn Books, 2002.

Li Dazhao. *Qingchun* 青春 (Youth) *Qingchun*. In *Xin Qingnian* 新青年 (New Youth) 2 no. 1 (1916).

Liu, Lydia He. *Translingual Practice. Literature, National Culture and Translated Modernity. China, 1900–1937.* Stanford: Stanford University Press, 1995.
Liu Junning. *Zhongguo, ni xuyao yige wenyi fuxing!* 中国你需要一个文艺复兴 (China, You Need a Renaissance!) In 南方週末 *Nanfang zhoumo*, December 7, 2006.
Löwith, Karl. *Meaning in History. The Theological Implications of the Philosophy of History.* Chicago: University of Chicago Press, 1949.
Lu Xun, *A Brief History of Chinese Fiction* 中國小說史略 *Zhongguo xiaoshuo shilue*. Translated by Gladys Yang and Yang Xianyi. Beijing: Foreign Languages Press, 1959.
Luo Zhitian. *Inheritance within Rupture. Culture and Scholarship in Early Twentieth Century China.* Translated by Lane J. Harris and Mei Chun. Leiden: Brill 2015.
Ma Junwu, *Xin xueshu yu qunzhi zhi guanxi* 新學術與群治之關係 (The Relationship between new scholarship and governing the people). In 馬君武集 *Ma Junwu ji* (Collected Works of Ma Junwu), Mo Shixiang (ed.). Wuhan: Huazhong shifan daxue chaubanshe 1991, 187.
Machiavelli, Niccolò. *The Prince.* Translated by W.K. Marriott. London: J.M. Dent & Sons, 1958. www.gutenberg.org/files/1232/1232-h/1232-h.htm.
Machiavelli, Niccolò. *Discourses on Livy.* Translated by Harvey C. Mansfield and Nathan Tarcov. Chicago: Chicago University Press, 1995.
Machiavelli, Niccolò. Dell'arte della guerra. In *Opere*, vol. 1, Corrado Vivanti (ed.), 527–705. Turin: Einaudi, 1997.
Maissen, Thomas and Barbara Mittler. Aus dem Dunkel ins Licht. Epochale Umbrüche in China und Europa. *Ruperto Carola Forschungsmagazin* 7 (2015), 16–25.
Marsh, David. *The Quattrocento Dialogue. Classical Tradition and Humanist Innovation.* Cambridge Mass.: Harvard University Press, 1980.
Masse, Marie-Sophie. Présentation. In *La Renaissance? Des Renaissances? (VIIIe–XVIe siècles)*, 7–28. Paris: Klincksieck, 2010.
McLaughlin, Martin L. Humanist Concepts of Renaissance and Middle Ages in the Tre- and Quattrocento. *Renaissance Studies* 2 (1988), 131–42.
McNeill, William H. *The Rise of the West: A History of the Human Community.* Chicago: Chicago University Press, 1963.
Menzies, Gavin. *1421: The Year China Discovered America.* New York: Harper Perennial, 2002.
Menzies, Gavin. *1434: The Year a Magnificent Chinese Fleet Sailed to Italy and Ignited the Renaissance.* London: HarperCollins, 2008.
Michelet, Jules. *Histoire de France*, vol 7: *Renaissance*. Paris: Chamerot, 1855.
Mittler, Barbara. *Dangerous Tunes. The Politics of Chinese Music in Hong Kong, Taiwan and the People's Republic of China since 1949.* Wiesbaden: Harrassowitz, 1997.
Mittler, Barbara. *A Newspaper for China? Power, Identity, and Change in Shanghai's News Media, 1872–1912.* Cambridge: Harvard University Press, Asia Center Series, 2004.
Mittler, Barbara. 'My brother is a man-eater': Cannibalism before and after May Fourth. In *Zurück zur Freude. Studien zur chinesischen Literatur und Lebenswelt und ihrer Rezeption in Ost und West. Festschrift für Wolfgang Kubin*, Marc Hermann and Christian Schwermann (eds.), 627–655. Sankt Augustin: Steyler Verlag, 2007.
Mittler, Barbara. *A Continuous Revolution. Making Sense of Cultural Revolution Culture.* Cambridge: Harvard University Press, Asia Center Series, 2012.
Mittler, Barbara and Thomas A. Schmitz. 'Gutenberg kam nur bis Gonsenheim' – Gründe, warum Gutenbergs Erfindung weder in China noch bei den alten Griechen eine entscheidende Rolle gespielt hat. Ein (nicht ganz ernstgemeinter) west-östlicher Dialog.

In *Die Innovative Bibliothek. Elmar Mittler zum 65. Geburtstag*, Erland K. Nielsen, Klaus G. Saur and Klaus Ceynowa (eds.), 193–209. Munich: Saur, 2005.

Moloughney, Brian. From Biographical History to Historical Biography: A Transformation in Chinese Historical Writing. *East Asian History* 4 (December 1992), 1–30.

Mommsen, Theodore E. Petrarch's Conception of the Dark Ages. *Speculum* 17 (1942), 226–242.

Muhlack, Ulrich. Mittelalter und Humanismus. Eine Epochengrenze. In *Staatensystem und Geschichtsschreibung. Ausgewählte Aufsätze zu Humanismus und Historismus, Absolutismus und Aufklärung*, 9–27. Berlin: Duncker & Humblot, 2006.

Müller, Gotelind. *Documentary, World History, and National Power in the PRC: Global Rise in Chinese Eyes*. London: Routledge, 2013.

Nakayama, Shigeru. The Chinese 'Cyclic' View of History vs. Japanese 'Progress.' In *The Idea of Progress*, Arnold Burgen, Jürgen Mittelstrass and Peter McLaughlin (eds.), 65–76. Berlin: De Gruyter, 1997.

Neddermeyer, Uwe. *Das Mittelalter in der deutschen Historiographie vom 15. bis zum 18. Jahrhundert: Geschichtsgliederung und Epochenverständnis in der frühen Neuzeit*. Cologne: Böhlau, 1988.

Nelson, Janet L. The Dark Ages. *History Workshop Journal* 63 (2007), 191–201.

O' Connor, Barbara. *Leonardo Da Vinci: Renaissance Genius*. Minneapolis: Carolrhoda Books, 2003.

Palmieri, Matteo. *Vita civile*, Gino Belloni (ed.). Florence: Sansoni, 1982.

Panofsky, Erwin. *Renaissance and Renascences in Western Art*. Stockholm: Almqvist & Wiksell, 1960.

Peng, Hsiao-yen and Isabelle Rabut (eds.). *Modern China and the West: Translation and Cultural Mediation*. Leiden: Brill, 2014.

Petrarca, Francesco. De vita solitaria. In *Prose* (*La letteratura italiana. Storia e testi*, vol. 7), G. Martellotti (ed.), 285–291. Milan/Naples: R. Ricciardi, 1955.

Petrarca, Francesco. Secretum, ed. E. Carrara. In *Prose* (*La letteratura italiana. Storia e testi*, vol. 7), G. Martellotti (ed.), 22–214. Milan/Naples: R. Ricciardi, 1955.

Petrarca, Francesco. *Epistulae metricae/Briefe in Versen*. Edited and translated by Eva and Otto Schönberger. Würzburg: Königshausen & Neumann, 2004.

Petrarca, Francesco. *Letters on Familiar Matters*, ed. Aldo S. Bernardo. New York: Italica Press, 2005.

Pignatti, Franco. Il dialogo del Rinascimento. Rassegna della critica. *Giornale storico della letteratura italiana* 176 (1999), 408–443.

Porter, Roy and Mikulas Teich (eds.). *The Renaissance in National Context*. Cambridge: Cambridge University Press, 1992.

Prazniak, Roxann. Menzies and the New Chinoiserie: Is Sinocentrism the Answer to Eurocentrism in Studies of Modernity? *Medieval History Journal* 13, no. 1 (April 2010), 115–130.

Rabb, Theodore K. *The Last Days of the Renaissance & The March to Modernity*. New York: Basic Books, 2006.

Raqs, Media Collective. On Curatorial Responsibility. In *The Biennial Reader: An Anthology on Large-Scale Perennial Exhibitions of Contemporary Art*, Elena Filipovic, Marieke Van Hal, and Solveig Øvstebø (eds). Bergen: Bergen Kunstahll, 2010.

Ranke, Leopold von. Über die Epochen der neueren Geschichte, *Aus Werk und Nachlass*, vol. 2, W. P. Fuchs and Th. Schieder (eds.). Munich and Vienna: Oldenbourg, 1971.
Roeck, Bernd. *Der Morgen der Welt. Geschichte der Renaissance*. Munich: C.H. Beck, 2017.
Rowland, Ingrid. The Intellectual Background of the School of Athens: Tracking Divine Wisdom in the Rome of Julius II. In *Raphael's 'School of Athens'*, Marcia Hall (ed.), 131–170. Cambridge: Cambridge University Press, 1997.
Rüegg, Walter. Das antike Vorbild in Mittelalter und Renaissance. In *Anstöße. Aufsätze und Vorträge zur dialogischen Lebensform*, 91–111. Frankfurt am Main: Metzner, 1973.
Rüsen, Jörn (ed.). *Time and History: The Variety of Cultures*. New York: Berghahn Books, 2007.
Said, Edward. *Culture and Imperialism*. New York: Vintage Books, 1993.
Sakai Tadao. The New Life Movement with Relation to the Neo-Confucian Culture in Modernizing China. *Proceedings of Conference on Chiang Kai-shek and Modern China*, vol. 3., 708–723. Taipei: China Cultural Service, 1987.
Salutati, Coluccio. *Epistolario*, Francesco Novati (ed.). Rome: Tipografi del Senato, 1893.
Schildgen, Brenda D., Zhou Gang and Sander L. Gilman (eds.). *Other Renaissances: A New Approach to World Literature*. New York: Palgrave Macmillan, 2006.
Schwarcz, Vera. From Renaissance to Revolution: An Internal History of the May Fourth Movement and the Birth of the Chinese Intelligentsia. PhD diss., Stanford University, 1978.
Schwarcz, Vera. *The Chinese Enlightenment: Intellectuals and the Legacy of the May Fourth Movement of 1919*. Berkeley: University of California Press, 1986.
Sichel, Edith. *The Renaissance*. London: Williams & Norgate, 1914.
Singh, Jyotsna G. (ed.). *A Companion to the Global Renaissance: English Literature and Culture in the Era of Expansion*. Malden, Mass.: Wiley-Blackwell, 2009.
Smith, Adam. *An Inquiry into the Nature and Causes of the Wealth of Nations*. London: W. Strahan and T. Cadell, 1776.
Spivak, Gayatri C. *Other Asias*. Oxford: Blackwell, 2008.
Stierle, Karlheinz. Gespräch und Diskurs. Ein Versuch im Blick auf Montaigne, Descartes und Pascal. In *Das Gespräch*, (= *Poetik und Hermeneutik*, vol. 11), Karlheinz Stierle and Rainer Warning (eds.), 297–334. Munich: Fink, 1984.
Stierle, Karl Heinz. Renaissance. Die Entstehung eines Epochenbegriffs aus dem Geist des 19. Jahrhunderts. In *Epochenschwelle und Epochenbewußtsein* (= *Poetik und Hermeneutik*, vol. 12), Reinhart Koselleck and Reinhart Herzog (eds.), 453–492. Munich: Fink, 1987.
Subrahmanyam, Sanjay. Connected Histories: Notes towards a Reconfiguration of Early Modern Eurasia. *Modern Asian Studies* 31, no. 3, (1997), 735–762.
Suleiman, Susan R. (ed.). *The Idea of Europe*, = Special issue of Comparative Literature 58, no. 4 (2006).
Summit, Jennifer and David Wallace (eds.). *Medieval/Renaissance after Periodization* = *Journal of Medieval and Early Modern Studies* 37, no. 3 (Fall 2007).
Tang, Xiaobing. *Global Space and the Nationalist Discourse of Modernity: The Historical Thinking of Liang Qichao*. Stanford, Calif.: Stanford University Press, 1996.
Tasso, Torquato. *Dell'arte del dialogo*, Guido Baldassarri (ed.). Naples: Liguori, 1998.
Tibebu, Teshale. The Orient. In *Hegel and the Third World: The Making of Eurocentrism in World History*, 230–296. Syracuse: Syracuse University Press, 2011.

Toynbee, Arnold J. *A Study of History*, vol. 9. London: Oxford University Press, 1954.
Varga, Lucie. *Das Schlagwort vom 'Finsteren Mittelalter.'* Baden: Rohrer, 1932.
Vasari, Giorgio. *Le vite de' più eccellenti pittori, scultori e architettori nelle redazioni del 1550 e 1568*, Rosanna Bettarini and Paola Barocchi (eds.), Florence: Sansoni, 1966–1987.
Verdon, Timothy. Pagans in the Church. The *School of Athens* in Religious Context. In *Raphael's 'School of Athens,'* Marcia Hall (ed.), 114–130. Cambridge: Cambridge University Press, 1997.
Vezzosi, Allessandro. *Leonardo Da Vinci: The Mind of the Renaissance*. New York: Harry N. Abrams, 1997.
Voltaire, F.M.A. de. *An Essay on Universal History: the Manners, and Spirit of Nations, from the Reign of Charlemagne to the Age of Lewis XIV.* Written in French by M. de Voltaire. Translated into English, with additional notes and chronological tables, by Mr. Nugent. The second edition, revised, and considerably improved by the author. London: printed for J. Nourse at the Lamb opposite Katherine-Street in the Strand, 1759.
Voltaire, F.M.A. de. *Le siècle de Louis XIV.* Paris: Livre de poche, 2005.
Wagner, Rudolf G. China 'Asleep' and 'Awakening.' A Study in Conceptualizing Asymmetry and Coping with It. *Transcultural Studies* 1 (2011), 1–136. http://archiv.ub.uni-heidelberg.de/ojs/index.php/transcultural/index.
Wakeman, Frederic. *Spymaster: Dai Li and the Chinese Secret Service*. Berkeley: University of California Press, 2003.
Wang Shou-nan. Chiang Kai-shek and the Promotion of the Chinese Cultural Renaissance Movement. *Chinese Studies in History* 21, no. 2 (Winter 1987–1988), 66–90.
Wang, Edward Q. *Inventing China through History. The May Fourth Approach to Historiography.* Albany: SUNY, 2001.
Wiele, Mignon. *Die Erfindung einer Epoche. Zur Darstellung der italienischen Renaissance in der Literatur der französischen Romantik.* Tübingen: Gunter Narr Verlag, 2003.
Wind, Edgar. *Art and Anarchy.* London: Faber & Faber, 1963.
Wright, Arthur F. On the Uses of Generalization in the Study of Chinese History. In *Generalization in the Writing of History,* Louis Gottschalk (ed.), 36–58. Chicago: University of Chicago Press, 1963.
Yu Ying-shih. Neither Renaissance nor Enlightenment: a Historian's Reflections on the May Fourth Movement. In *The Appropriation of Cultural Capital: China's May Fourth Project*, Milena Doleželová-Velingerová and Oldřich Král (eds.), 299–326. Cambridge: Harvard University Press, 2001.
Zhao Jiabi. Preface to *The Great Series of China's New Literature* (*Zhongguo xin wenxue daxii* 中國新文學大席), vol. 1. Shanghai: Liangyou tushu gongsi, 1935.
Zhou Gang. The Chinese Renaissance, a Transcultural Reading. *PMLA* 120, no. 3 (May 2005), 783–795.
Zhou Gang. Other Asias, Other Renaissances. *Concentric: Literary and Cultural Studies* 34, no. 2 (September 2008), 87–100.
Zhou Gang, *Placing the Modern Chinese Vernacular in Transnational Literature.* New York: Palgrave Macmillan, 2011.
Zhou Zuoren, *Kukou gankou wenyi fuxing zhi meng* 苦口甘口文藝復興之夢 (The bittersweet Dream of a Renaissance), Shanghai: Taiping shuju 1944.
Zhu Jinpan. The Chinese Renaissance. In *Taizhong* 台中 (Canton) 18 (1930), 56.

Zhu Weizheng. China's Lost Renaissance. In *Coming Out of the Middle Ages: Comparative Reflections on China and the West.* Translated and edited by Ruth Hayhoe, 188–97. Armonk, NY: Sharpe, 1990.

Index of names and places

Abelard, Petrus   193
Adelman, Jeremy   149
Adige   172
Aachen   68
Alanus ab Insulis (Alain of Lille)   69
Alberti, Leon Battista   66, 73
Alcibiades   80
Alcuin of York   68
Alexander the Great   40, 54
Ampère, Jean-Jacques   53
Anderson, Kyle D.   113
Anhui   216
Antiquity   15, 18f., 28, 30, 40, 54–56, 59–61, 64, 67–69, 78, 83, 95, 100, 124f., 128, 131, 143, 161
Antwerp   192
Aretino, Pietro   66
Arezzo   172, 174
Aristotle   39, 63, 72, 79f., 185, 193
Arquà Petrarca   175
Assmann, Jan   155
Athens   68, 72, 79, 167
Augustine of Hippo   28, 39, 57, 65, 67, 193
Augustus (Octavius, Gaius)   37, 40, 54, 68, 171, 186
Averroes   193
Avignon   63, 72, 167, 172f.

Baghdad   6
Bai Juyi   196
Balzac, Honoré de   53
Ban Gu   196
Barbaro, Ermolao   72
Baron, Hans   66
Bartolus de Saxoferrato   78
Basel   188
Bayle, Pierre   60, 129
Bede the Venerable   37
Beginning of the Great Revival 建黨偉業 Jiandang weiye (Feature Film)   106–108
Beijing   93, 106, 108
Belon, Pierre   59
Belting, Hans   6

Bembo, Pietro   65
Bentley, Jerry   4, 116
Biondo, Flavio   61
Blue Shirt Society 藍衣社 Lanyishe   102, 108
Blumenberg, Hans   13
Boccaccio, Giovanni   17, 175, 193
Bonaparte, Napoleon   40, 96
Book of Songs 詩經 Shijing   196
Boston   215
Boucheron, Patrick   6
Boxer Rising 1900   202
Bracciolini, Poggio   66, 73, 175, 191
Braunhemden   102
Bruni, Leonardo   57–59, 65f., 172, 177
Brutus, Marcus Junius   171
Buddha (Siddhartha Gautama)   155
Burckhardt, Jacob   29, 53–55, 83–87, 92, 108, 118, 123–125, 130, 189
Burke, Peter   5, 138, 150–152, 154
Bussi, Giovanni Andrea   59
Byzantium   127

Cabot, Sebastian   192
Caesar, Gaius Julius   54, 171
Caligula (Rome)   173
Cao Xueqin   196, 198
Cape of Good Hope   192
Casavecchia, Filippo da   182
Castiglione, Baldassare   66
Cathay   90, 199
Caxton, William   192
Charlemagne   40, 68
Charles V (Holy Roman Empire)   40, 54, 194
Charles VIII (France)   54, 194
Charter 08 (Manifesto)   105
Chaucer, Geoffrey   194
Chen Duxiu   90f.
Chen Xiaomei   113
Chiang Kaishek   102, 107f., 110
Chicago   85, 215f.

Index of names and places

China 5, 7, 11 f., 14–18, 20, 22 f., 25, 28 f., 33, 37, 40, 45, 47–49, 83–86, 88–99, 101 f., 104 f., 107–110, 112–116, 123–126, 130, 133–135, 137, 139 f., 142 f., 145–147, 155, 161–163, 189, 197 f., 200–206, 209, 212–218
Chinese Communist Party 84, 92, 105, 134, 138, 145 f.
Chinese Dream 中國夢 Zhongguo meng (Xi Jinping) 110
Chinese Enlightenment (see also Chinese Renaissance, Chinese Student Movement, May Fourth Movement, New Culture Movement) 116, 163
Chinese Nationalist Party 國民黨 (Guomindang) 102, 212
Chinese Renaissance (see also Chinese Enlightenment, Chinese Student Movement, May Fourth Movement, New Culture Movement) 12, 20, 84 f., 89 f., 94–96, 98, 102, 104, 106–109, 111, 114, 130, 133, 135, 138, 142, 145–147, 163, 200 f., 205, 207, 211–215, 216–218
Cicero, Marcus Tullius 57, 69–72, 74, 90, 124, 168 f., 171, 173–177, 184–187
Claudius (Rome) 173
Cleanthes 166
Cologne 184
Colonna, Agapito 57
Columbus, Christopher 54, 127, 192
Condorcet, Nicolas de 42
Confucius, Kongzi 17, 104, 156, 216
Conrad, Sebastian 7, 27, 49, 110, 140
Constance 177 f.
Constantine the Great 41, 56, 60, 174
Constantinople 190
Cooper, Frederick 117
Copernicus, Nicolaus 54, 127, 192
Crotone 179

Dante Alighieri 16 f., 69, 75, 80, 90 f., 95, 174 f., 181 f., 189, 193–195, 199, 206
Datongshu 大同书 Book of Great Unity (Kang Youwei) 46
Democritus 178
Denkzwang (Ludwik Fleck) 48, 113 f., 145
Després, Josquin 53
Dewey, John 85
Dikötter, Frank 140
Diocletian (Rome) 174
Diogenes 80, 178
Dionysus Exiguus 37
Dolabella, P. Cornelius Lentulus 171
Dolce, Lodovico 65
Domitian (Rome) 173
Drake, Francis 192
Du Fu 196 f.
Duara, Prasenjit 96
Dunlop, Anne 6
Dürer, Albrecht 59

Eisenstadt, Shmuel 27, 49
Empress-Dowager 202
Engels, Friedrich 16, 43
England 91, 127, 174, 189, 194, 199 f., 211
Erasmus of Rotterdam 28, 66, 74 f., 128, 184, 191
Euclid 78

Falungong 法轮功 (Dharma Wheel Practice) 107 f., 110
Farago, Claire 6
Federigo da Montefeltro (Urbino) 76
Feltre, Vittorino 78
Ferguson, Wallace K. 29
Ferrara 11, 109
Ficino, Marsilio 79 f.
Finland 25
Flaccus, Gaius Valerius 177
Flasch, Kurt 3
Fleck, Ludwik 114
Florence 6, 11, 54, 108 f., 165, 172, 180, 183
France 53–56, 60, 63, 75, 91, 109, 127, 171–174, 180, 189, 191, 194, 199, 209
Francis I (France) 194
Frederick II (Holy Roman Empire) 193
Freiburg 187
Froben, Johann 184
Fu Sinian 93

Galba (Rome) 173
Galilei, Galileo 54, 192
Gamsa, Mark 119

Genoa 165
Germany 40f., 63, 102, 109, 127, 189, 194
Geta (Publius Septimius Geta) 180
Giorgione (Giorgio Barbarelli da Castelfranco) 78
Gluck, Carol 49
Goddesses Nüshen (Guo Moruo) 17
Goethe, Johann Wolfgang von 28
Gongyang Commentary 公羊傳 *Gongyang zhuan* 46
Goody, Jack 5, 26, 29, 116, 142, 146, 153
Gordon, Charles George 201
Gregory I (Pope) 64
Grotius, Hugo 129
Gruzinski, Serge 6, 153
Guan Hanqing 198
Guangxu Emperor 202
Guangzhou (Canton) 105
Guo Moruo 17
Gutenberg, Johannes 192

Hadrian (Rome) 173
Han Han 107
Han Yu 196f.
Hang-Chow 杭州 Hangzhou 204
Haskell, Caroline E. 214
Haskins, Charles Homer 29
Hawkins, John 192
Haydon, Eustace 214
He Xin 105
Heavenly Kingdom 太平天國 *Taiping Tianguo* 47
Hegel, Georg Wilhelm Friedrich 42, 47f., 96
Heresbach, Konrad 188
Hesiod 38f.
Hitler, Adolf 102
Hobsbawm, Eric 125
Hong Kong 138
Hong Xiuquan 47
Horace (Quintus Horatius Flaccus) 68, 72
Hu Jintao 107
Hu Shi 15f., 18, 85f., 88–90, 95, 97, 99, 101, 104, 107, 123, 131, 151, 195, 200, 214f., 218
Hu Zanyun 17
Huang Shi 17

Huang Yuanyong 204f.
Huizinga, Johan 4, 11, 20
Humanism (Chinese) 考證學 *Kaozhengxue* (evidential learning) 152

Ignatius of Loyola 33
India 115, 139, 192, 208f., 211
Ireland 25
Italian Travelogue 義大利遊記 *Yidali Youji* (Kang Youwei) 16
Italy 5, 11, 16, 22, 34, 41, 54–56, 58, 63, 72, 86, 90, 103, 108f., 127f., 139, 165, 172, 174, 179, 189–191, 194f., 199

Japan 33, 49, 93, 202f.
Jenco, Leigh 150, 153
Jiang Fangzhen 18, 108
Jiang Zemin 105, 107, 110
Julius II (Pope) 79

Kang Youwei 16, 46–48, 100
Keazor, Henry 48
Kelly-Gadol, Joan 5
Korea 211
Koselleck, Reinhart 3, 111, 117
Kranenburg 184
Kublin, Hyman 215, 218
Kuhn, Thomas 114

Lacroix, Paul 54
Lactantius (Lucius Caecilius Firmianus) 173
Laozi 155
Leonardo da Vinci 138f.
Li Baojia 198
Li Dazhao 92
Li Hongzhang 201
Li Ling 196
Li Mengyang 199
Liang Qichao 16, 47f., 92, 100
Liang Shuming 207
Lipsius, Justus 129
Liu E 198
Liu Junning 105
Liu Yong 196
Liu Zongyuan 196
Livy (Titus Livius) 76, 183f.
Louis XII (France) 194

Louis XIV (France)   54
Luther, Martin   17, 33, 54, 90f., 95, 128, 199

Ma Junwu   100
Machiavelli, Niccolò   39, 58, 75f., 128, 180f., 183
Manchu Dynasty   47, 204
Mandate of Heaven 天命 tianming   39, 45, 127
Manutius, Aldus Pius   193
Marcellus, Marcus Claudius   73, 176
Mark Antony (Marcus Antonius)   171
Marx, Karl   43, 47f.
May Fourth Movement (see also Chinese Enlightenment, Chinese Renaissance, Chinese Student Movement, New Culture Movement)   84, 104, 106, 116, 123, 126, 130, 145
Mayence   192
Medici, Giuliano de'   182
Melanchthon, Philipp   28, 59
Mencius   45
Michelangelo Buonarroti   60, 87
Michelet, Jules   53f., 85, 108
Middle Ages   11, 14f., 19, 25, 29f., 37–39, 54, 56, 59–61, 64, 67f., 83, 85, 90, 96, 115, 125, 127, 139, 143, 190f., 199
Ming dynasty   91, 196, 198f.
Modern Age, Modernity   19, 115–117, 124f., 131, 143, 161
Mona Lisa   139
Montgenèvre   165
More, Thomas   66
Mussolini, Benito   103

Nanjing   125, 201
Naples   11, 108, 165
Narni   173
National Essence Movement 國粹運動 Guocui yundong   99
National Essence Scholarly Journal 國粹學報 Guocui xuebao (Journal)   102
National Renaissance 再生 Zaisheng (Journal)   102
Naumann, Hans   29
Nebuchadnezzar II   40
Nero (Rome)   173
Nerva (Rome)   173
Netherlands   109, 129, 191
New Culture Movement (see also Chinese Enlightenment, Chinese Renaissance, Chinese Student Movement, May Fourth Movement)   12, 14f., 17, 22, 33, 84f., 88–100, 104, 106, 114f., 118, 124f., 130, 133, 136, 140, 142, 145f., 156, 162, 189, 200
New Historiography 新史學 Xin shixue (Liang Qichao)   16, 47f.
New Life Movement 新生活運動 Xin shenghuo yundong   104
New Tide 新潮 Xinchao (Journal)   93
New Youth 新青年 Xin Qingnian (Journal)   90, 92, 102, 210
Niccoli, Niccolò de'   177
Nietzsche, Friedrich   207

Occidentalism   113, 137
Orientalism   113
Orosius, Paulus   39
Otho (Rome)   173
Ouyang Xiu   196f.
Ovid (Publius Ovidius Naso)   38f., 41, 75, 128, 181

Padua   168, 175
Palmieri, Matteo   58, 76, 178
Panofsky, Ervin   21
Paratico, Angelo   138f.
Paris   40, 78, 97, 214
Patzelt, Erna   29
Pedianus, Quintus Asconius   177
Pericles   54
Persia   40, 211
Perugino, Pietro   80
Petrarca, Gherardo   172, 174
Petrarch (Petrarca, Francesco)   54, 56–58, 60, 66f., 70–72, 75, 172–175, 181, 193f.
Pico della Mirandola, Giovanni   79
Pithou, Pierre   59
Plato   65, 68, 70, 79f., 169, 185, 191
Poland   25
Polybius   39

Pompey (Gnaeus Pompeius Magnus)   171
Pound, Ezra   195
Priccardus, Leonardus   188
Probus (Rome)   174
Ptolemy, Claudius   80, 127
Pulice da Vicenza   168
Pythagoras of Samos   169

Qing dynasty   28, 99f., 140
Qu Yuan   196f.
Quintilian (Marcus Fabius Quintilianus)   73, 169, 176f., 187, 191

Rabelais, François   189f., 194
Ranke, Leopold von   43
Raphael (Raffaello Sanzio da Urbino)   60, 79f., 81
Records of the Grand Historian 史記 Shiji (Sima Qian)   196
Rhône   167
Rieti   173
Roeck, Bernd   6
Rome   11, 28, 38, 40f., 54, 56, 60, 68, 72, 79, 108, 137, 167, 173f., 177, 180, 182
Russia   203, 211f.
Russo-Japanese War 1905   203

Said, Edward   111, 113
Sainte-Beuve, Charles-Augustin   53
Sallust (Gaius Sallustius Crispus)   41
Salutati, Coluccio   66, 72
San Casciano in Val di Pesa   181
Schiller, Friedrich   28
Schwarcz, Vera   115, 130
Seneca (Lucius Annaeus Seneca)   70, 168, 170, 173, 187, 191
Septimius Severus (Rome)   174
Séré, Ferdinand   54
Severus Alexander (Rome)   174
Sforza, Francesco (Milan)   63
Shakespeare, William   194
Shandong   211
Shanghai   17, 104, 204, 217
Shi Nai'an   196, 198
Shiritan 十日談 (Giovanni Boccaccio, Decamerone, in Chinese translation by Huang Shi and Hu Zanyun)   17

Sichel, Edith Helen   86, 89, 118, 124, 189, 195
Sigonio, Carlo   65
Sima Qian   196
Sima Xiangru   196
Slavonia   174
Smith, Adam   41, 47
Socrates   65, 80, 178, 185
Sodoma (Giovanni Antonio Bazzi)   80
Solon   78
Some Modest Suggestions on Literary Reform 文學改良芻議 Wenxue gailiang chuyi (Hu Shi)   90
Song dynasty   196
Sorgue   72, 166–168
Spain   127, 173, 189
Speroni, Sperone   65
Spring and Autumn Annals 春秋 Chunqiu   46
St. Gallen   73, 177
Stendhal   53
Stierle, Karlheinz   64
Su Shi   196
Su Wu   196

Taiping Rebellion   201, 203
Taiwan   93, 104, 108
Tang dynasty   196
Tasso, Torquato   65
The Scholars 儒林外史 Rulin waishi (Wu Jingzi)   198
Theodosius I   41
Thomas Aquinas   67
Tiberius Claudius Nero   173
Tibullus, Albius   75, 128, 181
Titus (Rome)   76, 173, 184
Tokyo   99
Toynbee, Arnold   5
Trajan (Rome)   173
Tschudi, Aegidius   59
Tsingtau 青岛 Qingdao   204
Turkey   115, 211
Tuscany   63

Ukraine   25
United States of America   85f., 217f.

Vadian, Joachim   59
Valla, Lorenzo   58 f., 65 f., 191, 194
Var   165
Vasari, Giorgio   60, 79, 99
Vasco da Gama   192
Vaucluse, Fontaine de   72
Venice   11, 109, 192
Vergerio, Pier Paolo   66
Verona   172, 191
Veronese, Guarino   73, 175, 178
Versailles   84, 102, 211
Vespasian (Rome)   173
Vespucci, Amerigo   192
Vettori, Francesco   75, 180
Vicenza   168
Virgil (Publius Vergilius Maro)   39, 69, 165, 173, 175, 191, 193 f.
Visconti, Gian Galeazzo   175
Vitellius (Rome)   173
Vlatten, Johann van   184, 187
Voltaire   16, 19, 54, 108

Wang Fuzhi   45
Weber, Max   31, 117
West Lake 西湖 Xihu   204
Wu Jingheng (Wu Zhihui)   209
Wu Woyao   198

Xi Jinping   109, 146

Xin Qiji   196
Xinjiang   146
Xinmin 新民 *The New Citizen* (Journal, editor Liang Qichao, 1902)   47
Xue Guangqian   104
Xunzi   196

Yang Xiong   196
Yangzi   201
Yao Nai   197
Yu Yingshi   15, 116, 118, 162
Yuan dynasty   90, 99, 196, 198
Yuan Shikai   204

Zanobi da Strada   165
Zeng Guofan   197
Zeuxis   179
Zhang Junmai 张君劢 (Carsun Chang)   102
Zhang Taiyan   99 f., 102
Zhou dynasty   27, 142
Zhou Gang   147
Zhou Zuoren   109
Zhu Jinpan   97, 213
Zhu Xi   196
Zhuangzi (Zhuang Zhou)   209
Zoroaster   80
Zuo Commentary 左轉 *Zuozhuan*   196

www.ingramcontent.com/pod-product-compliance
Lightning Source LLC
Chambersburg PA
CBHW031806220426
43662CB00007B/545